What others are saying about
THE COVER DOG

"Oros' conversational manner and intentional disregard of formality allows him to jump off the page as a lovable and entertaining character."
Kyle Strickland
The Park Record

"Tony Oros will be replacing Gore Vidal in the salons of Soho in no time."
Terry Burden
TV host, Park City Television

"This book is more anticipated than the Facebook IPO.'
Kevin Kennedy
Park City local

"Tony is funnier than me a
most of the comedians I know…
Fuck you, Tony."
Guy Seidel
Actual comedian

THE COVER DOG
TRUE TALES OF ENTERTAINING THE PLANET

WITH
TONY OROS

COVER AND BOOK DESIGN
Cheryl Roder-Quill

CO-EDITORS
Cheryl Roder-Quill & Kim Curran

COVER PHOTO TREATMENT
Kevin Taylor

BACK COVER PHOTOS
Natalie Cass
Teresa deWilde

For additional information address:
Park City Productions
PO Box 981011
Park City, UT 84098-1011

tony@parkcityproductions.com
www.parkcityproductions.com

tony@thecoverdog.com
www.thecoverdog.com
www.thecoverdog.wordpress.com

Book design
angryporcupine*design
www.angryporcupine.com

Website
C&S Creative Services
www.cscreate.com

Cover photo
Kevin Taylor Visuals
www.kevintaylorvisuals.com

Cass Studios
www.cassstudios.com

Teresa deWilde
Egyptian Theater

Lyrics reprinted by permission

Some names have been changed to protect the idiots.

TABLE OF CONTENTS

INTRODUCTION

In April of 2003, after splitting time between Los Angeles and suburban Chicago, I relocated to Utah. The people of this state opened their arms and hearts to me, allowing me the opportunity to entertain them, teach their children, and make them laugh. Many a new friend or client has inquired into the strange path that brought a militant secularist entertainer to this right-leaning corner of the Intermountain West.

In January of the previous year I jogged a quarter mile though residential streets of San Jose, California, relaying the Olympic Torch up to the Games in Salt Lake and Park City. By both a fluke of the booking gods and an influx of post-Olympic capital, some months later I would gig in Utah for the first time, and soon she would suck me in. This compilation of tour journals, musings, blogs, and silliness is dedicated to my adopted tribe, these Utes and Parkites. This is my love song to Utah.

Very few of the pages to follow would be possible without the influence of my late grandfather Lewis Popp, who gave me the tools to explore the planet bravely and on my own terms. Lew was a strong and quiet teacher. Never a musician and rarely a clown, he was nevertheless invaluable to all I would pursue.

I have been aurally re-telling some of these stories for years — to friends and family, and at times between songs during my live performances. Other bits, I've never explored until now. Muchluv to my creative team Cheryl, Karla, and Kim. It has been a fantastic ride, grabbing all these disparate tales from my skull (or from my travel journals) and getting them down in some semblance of permanence.

And besides: Sarah Palin wrote a book, so can I! (I briefly considered that for my title.) I should probably read her stuff before criticizing. But then again, if I want to read children's books, I'll visit my niece.

Overseas and over the years, with the help of my cadre of knuckleheads, I've had the honor of entertaining countless service people in shitty places; this work is my salute to them and all they do.

Onward!

- Tony O

WILL SING
FOR LIFT PASS

"Thank you folks for being here tonight, my name's Tony. Let me know if there's anything you'd like to hear. Send me up the dreaded Request Napkin. I also do telepathic requests, so start thinking really hard. But I don't do any James Taylor, per my ban on bald guys... ok maybe some Phil Collins. And I don't play any hair metal, as I need twice the compensation to hit my costume closet and let's face it — without the spandex and schtick? Those songs just suck.

"But give me three artists and I can probably do one. And thanks for drinking with us here, and not with the assholes up the street... By the way, I'll be up the street tomorrow at The Sidecar Bar."

. . . .

25 October 2009, Park City, Utah: A resort town shoulder season amidst the global economic downturn. I had just returned from a brief casino run in Las Vegas with my U2 tribute Rattle & Hum. We usually hop the 75-minute flight back and forth from Salt Lake International, but on this weekend we opted instead for the six-hour drive. I rode down and back with my drummer Cam, shuffling comedy CDs through the gorgeous desert landscape. I arrived napless at my weekly steakhouse gig to find only two tables quietly conversing near the piano bar.

I was a good hour into my acoustic set. No one had looked in my direction or requested a thing, so I was deep into esoteric float-mode. I was dedicating songs in my head — singing obscure album cuts to friends and family in absentia that dig the stuff I dig. While simultaneously filtering my selections to create an unobtrusive atmosphere for all of our four diners, I was scrolling through the iPod in my skull, thinking: *Who would dig THIS tune right about now?*

3

Elbow — "The Fix" and "Fugitive Motel," for brilliant photographer and über-professional bartender Kevin, and for my best friend Karla in LA, who introduced me to that fantastic British band.

Jeff Buckley's ethereal arrangement of Leonard Cohen's "Hallelujah" was next on the playlist.

Catherine Wheel —"Mad Dog," for one of my first Ute friends, Anmaree.

Ray LaMontagne — "Empty," during which I floated love to my dear friend Meg somewhere far up in the Canadian wilderness.

Martin Sexton — "Black Sheep," for my buddy JB and for tonight's hostess Hillary, a huge Sexton fan.

Ours — "Ran Away to Tell the World"

> *"Don't spend your whole life waiting for your whole life."*

At this point in the evening I made eye contact with the two ladies closest to me at the piano bar. One asked if I was playing original tunes.

"No," I answered her off-mic. "But they are some of my favorite covers, which are pretty obscure."

They were in town from Wyoming, an hour or so from Park City up the Interstate 80. My buddies and I had recently played a corporate gig as Mullet Hatchet (Southern Rock Redneck Re-View!) at the Four Seasons in Jackson Hole. It was for some FOX network affiliates, actually. We wrote extra money into the contract after I was told to back off the Sean Hannity jokes.

"I can get to some hits if you'd like," I offered one of our Wyoming cowgals.

"No, no, keep doing what you're doing," she said.

I immediately realized I was inadvertently steering my head into sing-along mode. I reconsidered the night's playlist and stopped for a breath and a sip of tea —never push sing-alongs to a room when you could be playing the stuff you'd do at home on a night off. This isn't a sprint, it's a marathon.

Our steakhouse soundtrack continued with:

Radiohead from their *In Rainbows* album — "House of Cards"

Pink Floyd — "Fearless," for my younger brother back in rural Illinois. Andy is a cop in the Midwest. He looks like Bears' middle linebacker Brian Urlacher and has admittedly no musical abilities whatsoever. It's trippy. One of us was the milkman's.

Travis — "Driftwood," prevalent on many a cassette mix on many a tour through kooky places: Korea, Germany, Iceland.

Stereophonics were introduced to me back in LA by producer and 80's Geek Show creator Matt Chidgey. Back in 2004 on their pre-UK run, 'Phonics gave Salt Lake City a free show at a local club. The crowd was sparse but in complete awe. I played a solo acoustic set to open their "unplugged" set. All of maybe 200 Utes sang along in disbelieving glee, while that very next week Stereophonics would headline the 60,000-seat Earl's Court stadium in London. They sold out two shows while few back here in The States gave a shit.

"Maybe tomorrow I'll find my way home."

Where to next?

John — "Norwegian Wood"

Bob Seger — "No Man's Land." Seger is one of my favorite vocal impressions. That one was for Pops back in Illinois. And for the guy in the Tigers cap who just walked in, now unsuccessfully hitting on one of our servers.

Jackson Browne — "The Road" and "Shaky Town." I spared the room my Inaugural Ball story on this night…

Colin Hay — "Overkill" and "Lifeline." And to whom am I now dedicating? Well, to Colin fucking Hay! My first concert experience wasn't Rush's *Power Windows Tour* at suburban Chicago's Rosemont Horizon with teenage bandmates Higgie and Erhart; Rush was my first show sans-parental units. The night before my first day of junior high, at the long-vanished Poplar Creek Music Theater my Pops and I attended Men At Work's *Cargo Tour*. Their opening band on that tour was??? Wait for it…

INXS! Yes, they supported Colin Hay back in the day. "Don't Change," baby! Oh. And don't asphyxiate yourself whilst punchin' the clown. Leave a good-looking corpse, sure. But maybe not with that particular outline. Hutchence was a fantastic frontman, but never my bag. When VH1 was looking for singers to audition for the band via their reality show, an industry friend approached me about the audition. It would require learning much material I was only casually familiar with and would require relocating temporarily back to Los Angeles from my newfound bliss in Utah. "How much does it pay?" I asked. "Nothing, unless you get the gig," I was informed.

I had just learned to ski. I was a big *no-buy*. Such "opportunities" are often referred to as Spec Gigs. This means, essentially — I *spec* I ain't getting paid.

My solo set at the bottom of Main Street segued into:

Kings of Leon — "Use Somebody," for our lovely hostess Aly.

Amy Winehouse — "You Know I'm No Good," because I knew Julia would start singing from behind the bar. Winehouse's *Back to Black* CD had been sitting on my bedroom stereo for a while when I got home from my Metal Show one Thursday and put it on — and repeated it until dawn. Amy Winehouse was the kind of musician I would have completely dismissed back in my twenties, soured by their public antics and/or self-loathing personas. But time has found me more forgiving to the few true Artists in a genre replete with copycats and rip-offs. If these people come across as flighty, so what? Thom Yorke and Beck hear stuff from other planets and they couldn't give a shit less if it displeases you.

As our Sunday night was winding down and the last table was hitting the tiramisu, in walks our local TV anchorwoman with friends in tow. The whole crew was "bubbly." The evening switches gears on a dime and it's GO TIME with the sing-alongs:

Manilow — "Can't Smile Without You"

Mellenhead — "Jack and Diane"

Neil Diamond — "Song Sung Blue," morphed into…

Glen Campbell — "Rhinestone Cowboy," perhaps the first song I ever sang to myself in its entirety, at age 5, on a neighbor's swing set.

"Ever notice that Glen Campbell and Nick Nolte have virtually identical DUI photos? Somebody get that cat a comb!"

Billy Joel — "Only the Good Die Young" for a Recovering Catholic, musically confessing along at the piano bar. Someone will inevitably ask me for "Piano Man." I just hold up my acoustic guitar, staring blankly at my requestor. Although one day I will improve my piano skills just enough to learn "Guitar Man" on the keys. Just to be an ass.

Next up:

The Boss — "I'm On Fire" for Anchorgirl's married friends, just arm's reach across from my duct-taped Martin DXME electro-acoustic.

Eagles — "Best of My Love"

Prince — "Purple Rain" from the Best Bad Movie Ever! And you gotta love a cat who'll change his name to avoid being fucked.

Louie Armstrong — "What a Wonderful World." I try to end most acoustic nights with the Stachmo. It's just undeniably *warm*, no matter how cynical you are or how crummy your evening was. I've had post-gig midnight meals in Kosovo with Louie on the Walkman, digesting the stimuli of singing for homesick soldiers. There's no better song to snap your universe back into place before you trudge back to a freezing Balkan sea-hut, or stumble down a ski town's Main Street, perchance to dream of bluebird powder mornings and one-hitters in the aspens.

"I don't do any Lenny Kravitz, folks. Not because he's ripped off Terence Trent D'Arby his whole career, but because he's slept with Lisa Bonet and I haven't."

One patron during Sundance 2010 sitting at the piano bar agreed with my deflection of the Kravitz request, so we sang along to D'Arby's "Wishing Well." We began discussing other unheralded records from the early 90's. I had recently touched up on "Waiting for That Day" from George Michael's *Listen Without Prejudice* album. Our tourist at the bar knew every lyric. I transitioned into The Stones' "You Can't Always Get What You Want" to pull our peripheral listeners back in.

My favorite request of all time is "Do your favorite song," which essentially means: You're the driver, we trust you.

I delve deeply into the material that truly moves me. However I have to dig deep to find it and it's still a delicious rarity when I do. I will cop to music snobbery, a la Jack Black in *Hi Fidelity*. But if you're a chef in a 4-star restaurant, chances are you're not wolfing down many Big Macs. At any given time, there are a dozen artists you've never heard of that could become your Favorite Band in the World. While DJ-ing at Park City NPR affiliate KPCW, I would regularly get calls of "Who was that last song? With the girl singer/sitar/etc.?" Often those have been the most satisfying moments in my workweek and karmic chubbies ensue.

- - - - - - - - - - -

If you're ever in the back of a club watching live music and think it might be clever to yell "Free Bird?" Trust me — it's not.

Request night eye-rollers also include the obligatory shouts for Jimmy Buffet. Despite years of my Pops' prodding, all I've bothered to learn is tired old "Margaritaville." Until I actually become a care-free 50-something parking my love handles on a beach somewhere, no thanks.

Ditto on James Taylor. I am aware that sitting here with an acoustic guitar I am somehow morally obligated to have at least one Taylor tune, but I just can't feel that guy's stuff. Call him "J.T." all you want.

"Sorry, ma'am. I don't have any. I can, however do Carly Simon's 'You're So Vain' if you'd like. She apparently wrote this song for a big movie star of the time… wait for it… that's right ladies and gentlemen: Ned Beatty. Now squeal like a pig! Squeeee!" *

A woman asks me during a gig once, "Hey can you play 'Old Man' by Neil Young?"

"No, sorry, I haven't learned 'Old Man' yet. But I have four other Neil tunes," I said.

"Aww! I want THAT one!" she huffed.

---

* *Yes, I know it was Warren Beatty*

"Listen, I only have 600 songs in my head, and I guess that's number 601."

I've got a weird head and a wacky job. Welcome to it.

ROCK AND ROLL REVELRY

I had been taking temp work around LA in the late 90's: stuffing envelopes at Polygram Publishing on the A&M lot, answering phones at Warner Chappell Music on Santa Monica Blvd. See: *bullshit*. I was surrounded by other part time musicians not quite living the dream, submitting ourselves to the daily tease.

Orange County guitarist Spark Myth had given my number to AKA Productions out of Upland, California, which sends entertainers overseas for The United States Department Of Defense. I'd recently obtained my first passport for a run through Norway with my original band Egodog and a subsequent Eurail excursion. The singer of Spark's classic rock band Sticky was unable to do a September run of two weeks through Bosnia and Kosovo, and would I be interested?

AKA PRODUCTIONS
CIVILIAN DOD
ENTERTAINMENT
CONTRACTOR
UPLAND CA

SPARK MYTH
GUITAR
COVERDOGS

I've been a news-hound from the womb. Before you could say "Radovan Karadzic," I was sold. The Pentagon's entertainment wings stretch beyond the famed USO, which brought Bob Hope to Germany, England, Korea, Southeast Asia, and also late in his life to Kuwait. A branch called United States Army Family & Morale, Welfare and Recreation Command (formerly just MWR) provides deployed soldiers and sailors with such distractions as fresh DVDs, video games, and pool tables. And under-the-radar bar bands from LA.

While today's pop/media stars are surgically dropped into our current war zones to lip synch, sign a dozen autographs and promptly fly out, MWR players eat, sleep and shower with servicemen and –women. As Bob Hope

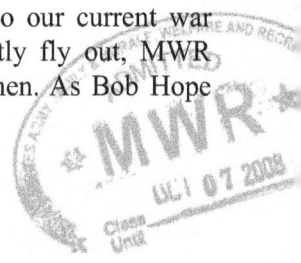

did nearly 200 times.

Sticky was renamed Rock Steady for my first Department of Defense tour, then soon after, The Coverdogs. I thought "Rock Steady" as a band name was a bit predictable. I figured, hell, we're just doing classic rock covers so let's go with that theme. I was also heavily digging a one-off album by a late 80's band called Riverdogs. The irony of it all is, I'm allergic to dogs. My face explodes like a balloon and my sinuses go ape-shit. Which makes it a drag to sing… Yet all my bands have this suffix. Go figure.

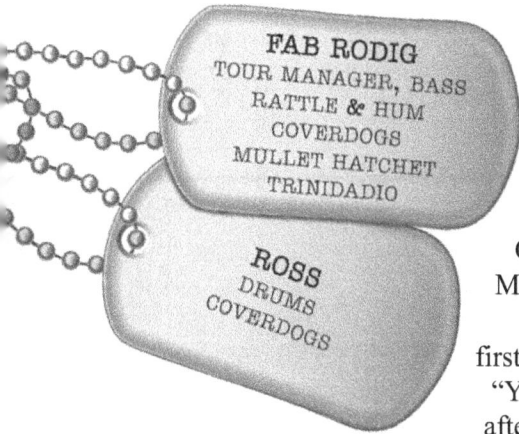

FAB RODIG
TOUR MANAGER, BASS
RATTLE & HUM
COVERDOGS
MULLET HATCHET
TRINIDADIO

ROSS
DRUMS
COVERDOGS

On bass and sound and Tour Manager duties through Rock Steady/Coverdogs' 1999 Balkan run would be a cat named Fab. It was a moniker he adopted through several DOD tours, and is decidedly *not* short for Fabio.

On drums we had Ross, presently of Sam Moore's band (Sam & Dave). A sweetheart of a cat from Northern Cal, one of Ross' first big tours had been with Kenny Loggins. "Yeah man, I was checking out of our hotel after the first stop of the tour. They hand me the bill and I was like, what are all the charges?"

"Mini bar, sir."

"What? There wasn't any bar in my room. I just ate some of the stuff that was left in the little fridge..."

After a day lunching and sightseeing in Budapest, Ross and I split a room at the Hotel Kapos in Kapesvar, Hungary. Taszar Base, a 20-minute bus ride from Kapesvar, was Stabilization Force's (SFOR) northernmost staging area for the Bosnian conflict. The women in the lobbies were stunning. And *working*. The restaurant menu was in Hungarian and German. The goulash sounded good but that'd be too clichéd. Hell, I'll just get the fish. Right? How much can someone fuck up fish? I was mid-psycho-nutrition phase and I would highly sweat these things. It was either comical or annoying as hell to my tour mates: "What is it today Oros, nuts and twigs?"

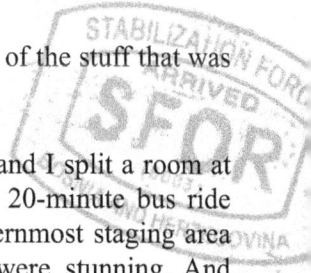

We were exhausted and jet-lagged and drifting off in our seats when the food came. *Jesus my fish is staring at me.* Contorting itself upward with eyes wide in horror, he looked like someone just pulled the hook out of his mouth and plopped him in the oil. As the band laughed aloud at my culinary quandary, I picked at the fried batter until I located a few flecks of meat before heading off to bed. The next morning, Ross and Fab were downstairs at *frühstuck*, munching toast and hard-boiled eggs. "Man, what's with that cat you bunked me with?" Ross asked Fab.

"Tony? Why?"

"The guy woke up screaming at like 3:00 in the morning. Freaked me the fuck OUT, man!" It's difficult forming a second impression when your first was night terrors. Yet for years I remained oblivious to my outburst. I even wrote in my tour journal that: "I finally got a good night's sleep."

Sorry Ross! Hit that mini-bar on me, buddy!

We set up and soundchecked in Taszar's MWR tent amidst ping-pong tables and video games. Spark found me a guitar tone (this process repeats every first soundcheck of every tour with whichever *actual* guitarist I'm playing with). Mid-way through the show as I'm addressing our GI audience, Ross spots his missing travel bag being brought in by our Point Of Contact, Mac. Ross sprints out from behind the kit, and hoists his suitcase over his head while the band led a soldier chant of "Swiss Air Sucks! Swiss Air Sucks!"

Our bus driver was Fritz (RIP). Fritzie was 100% German but he could've been a stunt double for Pat Morita. A little sweetheart, driving us through the countryside pointing and yelling, "Moo cow!" And ooh my, the Euro-funk! Unsuccessfully masked by cheap Duty Free cologne. I hate to rip on a brotha's B.O. after he's passed but *yikes*.

My first morning in Bosnia-Herzegovina found us at Camp Demi outside of Kladanj. Yes, "Demi" per *G.I. Jane* apparently.

I rubbed my eyes and looked at my watch: 6 AM. I sat up, straining to hear what I thought was... *huh?* Ross sat up too.

"Hey Ross... is that... Journey?"

They were playing "Stone In Love" through the camp PA. *For revelry.*

Rock.

The previous afternoon we were given a VIP tour of the camp, even trying our hands at tank simulators. I was coming down with a nasty case of the Bosnian Crud, a notorious deployment malady with a multitude of mutations, mine being a particularly brutal head cold I would sing through for six straight nights.

We had set up the PA in the late afternoon sun and were sitting on the edge of the stage when a green bus pulled up. They were the new arrivals from Kansas. Kids in Battle Dress Uniforms (BDUs) piling out, packs in hand, seating themselves on chairs set up for tonight's show. The Commanding Officer (CO) appeared and addressed the group. He was about to give the "Welcome to Bosnia" speech — and we were there to hear it. The CO belted out something to the tune of:

You will be here for nine months. That means a Bosnian winter. Not unlike Chicago or Buffalo. Your latrines are located at the end of the sea huts. Anyone caught pissing in a water bottle will be knocked down...

He meant they would be "knocked down" a rank; his point was not lost on any of them. *You're in Bosnia. Prepare to be miserable.* One young Black kid in the front row was dabbing his eyes.

Our first performance in The Balkans was inspired, high-energy: Foo Fighters, Bad Company, and Led Zeppelin despite my head cold. Even some of the jet-lagged newbies were digging.

First performance in a combat zone. *Check.*

My departure from Camp Demi, however, was less than heroic. If DOD entertainers are admonished about one thing repeatedly and sternly, it's DON'T LOSE YOUR SFOR ID! We were issued identification badges in Taszar, which we hung around our necks everywhere, outside of the showers or the stage.

Ok, it's kind of cool to wear them on stage.

After our second night's show, some of the troops wanted to show the band

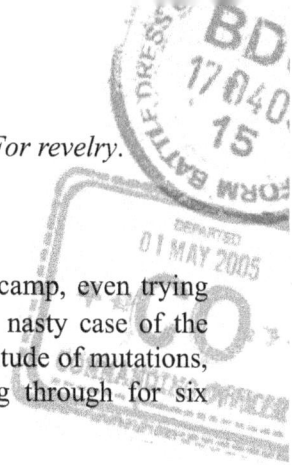

around camp. "You want to see the inside of an M1 tank?"

Shit yeah!

"I'll go get the keys."

There are KEYS?

We took turns climbing into that enormous, million dollar killing machine. "If I just put this in drive and pointed forward, we could plow through the whole camp," one of our soldier guides told us. "Go ahead, fire it up! That switch here, then press that button." I did as instructed and the whole thing started shaking; it sounded like I was strapped under a 737 — just *awesome* to feel. Fritz had our bus fired up, too, so we couldn't goof off for too long. As we boarded the bus and headed towards the camp gate, we got out our SFOR ID badges… Well. The rest of the band did.

I patted myself down and turned to our Tour Manager / bassist Fab, "Um… Houston?"

Fritz backed up and I hopped out, yelping for the tank drivers who'd just waved us off. I caught them just in time. I certainly didn't want to march into the CO's office and expose his tank crew as show-offs. Or myself, as an utter putz. I headed back to the line of tanks with our hosts in tow. Sure enough, next to the seat of my M1, was the Oros ID.

Disaster averted, it was on through the rest of the Bosnian camps: McGovern and Dobol, as well as Eagle Base. There were many Russians at Eagle during my first few tours through Bosnia. I dug the hell out of their regulation blue and gray horizontal striped undershirts and I tried unsuccessfully to wrangle a trade. "Anything I'm wearing. Yes, for a t-shirt. *Da!*" They didn't understand me and I failed to acquire any Russian government issue. No better luck finding a German to give up his cammo, either. German BDUs have the coolest pixelated design, and I scoured PXs all over SFOR looking for a jacket when I couldn't trade a soldier for his.

We gave Comanche Base an energetic outdoor show after a tour of the Apache helicopters on the flight line. The crew proudly told us that with Apaches' technology, "We can just lift a bit off the tarmac, fire a guided missile that'll go over that mountain and hit a tank three miles away. Then we drop her back down and go have lunch." I turned to Ross and asked him half-jokingly, "Why do people still fuck with us?" (Answer: Because we hadn't yet anticipated passenger airliners being flown into skyscrapers.)

The Coverdogs took in their sights of Sarajevo such as the media building — its interior still exposed by bomb craters — and the street corner where Ferdinand (Archduke Franz, not the band) was assassinated in 1914, provoking World War I. I'd learned, via my Polish grandmother, how passionately and stubbornly Europeans could hold long-term grudges. The heir to the Austro-Hungarian throne was killed with the backing of Serbian nationalists and folks over there are still quite pissy about all of it. Kosovo is even worse, with the grudges older and deeper.

German Panzers rumbled down side streets of Sarajevo in an impressive and intimidating twist on traffic congestion, passing churches, mosques, and bombed-out apartment buildings. Civilians had been shelled mercilessly from the hills around Sarajevo during the war earlier that decade, with their food, water and fuel being cut off by the surrounding army. An Olympic city starving, bleeding, and under siege. Residents had to bury their family members in apartment block courtyards because the Serbian forces would lob mortar shells down upon funeral processions. When people attempted midnight, candle-lit services, the Serbs would just aim for the candles.

Here we were at the center of one of the century's nastiest conflicts, brought from The States to sing Tom Petty tunes to troops from multiple countries, who were stationed here to keep a lid on this recently bloody corner of Europe. We left with pockets full of company coins, given to us in appreciation for coming to entertain them.

1st Battalion, 12th U.S. Cavalry. ALWAYS READY!

And we were made "Honorary Chargers."

Troops told us that if you're in a bar talking about which unit you served with, and another vet of that company produced his coin, you were obligated to show yours. Or buy the bar a round. Being given company coins was a touching tradition that would occur throughout my MWR tours.

RUNNING ON ANGSTY

Let me preface by saying I really dig Jackson Browne. *Running on Empty*? BEST road-album of all time. Dug it with my Pops as a kid, toured with it on many a Walkman. Ok…

18 January 2009: I was warming up the pipes at home when Utah radio star DJ Marci called with a "crazy question." After leaving her mid-day slot at The Blaze in Salt Lake a few years before, Marci had gone to KDKB Phoenix, then to K-Rock in New York City. She was now doing the afternoon drive-time shifts at The Globe in Washington D.C. with long time jock/celeb Surf who was MC-ing the Blue Diamond Inaugural Ball at the Smithsonian Natural History Museum. Marci had two tickets and would I like to go?

Damn. But it's Sundance Week… Gigs everywhere… Quandary!

I had long been on the Barack-Wagon, for his policies and in Bear-fan brotherhood. I'd also loaned him my small PA system during his August 2007 campaign stop in Park City:

ME: There's a lot of people filing in, do you need my PA? I did a wedding last night and it's in my truck.

CAMPAIGN MANAGER: No, we have a soapbox and a bullhorn.

Huh? *Soap box and a bullhorn*??? What, are you running against William Howard Taft?

Within an hour the crowd at Olympic Park was reaching a thousand, Barack's limo was heading up the I-80 freeway, and we were dashing for my truck. Obama's DNA is now forever on my microphone… Ok that sounded weird. But I did get the opportunity to shake my candidate's hand and wish him luck with the shit-storm he was aspiring to clean up.

Obama's Inauguration Week fell right in the meat of Sundance when I usually work about 18-20 gigs over that two weeks, so I was extremely conflicted about the trip. Plus, one of the bands Fab and I book through Park City Productions was doing their first corporate gig — for the Sundance Institute.

Besides, where am I getting a *tux* on a Monday night in Park City?!

Randy Barton was mid-shift at KPCW (.org and 91.9 FM) while I was en route to my acoustic night at the steakhouse. Randy gave a smoothly segued baritone shout-out to Park City and the Wasatch Back: "I've done some strange public service announcements in my day but this one is up there — a man in search of a tuxedo!"

I awaited calls mid-gig with my cell phone between my legs and set to vibrate mode... Ok that sounded weird too. But a few hours, emails and text messages later, I was ending my set and running across town for a loaner tux. *Thank you*, Alice and Mark and all who called to help! This town just keeps on giving. More texts to sub out my Tuesday and Wednesday gigs, three hours sleep and then an early flight into Baltimore. Cab to the suburbs and time to get dolled up with one Ms. Classic Rock D.C., Marci Wiser.

No small factor in this adventure was that for all the far-off and funky places I've been, this was my first time in our nation's capitol. After that election, it felt very much like *my* nation's capitol. I won't turn this into an Obama love-fest, but of the two choices the electoral college shoved at us in 2008, the politician I voted for had the more forward thinking ideas (bullhorn excepted) and for once, my country chose not to vote out of fear. I make no apologies for being objective and capricious in my patriotism. When we sit on our asses and spew about how great we are? That's not my country. But when we take all of our talk about progress and opportunity and actually act on it, then I get weepy. And preachy, apparently.

Ok...

Have I mentioned how much I love and respect Jackson Browne?

The Washington Metro system had its largest ever numbers that Tuesday and it seemed almost everyone on the line was Black Tie. People from all over, of all ages, dressed to the nines. Marci and I sat by two older couples en route to the Illinois Ball. Inauguration Day was frigid, even for this Chicagoan-cum-Ute.

We're chatting with any and every stranger, bundling up as we ascend the steps from the subway, when I'd forgotten — we were de-training at the National Mall. Beautifully lit up, the Washington Monument stood majestically to my left and the Capitol to the right. This was my first sensory experience in D.C.

We found our way into the museum as various speakers were taking turns on stage. Marci spotted Surf and her 94.7 The Globe peeps while I wandered the room, chatting with my fellow Americans: "You're orthodontists, no shit? Me? Oh, I wear wigs and sing AC/DC songs."

Back in Utah, Fab was holding down our Park City Productions reigns at the Sundance party. I was texting him for updates while snapping pictures and taking in the scene around me. At one point I was upstairs gazing at the Hope Diamond, dying to break into a conversation with Dennis Kucinich who stood right behind me. But I sadly wussed out. I'm easily intimidated by people I truly respect — if I ever meet Sir Paul or John McLaughlin, I am sure to soil myself.

Graham Nash was playing and he had the whole room on sing-alongs. Wow, that guy's career bookends: from Woodstock to Barack!

I crept up to stage right a few songs into Jackson Browne's set. I'd seen him years ago in LA in my 20's, albeit from the Universal Amphitheatre's nosebleed section. When I was 11, my family was vacationing at Wisconsin's Alpine Valley Resort (the closest thing to skiing in Bear/Packer land). In the lobby for checkout that Sunday morning, my musically astute mother quietly nudges my brother and me: "Those guys with the guitar cases, on the couches? That's Jackson's Browne's band. They played here last night."

My Ma. She partied with Pablo Cruise.

Guitarist Mark Goldenberg was killin' it at the museum. I shot some video, just for the moment. I was a fan and an American, not an entertainer, on this night.

- - - - - - - - - - -

Forward to a few days later. I'm home and loading the images onto my Mac. The song was "Doctor My Eyes." There were three women next to me posing for a picture, their backs to the stage. And there I was, filming away. So I'm watching the footage... And I'm watching Jackson's face... He mouthed something... And he was clearly not happy.

I had pissed off Jackson Browne.

Either it was me, or the chicks behind me. But I'm pretty sure he was scowling at me.

So allow me now this opportunity to apologize to Jackson Browne and band, if I in any way stepped on your vibe: The footage was for my own personal use and I never posted any of it on line nor did I ever intend to. I didn't notice at the time, but you guys were irked.

Then again, every time I get on a stage I expect — as a default — that someone is filming. Difference being however, that sometimes when I see a camera, I pucker and tweak my nipples.

But thank you, sir. For your years of activism, and for the bus shifting gears on "Nothing But Time."

    "And at the moment that my camera happened to find you..."

TIME CAPSULE

Pops had a wedding band in the 70's. They were extremely part-time and occasionally competent. Band names would come and go: Equinox, Now & Then... Time Capsule! But those band members were static: Pops, neighbor Bill, Al Seavers on guitar, and big Rich on drums. Rich was an enormous man and would eventually die from complications due to his obesity. Al was a smooth, jazzy guitarist with a beautiful f-hole Gibson. I timidly picked Al's brain on the rare occasion their rehearsals landed in our kitchen.

I find myself awed at the resources available to today's teenage and pre-teen musicians: School of Rock and their competing programs, instant access to chord charts and tutorial videos on line, not to mention the advances in gear. In my early years I was lucky for five minutes every three months with Wedding Band Al. Or, for a short stint, acoustic guitar lessons with Sister Carol at Our Lady of Good Counsel, who just couldn't cop any feel whatsoever.

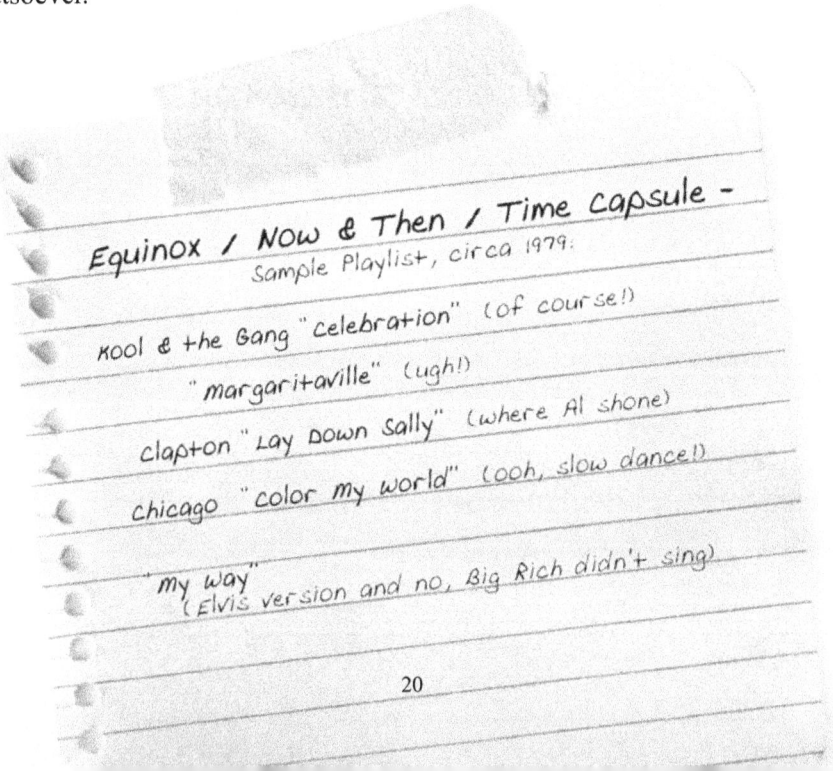

Equinox / Now & Then / Time Capsule -
Sample Playlist, circa 1979:

Kool & the Gang "Celebration" (of course!)

"margaritaville" (ugh!)

Clapton "Lay Down Sally" (where Al shone)

Chicago "color my world" (ooh, slow dance!)

"my way"
(Elvis version and no, Big Rich didn't sing)

Equinox / Now & Then / Time Capsule -
Sample Playlist, circa 1979:

"Born to Be Wild"
  cause they were rebels, apparently.

  Commodores were HUGE back in '79!
"Three Times a Lady"

Pops was rocking some Tom Jones!?
  "Green Green Grass of Home"

"Soul man" likely the Blues Brothers version
because after all Pops' band was hopelessly white.

Bachman Turner Overweight
  "Takin' Care of Business"

They didn't gig often, maybe two a month during the summer wedding season. But when they did I'd tag along, humping gear and watching Pops work a crowd.

I would be remiss not to mention Bill's instrument. He was the accordion player.

Now, if these four dudes were to approach me for bookings in Park City, Utah, guess who's the first guy on the chopping block? And I'll give you a hint: it's not even the 300-lb drummer with the inguinal hernia.

Accordion!

Bill carried all the piano parts and was handy when drunk Polacks needed to dance, but that visual alone was a buzzkill. Unless you're at a Klezmer festival, no one gets laid to an accordion. Not even accordion players. When I got a bit older I had my first sit-in with my Dad's barn-burner of a wedding outfit. I gave The Stones a go, with "Honky Tonk Woman." Accordion Bill was sitting back by the old purple padded dinosaur powered mixer. He kept turning my volume pot down. He later told Pops I was "pitchy."

For the record, I'm sure I was. But I was fourteen. And that guy still plays the accordion.

Pops had it goin' on there for about five minutes back in the day: White guy Afro, butterfly collars, the Robert Blake *Baretta* brim. I've seen pictures. Pops was fly! Nowadays it's baseball caps and Dockers. *"Wha' happened?"*

· · · · · · · · · · ·

My childhood obsession with everything Beatle was at full throttle. I'd been instinctually memorizing song lyrics since hearing "A Hard Day's Night" on WLS AM at age seven (Larry Lujack's *Animal Stories*? Old-school 312, testify!). I would kill time in my classes drawing the Fab Four from photos in the stack of Beatle books I had assembled. You'd have thought it was 1964, my immersion was so complete.

On the morning of 9 December 1980, I was making my daily two-block trek to Bardwell Elementary, the enormous, imposing brick school at the end of our street. My quiet neighbor buddy just could not comprehend why I was upset.

"But, John Lennon! Some guy shot John Lennon, Chris!"

That next frigid Sunday, WLS Chicago was broadcasting all Beatles, all day as a candlelight vigil was held in Grant Park. I sat somberly attached to my clock radio and cassette recorder, taping the coverage and supplementing my collection with any Beatle tracks I didn't already own on vinyl. I remained depressed for a solid month, only my parents and Aunt Linda understanding why. I had been repeatedly spinning the *Double Fantasy* LP and I had to stop listening to "Beautiful Boy" because John's lyrics were just too heavy.

Yet, even as a ten year old grieving fan, I was perturbed at the John song / Yoko song / John song arrangement of that record. Come on, guys! That's musical blackmail, I don't want to listen to his wife! Love is deaf, apparently. What's Japanese for "suck"?

22

I spent my pre-teen summers playing little league baseball in the evenings, but my days found me planted firmly in front of new cable channel MTV, soaking in everything their programmers could muster during those first few seasons. Not only "back when MTV played music," but back when there weren't enough true promotional videos to fill a 24-hour rotation; they aired songs from full concert films: Rush's "Limelight" and "Red Barchetta" from *Exit...Stage Left* and Triumph tunes from the *Allied Forces Tour* — what a drag to be the second greatest power trio in Canadian musical history!

I couldn't wait for the Journey selections, circa *Escape*. Sure, you're sick to death of "Don't Stop Believin," but that's not Journey's fault.

The Clash's "Rock the Casbah" (it looks like the bassist has that one word in the chorus wrong...).

J. Geils Band — "Love Stinks," with the drummer playing a fish.

David Bowie — "Ashes to Ashes" (yes, that's a pink tutu and a bulldozer).

"Who Can It Be Now?" was a fave in spite of the ribbing my affinities took from the "potheads" down the block who cranked the *Highway to Hell* album out their bedroom windows as their dysfunctional family screamed obscenities at each other. Meanwhile, I was happily ensconced in pop and classic rock stimuli:

The Who was pressing on after the loss of legendary train-wreck drummer Keith Moon, with a shorthaired Daltrey wailing away on "Another Tricky Day."

Missing Persons and Bow Wow Wow videos provided many an early stiffy.

Many of the videos in rotation were actually shot on video and my, the cheese factor! I was hooked!

The Waitresses — "I Know What Boys Like." You intentional bitch!

Ma would make me change the channel if she walked in during John Cougar's "Hurts So Good" video. Apparently because of the leather and chain-clad extras, table dancing in the sleazy roadhouse. Biker bondage!

"Burning For You" — no Blue Oyster Cult allowed at Casa Oros, either.

Well, there were flames, after all. That's an implicit endorsement of Satan, right?

Ma wasn't a big Bible-thumper. I know now, she wasn't really buying all that puritanical shit. She was just defaulting to age-old, clichéd moral standards to maintain some sanity around the house.

Billy Squier — "The Stroke," with its music industry double entendres eluding me as a preteen.

My twelve-year old reaction first seeing Van Halen's "So This Is Love" video, Diamond Dave wobbling around stage with a half-drunk liter of whiskey:

> *"What a dick."*

Secondary reaction:

> *"I wish they'd play that U2 video again."*

The parental units would have small gatherings at our big scary old house on Sexton Street, with late night sing-alongs to Eagles and Doobie Brothers records. Oh and there were doobies, all right. Although to their credit I was unaware they partook in the ganja until I was years older. Well. Thanks to Bear Stearns and AIG, people won't have to hide it for long. We'll take that tax revenue now, please. *Smoke up, Johnny! Our bridges are collapsing!*

Pops sold cable TV around Aurora in the earliest days of the industry. We had that big, ugly converter box atop the tube in our living room and a "remote control" that required a fifteen-foot cord. Weekend late night viewings of HBO gave me an early and rare window into a foreign counter culture. Sure, I'd catch the fantastic feature films that HBO rotated. *Humanoids From the Deep,* anyone? But Pops and I would really look forward to their weekly comedy specials:

Robin Williams, coked out of his mind and brilliant.

George Carlin, the Master, taking the baton from Lenny Bruce and paving a path for Bill Hicks. *On Campus, At Carnegie!* Forget about "Stuff" man, this guy was on my TV talking about "Bullshit!" Carlin's last Utah show in May of 2008 remains perhaps my top concert experience ever. Thanks to KBER

101, I was literally front row, center. George Carlin's sneakers were just inches away. I was in heaven all night.

Age 10, on the living room floor at Sexton and Simms, I was planted on my elbows in front of the *5th Annual Young Comedians Show*. Again, with my shitty little cassette recorder at the ready:

Paul Reubens rocked a character named Pee Wee Herman and a doll named Hugo that hypnotized audience members.

A pre-*Roger Rabbit* Charles Fleicher informed me that on a recent National Geographic episode, "Jacques Cousteau said the vagina of a tuna fish smells like a human being." As with the lyrics to Jackson Browne's "Rosie" I had absolutely no idea what he was talking about. I committed Fleicher's brilliant "Moleeds" kit to memory and somehow convinced my 7th grade science teacher Mrs. Wilson that it was relevant enough to present to the class. Particle-centric comedy at 10 AM on a Monday. The balls! They just stared at me like I was speaking Swahili.

Mrs. Wilson was all right for a meagerly paid public school teacher. She was one of those adults who refused to be out-clevered by a fourteen year old. I caught her returning from the bathroom and asked her if everything came out ok. "Sure," she deadpanned back at me, "It was only pee."

Those were the redemption years for *Saturday Night Live* after some really un-funny seasons following the original "Not Ready for Prime Time Players." Pops had played high school football against the late John Belushi, but in junior high I was busy memorizing skits by Eddie Murphy and impersonating characters by Billy Crystal and Christopher Guest.

"Boy I hate when that happens, Willie."

I listened to Dr. Demento, religiously every Sunday evening.

"Roly-poly fish heads, eat them up, yum!"

My annual birthday and Christmas gift requests for Beatle records were supplemented with comedy albums as well. Bill Cosby's *Why Is There Air?* and *To Russell, My Brother, Whom I Slept With*. My brother Andy and I stayed up late in my room, spinning Cheech and Chong's *Still Smokin'*, a present from my Aunt Linda. Being Ma's older sister gave Linda a bit of leeway placing such heresy under our Christmas tree. She was a grade school teacher and always provided me with a non-condescending ear. Years later she would nominate me for the running of the Olympic Torch after I visited her school and explained my Department of Defense travels to her 3rd graders; we studied the huge world map and passed around my company coins.

Aunt Linda provided me with a bulk of my Beatle LPs, many handed down from her college friend Bob Dicks whose name was magic markered on many album sleeves, providing Andy and I with endless giggles. I had the 1964 two record set from VeeJay Records, *The International Battle of the Century: The Beatles Versus The FOUR SEASONS*!? Complete with a "score card" on the back cover so you can compare the bands. Just a touch myopic, no? "YOU be the judge and jury!"

Christ, that Frankie Valli stuff. There's even a tribute show to them in Vegas. I'll take the hot fireplace poker in the eye, thank you. Music didn't get much whiter than that crap. Nostalgia for people who fondly remember poodle skirts and segregation.

WHEN MONKEYS FLY OUT MY BUTT

Born and raised in Aurora, Illinois. Yes of *Wayne's World* fame, only less interesting. Oh, and with more crime. A nice place to grow up, and a better place to get the fuck out of. In junior high I hung out mostly with Rich and Brian. We argued Marvel Comics incessantly (Al Milgrom is drawing the *Secret Wars* Mini-Series sequel, you gotta be shitting me). We were one each: a Black, a Mexican and a Polack, thus providing fodder for ninety percent of pubescent hallway jokes. We were the United Nations of K.D. Waldo Jr. High. We were The Knights of Jamalot.

Rich and I recently found each other on line. Following a stint in the Marines, Rich had entered a Christian ministry of some sort. Below is our IM chat. I asked him about our third amigo, Brian:

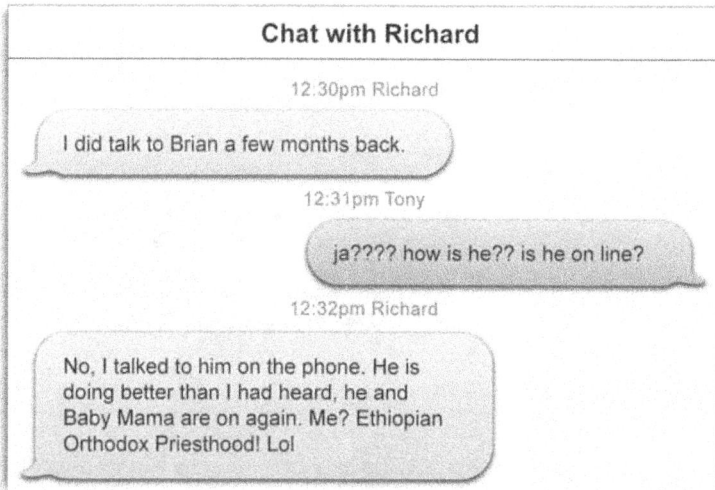

Chat with Richard

12:30pm Richard

I did talk to Brian a few months back.

12:31pm Tony

ja???? how is he?? is he on line?

12:32pm Richard

No, I talked to him on the phone. He is doing better than I had heard, he and Baby Mama are on again. Me? Ethiopian Orthodox Priesthood! Lol

Chat with Richard

12:33pm Tony

WHAA (Kristi) well good 4 them

12:34pm Richard

Yep. How about u, doing the "Big Love" thing out there? Lol

12:35pm Tony

strangely, polygamy is the one tenet of Mormonism I agree with; it's an evolutionary thing; WE ARE MONKEYS. So FUCK, monkeys! Because we are DESIGNED TO!

12:36pm Richard

Hell, I don't want to think about ONE wife, let alone MULTIPLE ones... Celibacy... unless Toni Braxton or Ashley Judd becomes available...

12:36pm Tony

bravo

12:40pm Richard

lol. We are more than apes, if we were just that; we wouldn't have the problems that we do.

12:41pm Tony

apes with the curse of self-awareness and nuclear weapons and superstitions........

12:41pm Richard

Naw, I am sure that chimps and even dolphins are self-aware. Our issue is that we have a nature that is beyond our physical one, beyond the temporal and spatial aspects of this actuality. I love animals. They are easy to understand. Ah yes. Our spiritual nature is elusive to most people because we severed our connection to its source.

Chat with Richard

12:44pm Tony

but. what of their "spirit"? is that the level u're referring to? ok, Ethiopian Orthodox.
RIDDLE ME THIS!!!!!!
Was Jesus of Nazareth divine?

12:46pm Richard

Divine as in God? Short answer, yes.
He is the physical manifestation of the spoken word of the Most High God.

12:47pm Tony

WAS MOHAMMED?
WAS THE BUDDAH???

12:47pm Richard

Nope, nor did either claim to be.

12:47pm Tony

so then, because of HIS CLAIM, he was???
WHAT outside of our DESIRE,
as MONKEYS, to LIVE FOREVER,
justifies a belief in an afterlife????

12:49pm Richard

Jesus did claim to be God, eternal. True.
Muhammad and Buddha did not, which is a statement of fact.

12:49pm Tony

agreed. I lean toward Buddhist teachings because he claimed no EXTERNAL knowledge
it was INTROspection
which is all we are - individual apes, hoping 2 live forever which we WILL NOT
THUS.... should we not aspire to making THIS planet more joyous??? but we don't, Rich
we blow each other up because we believe in different gods sorry Rich. But THAT is why I am Agnostic. Because WE DON'T KNOW.

Chat with Richard

12:54pm Richard

I don't believe religion is the source of the wars between people, an excuse at best... Jesus taught a message that was about change from within, spiritual rebirth to reconnect us with our spiritual source, as we seem to allow our carnal nature to rule us. Take chimps, why do they kill each other? They are every bit as warlike as we are. I don't see churches, temples or mosques amongst them, We kill each other because we allow our NATURE (the one we share with Chimps) to rule us.

12:56pm Tony

I concur. We kill each other when we are IRRATIONAL

12:57pm Richard

Not exactly, I can think of quite a few rational reasons to have to kill.

12:57pm Tony

apes are not (yet? Darwin??? Persecuted by RELIGION) rational beings.

12:57pm Richard

Rationality is part of our psyche

12:57pm Tony

not exclusively, Rich... RIGHT

12:58pm Richard

cannot be utilized effectively apart from our emotions.

12:59pm Tony

could we not become more rational?? Part of rationality is that a woman cannot be impregnated by an angel. "Maybe a Jewish minx lied." - Christopher Hitchens

---

Chat with Richard

1:02pm Richard

Rationality is overrated.
It is subjective.
Not objective.

1:03pm Tony

WHAT? SCIENCE allows itself the
HUMILITY to correct itself. Does
RELIGION???

Richard has gone offline

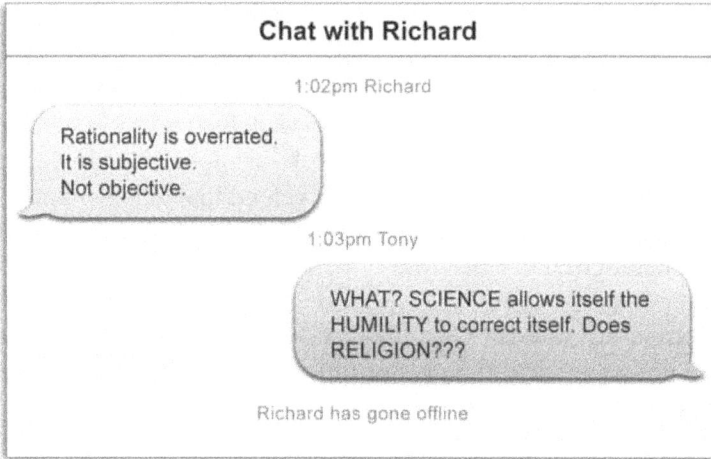

At that point, Rich went offline, though certainly not for want of intellectual courage.

Some two-plus decades ago in junior high Rich and I developed our debating skills via the Marvel Comic universe: the properties of adamantium, the feasibility of molecular teleportation, and alternate planes of reality. Here we were, catching up in our late 30's, substituting "X-Men" and "Alpha Flight" with "God" or "Jesus," still speculating about ambiguities.

. . . .

One summer night my step-uncle Jim brought over shrimp cocktail to a family bash and was just raving about a new sitcom that my parents absolutely needed to watch. It would be an oversimplification to describe Uncle Jim as "Louie DePalma-like," but he did turn my family on to *Taxi*...

Jim sold industrial cleaning products. One day he and my Uncle Action Jackson were driving towards the tiny airport at Freeport, Illinois. Jim said he had a meeting at the airport bar, to come on in, he'd only be a minute. When they reached the front door, Jim turned to Action and said, "No matter what happens just go along with this." I can only imagine the sinking rock in Action's gut.

Jim sits next to the guy waiting at the bar who immediately begins a loud and nasty tirade: "You son of a BITCH! That crap you sold me tore up all my floors! Give me my money back," etcetera and so on.

Jim quietly ingests this stream of abuse and profanities. He turns slowly on his bar stool, sticks his finger in Action's face and says, "Goddammit Action. I warned you about which stuff to use on this kind of job. Son of a bitch! How many times now? Shit! Just... Go wait in the car!" Stunned, Action could only obey, though it doubtlessly killed him. Family legend has it however, that not only did Uncle Jim *not* refund that client's money, but that he also sold the schmuck extra supplies to fix the initial mess. The client may have even apologized to Uncle Jim.

Jim had dated my paternal Grandmother. At family gatherings, my Grandma O. would press me with, "You know Jim's nephew is a really good drummer. You two should get together." Higgie was a year ahead of me. Our paths only rarely crossed, having different towns and schools. *Yeah*, I thought. *He probably sucks.*

Over at Camp Hig, the opposite exchange was occurring. "Yeah," he told Uncle Jim, "that guy probably sucks."

Higgie and I eventually did get together in a suburban garage, via a mutual guitarist. Erhart had a Les Paul and worshipped Jimmy Page. Most of our set was either Led Zeppelin or Rush, and we wondered why the chicks in our school didn't give a shit. There was a strobe light and pot-filled rehearsals. Endless loops of *The Song Remains the Same* on VHS. There were arguments about nothing. Then, eventually, gigs at the church fair to cringing Catholic passersby. We were searching high and low for band names and I was hanging in Action's back yard one Sunday, raking leaves.

"Action, we need to change our name. We have zero ideas."

"Do what Lynyrd Skynrd did. They named it after their high school gym coach."

"We're in private school, we don't have gym class, actually."

"Well then, what about your music teacher?" Action said.

"Norbert Rozanski?" I asked.

He didn't miss a beat: "There you go!"

I wisely eschewed Action's suggestion; surely there would have been intellectual property issues. Although a few years later during music school out in Hollywood I would take liberty with two names of Action's friends, performing briefly as Jim Schwebke and The Groin Pulls, then as Randy Hesselbaum and The Butt Crumbs. Your checks are in the mail.

Good old Mr. Rozanski. "I know that you're in a band with Erhart. Why don't you ever try out for any school musicals?"

Because you were doing *Bye Bye fucking Birdie*, Norb.

I loathe musicals and always have. Sorry. Just when you start to give a shit about a story line or a character, they break into a fucking song. Then that's not enough, they have to start dancing. Sweet Jesus make it stop.

But I was still open to being a team player and I countered to Aurora Central Catholic's music teacher: "I have an idea, Mr. Rozanski. Let's do *TOMMY*!" The theological metaphors in The Who's first Rock Opera were obviously known to Norb, and he nixed that idea post-haste.

I tried again: "Alright then. The school band has a horn section. Next assembly, just have them learn The Honeydrippers' 'Rockin' at Midnight' and my band will learn it too. I'll sing the Robert Plant part!"

Well that didn't happen either. But hey, be true to your school, right?

Our first garage band's gig was at a little all-ages dive out in the country. The owner of The Getaway Lounge in Yorkville made us audition for him on a Sunday afternoon. For four hours. For free... Now that I think about it? Smart guy. An interested batch of our Aurora Central Catholic High School mates were in attendance. As well as a smattering of dubious local farmers. Booked as Mystic Fury (forgive us, we were 16 and really, really into Rush) our trio was mid-Zeppelin with "Whole Lotta Love" and most of the young crowd was digging. Hig, Erhart and I knew The Fury (or Mystic *Furry* per Efrain Perez in homeroom) was far from its epic aspirations, but I hit the a-capella break:

> *"Wayyy down inside, woman, youuu neeeed..."*

One guy standing toward the front broke the silence with "This band SUCKS!"

I continued screeching into: *"Luuuuv,"* and the band kicked back into the Bonham/Page riff, while I angrily flew him the Bird, drawing — sadly — our biggest cheers of the night.

In retrospect, I must say, Mystic Fury certainly did suck.

I cringe at my vocal inabilities back then at sixteen. A Higgie family friend was a vocal instructor and I was offered an introduction. But in youthful insecurity I was offended, and blew the opportunity. Although in a few years I would learn how to belt with some competence at Musicians Institute, I wouldn't truly learn how to utilize my instrument until studying bel canto with renowned LA vocal coach Ron Anderson in my 30's.

Spring 1988: Late in my senior year at Aurora's best option outside of gang-ridden public schools, our history teacher was going up and down the rows asking us to declare where we would be attending college the coming Fall.

Southern Illinois, eh? Nice. University of Illinois in Chapain? Nicer. "Waubonsee Community College" was a popular answer, but somewhat looked down upon at our college-prep high school.

My answer that morning was, "Musicians Institute, Hollywood California."

I was surprised that many of my classmates were surprised. But I had seen MI's ad in the pages of Guitar Magazine (WHAT? They voted Geddy Lee #5 best bassist and Nikki Sixx #1? The injustice!). The print ad read: "You gotta know the rules before you can break 'em." The accompanying picture was a wild-eyed Billy Sheehan ripping the strings off his bass. Gimme THAT.

My folks somehow found the bread, I sent a demo tape, and all was locked. All I had to do was maneuver through my remaining months as a square peg in that "Teenage Jail."

During an April assembly our principal was railing, not very subtly, on seniors who were trying to grow their hair long in anticipation of the approaching summer. The row in front of me instantly spun around with huge grins and I was wound tight enough not to see the humor in the moment. Months of frustration and teen angst were already at critical levels. Leaving the auditorium in a crowd toward 3rd period I apparently railed off an impressive tirade of expletives, which I do not recall, although I do vaguely remember heaving my books violently against the stairwell wall in the process.

Sociology teacher/football coach/Beatle fan Bob Padilla snagged me by the arm and yanked me into his classroom. "What the FUCK are you doing?" He was livid, but could see that I was out of my head for a few seconds there. I remember spewing something about being "...done with this place, tired of taking shit, I'm out of here," etcetera. "I know what I want to do and it has *nothing* to do with this place!"

Coach Padilla had sat down in his chair and was nodding empathetically. I was panting heavily and looking over my shoulder for the arrival of the Catholic Gestapo.

"Look Tony. You're almost there." He lit up a Marlboro Red. I still have no idea how he got away with blazing up in his classroom between periods. "Just hang on a little longer, graduate and then get out of here. Do whatever you have to do. But what you have to do today is calm down. And graduate."

There were a couple bastions of sanity at that Conformity Factory to whom I am grateful. Guidance counselor Mrs. Vance was sage enough not to dissuade me from my path and impressed me with her knowledge of Rush lyrics. Coaches Padilla and Lindo gave me a benefit of the doubt I sorely needed, though I never did sports in high school.

I intended to. Really, I did. I had transferred from public schools for my sophomore year, a move that made me ineligible for any private school sports for twelve months. I had been enjoying baseball during my summers, and I attended the first ACC tryout, even though I wouldn't be allowed to play. My high school had a rich boys baseball tradition, of which I was aware. But at that first tryout/practice, we were addressed by a coach I hadn't met: "This is Aurora Central Catholic, people. You're not here to have fun. You're here to win. If you want to have fun, go play for East High."

Well *up yours*, I thought, and never returned.

Fucking herd mindset. Loyalty for sake of loyalty. Sacrifice for the sake of sacrifice. Us against them. Fear and all of it. It just beats the shit out of kids that are cursed with that pesky inclination to think for themselves. My buddy George and I hung out at Ach & Lou's Pizza on Friday nights and made snide comments to classmates as they bummed out after varsity basketball losses. If you can't beat 'em, join 'em. And if you can't join 'em, fuck 'em.

Early in that school year I'd borrowed a cassette tape of Roger Waters' first solo album, *The Pros and Cons of Hitch Hiking* and went to the school office to make a copy of the lyrics on the tape sleeve (no Google back in the day, kids). And Jesus, the grief I took from this old bag in the copy room. The cover's artwork is a cartoon depiction of a nude woman, her back to the camera *with* her ass blocked out, doubtlessly for the benefit of Waters' uptight record buyers over here in the States. Like office lady here. These people just couldn't relax. Sex is bad, fear it. We wonder why we're fucked up.

Brilliant album, incidentally: *Pros & Cons*. That record made me understand the "Clapton is God" graffiti back in Yardbird-era London. His Strat just weeps through Waters' dark and personal travels. Eric Clapton even toured along for that release. Fantastic, underappreciated stuff, even for many hardcore fans of The Floyd.*

While living in Utah two decades later, I began receiving emails from my Catholic alma mater. Most of them advertised fund raising events. One had a pirate theme, ostensibly to piggyback off Disney's Johnny Depp movie, very popular at the time. That place was still trying to milk us. The nerve! I was in my 30's and still trying to shake their Invisible Man following me around and reading my thoughts. I was moved to write the Alumni Staff. I replied:

From: Tony Oros
Subject:
Date: Sep. 2007
To: Aurora Central Catholic Alumni staff

Dear Sir or Madam!

As Aurora Central Catholic Alum and an active member of the Church of the Flying Spaghetti Monster I take offense to your "Pirates of the Caribbean" event, scheduled for 28 September, 2007. All Pastafarians hold Pirates sacred, as we have been taught that the decline of pirates on modern seaways is the cause of global warming. Piratism is thus, an intrinsic part of my religion and I demand an apology from Aurora Central Catholic Church and the Illinois Archdiocese for the insensitively Pirate-themed fundraiser, to which we Pastafarians take umbrage.
- RAmen, T

---

* *That said, Clapton's Unplugged over U2's Achtung Baby for Album of the Year Grammy back in 1993? I call bullshit of Milli Vanilli-esque proportions.*

No apology came. But I didn't send Benedict XVI and his minions any donations either. No cash for you, buddy! At least the Mormons have the balls to say it up front: *give us 10% or you're fucked!* The Catholics just guilt it out of you. They pass around that little basket at the end of mass and you're a dick — even when you're a kid — if you don't drop something in there. *But I need to buy baseball cards dammit!*

Higgie and I worked day jobs that post graduation summer of 1988, saving bread for our upcoming year at music school in LA. He joined the workforce via his mother those three months at Valley Rivet Company, which inevitably led to a series of "Your Mom's a spot welder" jokes. We rehearsed with local guitar wiz Hatz and bassist "Poor" Eddie out at old Book Farm. Rick Book was in a local blues bands and his family owned much farmland out past the Fox Valley Mall. He converted a small barn into a recording and rehearsal studio. We were soundproofed and miles away from anything. I wondered to myself what the white powdery residue was, lodged in the crevices atop the Peavey bass cabinet.

Friday night rehearsals began humbly in late May. Four guys, some beer and some Dio tunes. My first day of construction cleanup was a Friday. I drove straight to The Barn after quickly showering off several inches of drywall dust. Having been unprepared for masks, I was still digging sheet rock out of my nostrils when I pulled up to an exuberant Higgie. "The new Queenryche album is out! *Operation: Mindcrime!* It's so good man, do you want to hear it? No?" I just wanted to lie down among the MGD boxes and rat droppings.

By mid-summer it was less practice than party. Word had spread around the greater Aurora/Naperville area and The Women had arrived. Groups brought their own beer and god knows what else in their El Caminos and IROCKs. There were bonfires. Dramas. Copulations. The girl who jacked a dog off. Much frilly stonewash. Hatz's black Dodge Charger, an undeniable pussy magnet in late 1980's suburban Chicago.

By late August, the summer of the barn was hitting a perfect climax. We'd built enough of a buzz every week to bring a scene, but the local fuzz hadn't yet gotten wind of us. Higgie and I were ready to start packing.

"I'm going to California with an aching in my heart."

HOLLYWOOD IN A NUTSHELL...
OR RATHER,
IN A SHELL GAME

Aurora to Los Angeles. Jesus! It was like they plopped us down into an episode of *T.J. Hooker*.

Drummer pal Higgie and local guitar hero Spank drove out to LA a week before my grandfather and I. There were few mushy goodbyes — the three of us were just itching to get out of the only town we knew. I followed with Lew in a big maxi van, crammed with all my belongings. I forced him to listen to my cassettes. These included the aforementioned band, Queensryche. The poor guy. "Is that a woman singing?" That was Grandpa's unobtrusive way of asking, "Will you give me a break with this noise?"

The two of us shared the driving through the desert to the Torrance, California home of Lew's youngest brother, the longtime Assistant Chief of Police. I caught up with Higgie and Spank in the San Fernando Valley for a few nights on Spank's bassist's floor in Granada Hills as we apartment hunted. Sam's un-amused roommate gave me my first heavy vibe in Cali. *"Who are these assholes on my floor, Sam?"* Higgie, Spank and I promptly settled in Beachwood Canyon, a midnight's hike from the Hollywood sign.

Bopping home down Hollywood Boulevard one evening, Higgie and I passed a shell game — a *literal* shell game. Several men were gathered, some playing, one dealing, one on the lookout for LAPD. Higgie and I studied the dealer, turning to each other in youthful enthusiasm: "Did you see it? Me too! I saw where it went every time! We've got this thing!" We raced to the Security Federal ATM on Cahuenga and promptly withdrew a small chunk of our summer's nest eggs. Our sprint from the ATM had included discussions of strategy. "Yeah we can't get too greedy. We should set a dollar amount then we quit when we hit that number." We were in.

Hustling back to the game (now on a different corner, hmm, no this isn't at all shady) we awaited our turn and plopped down our cash for round one. Our dealer showed us the bean, so to speak, and began whipping shells in semi-circles before us. Higgie and I both eyed our shell. The shells stopped and we agreed: *That one.* He lifted our choice, and lo...

Nada. No bean. LOSERS!

"Next up!" This guy scoops our money while my drummer and I stumble backward, dazed and speechless. It was one of those beautiful Light Bulb moments: *Oh... THIS is what the planet is about, and I don't know what the fuck I'm doing.*

Classic.

Our subsequent years in Los Angeles were essentially an extended replay of that shell game: endless mailings of press kits, writing checks for "radio promotion" (see: payola) and kissing up to "baby" A&R people: *Whose dick do I have to suck to get this career going, dammit? Where's that dick, under this shell? THIS one?*

Late 80's, Los Angeles: We were flyering The Sunset Strip on weekends. There was Aqua Net and ramen noodles. The blinding pursuit of the Major Label Deal...

"Hey ladies, our band is playing FM Station next Tuesday. Here's two tickets!"

Chick reaction?

"The Valley? Um, yeah we're busy."

Hollywood. There were clowns all around. Midnight omelets at Rock n' Roll Denny's, sitting across from the Izzy Stradlin look-alike. Really. There was some schmuck hanging about who looked and dressed like the Guns n' Roses guitarist — their rhythm guitarist, mind you — and he just sat in a booth by the door, letting clueless metal-bimbos talk to him. Terrifying.

"Where is Harrison Ford? Cause this must be Bladerunner."

Hollywood at 4 AM smells like jasmine and lawn fertilizer.

Our new buddies had a repugnant single apartment a block off Hollywood Boulevard. The building was named The Nirvana, years before anyone was ready for Kurt Cobain. We were all attending Musician's Institute (MI) down the street. Just turn right at the Scientology Building where shady cats in ties offer free "personality tests" with one inevitable conclusion: *You need a religion invented by a sci-fi writer.*

MI was a completely vocational school and geared mostly for rock n' roll. They had a respected jazz program that attracted players from every funky place imaginable: Japan, Israel, Mississippi. But it was their rock program, especially Guitar Institute, that lured the bulk of students to LA in the era of Paul Gilbert's million-mile an hour soloing. *What? You can't arpeggio sweep 64th notes? Poser!*

My first vocal training was with Tim Bogert. The school's elder statesman, Tim gave both bass and vocal lessons. One bass class ended with a Q&A. The room was full of longhairs, noodling on Iron Maiden riffs while grilling the former member of Vanilla Fudge and Beck Bogert & Appice for info.

"Who do you think is the most underrated bassist ever?" one student asked Tim.

"Paul McCartney." Tim didn't hesitate. "Listen to him carry melodies with his bass lines. 'Silly Love Songs?' Genius!" Half the room was expecting some props for Jaco Pastorius or Steve Harris. But I could dig it.

In a flurry of first semester vocal whoring, I jammed with anyone who approached me. One ephemeral project consisted of an Yngwie Malmsteen devotee from Japan. He had Yngwie's silk shirt and played the same cherry red Stratocaster, which he spun around his shoulder in a perfect send-up. We called him "Chingwie Chongsteen" behind his back. *Class.*

Another student, an aloof, quiet but annoyed drummer sat in the back of all the performance classes but never got up to play. The first few weeks went by with him just sitting in the back row looking bored, until an instructor called him out, informing him that at some juncture he must get up and actually play his instrument in class if he wished to pass the course.

"Ok," he said. "But when do I get to tour?"

The class went silent as he continued in all seriousness. "When do I get the record deal?" He was summarily pulled aside and... counseled. He didn't return.

On the opposite end of the get-it scale was drummer Ray Luzier, green from the farmlands of Pennsylvania. We never saw Ray at parties or out socializing. He went directly from drum lab to class, back to apartment with fellow percussionist Jorge Palacios. Ray was the first of us to land a gig that year, for guitar-intense Shrapnel Records. Subsequently he would join the David Lee Roth Band, then form Army of Anyone with Filter singer Richard Patrick and Stone Temple Pilots' brothers Robert & Dean DeLeo. Eventually Ray landed the drum slot with the unapologetically heavy Korn. Both Ray and Jorge are cover show veterans. Years after schooling together, the three of us began hooking up again while playing in Utah, San Diego, and a two-month run of weekends in Vegas. Ray was still enjoying an occasional silly wig show. It was probably a nice break from his regular onslaught of musical seriousness.

Musicians Institute had rehearsal rooms and was open 24/7. You could always find some temporary project hacking through Rush tunes at 3 AM on a Tuesday. Such jam sessions were made more the adventure by their compulsory midnight strolls though downtown Hollywood with a $600 guitar strapped to your hayseed ass. During the 1980's Hollywood was well visited by tourists yet seriously neglected by the Tom Bradley Administration, with junkies and sometimes dangerous homeless staking their incoherent claims. MI students were familiar with the regulars: Elephant Man, with his swollen and discolored clubfeet, and Jumping Bean, a small Black kid with pungent dreadlocks who would occasionally stop before a store window and hop up and down in place for a few minutes, staring intensely at his reflection.

You'd find yourself speculating about these guys' pasts: families, former professions, and aspirations that brought them to Hollywood. I mean, maybe they drove a big old van out from somewhere, packed with guitars and dreams of stard... *oh shit!*

The foot traffic on Hollywood Boulevard wasn't always menacing. One afternoon Bo Didley stopped a student and inquired about all the "cats carrying guitars." When told about the music school around the corner the blues legend wandered into the main performance room, M-100, where a jazz percussion class was in full, uh... *swing* on stage. Invited up by a surprised staff, much comedy ensued as Bo tried to teach his famous "Who Do You Love" beat (see also U2's "Desire," Guns n' Roses' "Mr. Brownstone" and most of George Thorogood's catalogue) to the class's Japanese drum instructor, who was far more familiar with odd-meter paradiddles than with Chicago Blues.

One afternoon I stopped by to see our bros at The Nirvana, no one was home and the door was locked. I turned to go and up bops this beautiful Mulatto girl — tiny skirt, crazy hair. Sold!

"Hi, I'm just waiting for Jeff and Mike," I stammered.

"Hi! I'm Candi. I live here. Wanna come in for a smoke?" She was gorgeous.

"Why yes… Yes I do."

She opened her door and the funk hit me like a fist. That place made my buddies' pad look like Martha Stewart's. Two steps in, what I could see of the carpet was vile. Half eaten food and strewn cigarette butts. I diplomatically shuffled some trash off a corner of the couch while she went to the kitchen, offering me a beer. Not a plain wrap, but close enough. Candi returned and picked up the pipe that had been hiding under a pizza box. She whipped the lighter out of her purse.

And then out came the *rock*. I dropped a crabcake in my pants, comforted in the knowledge the stench would go unnoticed. "Um yeah, ok. You know, I was kind of hoping for pot. I'm good on that today."

She shrugged and immediately indulged.

"Yeah, so. Tell Jeff that T stopped by, ok?" I probably left the beer in a cloud of dust.

The Nirvana's walk in closet was serving as Jeff's room but Toledo Tom needed his space, too. Since nobody would volunteer to take the garbage out, Tom began slowly accumulating empty cardboard beer cases. Most of the walls comprised either of Milwaukee's Best or Ralph's plain wrap, blue label (quality guaranteed*). Taped together floor to ceiling, this gave Tom his area so the three could share the single without the constant desire to throttle each other. Tom's room lasted until one early morning when Mike and Jeff crept up to the walls, grabbed its corners and began violently shaking while shouting "EARTHQUAKE!" Little Tom blasted though his living room wall into hysterical howls, irreparably destroying his home. But Jabba the Trash Heap kept growing, and alarmingly contained not just benign recyclables but also perishables. Higgie and I eventually stopped making the trip across Hollywood to The Nirvana, no matter now much pot they'd lucked into. Mike and Jeff would move into a dive a few blocks away with Rog. The toilet clogged and no one could fix it. But I guess *when you gotta go...* and they kept going. Not even their cat would enter the bathroom after a while. Eventually a shovel was brought in.

That stray cat. They didn't even name the poor thing. These guys were creative as hell but just called their cat "Kitty."

Jeff was Staten Island. Higgie and I knew nothing about New York. But Jeff's accent was beautiful. "It's so *weeed*," He told my deep-dish enunciating drummer, "Yous guys got no accent at all. You could be a *spoaatscastuh!*"

Mike was from upstate New York. These two brilliant idiots had attended Berklee School of Music together, and were close from a few brief but lean and educational years in Boston. Mike was a fantastic guitarist. To my knowledge he never attended a class at MI. Yet he'd stroll in at semester's end and ace every exam. Eventually he would get bored with rock, start listening to John Scofield (naming his dog after the jazz guitarist) and become a respected fusion player, getting written up in Guitar Magazine. Fortunately Mike never sought bragging rights. All his old rock buddies undoubtedly glossed right over any jazz articles. *Jazz? Fuck that! Look, Mick Mars discusses his distortion tone!*

One night, Jeff, Mike and Mike's girl Jess were lying around the apartment. It was Jeff's birthday and they were drinking more out of boredom than celebration... *Hey! We're stranded two thousand miles from home, with no money and no hope. Pass me another generic beer!* Mike was first to bed with Jess following. Jess was the daughter of a respected classic rock veteran, although at the time her family ties were thin and she rarely discussed her father or older brother (who would later achieve the record deal pipedream in that late 90's post-Wallflowers nepotistic signing flurry). Jess was a welcome addition to the circles; unobtrusive and offering a sometimes gravely needed female perspective. Her *one of the guys* status paid dividends for the birthday boy that night. Mike, in his perpetual lack of financial options, sent Jess into Jeff's room with a candle and a surprise birthday hummer.

Tales such as these amazed Higgie and I, still sheltered and sexually ignorant in our late teens. Our part time roommate at Beachwood (as well as my bass instructor back in Aurora) was Spank. He had a guitar with a Nagel face painted on it. His group had just won a local battle of the bands sponsored by LA's biggest metal station, the mighty Pure Rock KNAC in Long Beach. Grave Danger was soon signed, yet kept playing mostly at FM Station in the dreaded San Fernando Valley. They were older guys, mostly from Aurora. We listened, mouths agape at their post-show stories. "I walked in and Spank and Bob have her half naked on the bed. So I whipped out my dick and she stares up at me and says, 'I'm not a whore!' and I said 'Hey, I just want a blowjob!'" And we were impressed. Sam's bass playing abilities were passable. But being tall with nappy, pseudo-Slash, jet black hair he looked the part, somewhat balancing the presence of Grave Danger's heavy Hispanic lead guitarist, which in late 80's Hollywood was a big elephant in the room. Sam blew our minds because he was in his thirties and he owned a skateboard. The anarchy!

Despite a big name producer and much LA hype, it was not meant to be for Grave Danger. The label deal they negotiated with MCA (Musical Cemetery of America, unless you happened to be Bel Biv Davoe). Guaranteed no promo money or even a release date for that matter, the album was shelved upon completion. "Shelved." It was a slow fizzle for Danger, as opposed to a big rumors-flying blowout with an A&R guy or label CFO. Grave Danger. Add to the long list of *Good Shit You'll Never Hear*.

Yet Higgie, Jeff, Mike and I pressed on undaunted. The brass ring was still hanging out there. Lesser idiots were grabbing it, why not us? With two drummers and no bassist among us it wasn't going to be the four of us as a unit. But we were sure — we were next.

We all graduated from MI, with Higgie and I staying in SoCal but most of our new mates returning to more familiar surroundings back east. Several years later I was watching local news up in the Valley, a few miles but seemingly eons from my Hollywood past. A report came on about a fire in an apartment building at Orange and Franklin Avenues. The fire was only the first blow. When the antiquated sprinkler system once activated, it refused to turn off again. The building was flooded, with residents sleepily mulling about out on the foul-smelling, freshly sodden lawn. The anchor continued, "The Nirvana Apartments on Orange Ave…"

During my first year at music school I flew back to see the family for the holidays. I booked a show with a makeshift suburban lineup and we double-billed with a Lynyrd Skynyrd tribute. Not a proper tribute Show of any casino caliber, but basically five guys with a bar band that said, "Hey let's drop the two Allman Brothers songs from our set." The venue was the old Romanian church hall where my parents were married. We lined up the PA system, did some promotion and covered everything — except security. The Old Style was flowin'. In the parking lot, my 70-year old Uncle Nick shot his mouth off and one of the Skynyrd guys laid him out. No charges were pressed, as my family likely knew he had it coming.

Pops and I would periodically road-trip around the Midwest in whatever crummy little ride he presently owned. Marshall Tucker Band and Eagles graced the cassette deck. "How about we hit U of I down in Champaign-Urbana?" And why not! We were surrounded by corn on all sides. Pops and I found a rock club where a local band had a chick singer ripping into Metallica covers between really dirty and humorous original material. The three of us started chatting after her set, and we all decided to lose Pops. Yes, including Pops. He could go find a Denny's or something. His son had work to do. She bid her band a quick farewell (I think they were fighting, go figure) and we headed out toward the street. We exited the club and I squinted in the streetlight — she had purple hair. Pops, when regaling that night to his buddies, still refers to her as "Joan Jett" but I don't think Joan was as pierced. This girl was more Jeanette Napolitano meets Dale Bozzio. We bid Pops farewell and took her car back to the motel. Whether from post-gig or post-playtime exhaustion we both drifted off and didn't wake until after sunup. At which time I opened the motel room door to find a scowling Pops, sipping White Hen Pantry coffee in his driver's seat. He'd been out there all night. I roused "Joan" and skulked into passenger seat of the Chevette for a very quiet ride home north to Aurora.

November 1989, Hollywood: I'm out of music school and out of money. Around Thanksgiving, I see a couple of guys in flannel living out of a trailer and setting up tenting on the corner of Franklin and Highland. John Lyons was the boss on the lot (though I'd later meet the owner of the franchise, the actual Mr. Greentrees who was as real-deal lumberjack as they come). Old man Lyons from Spokane was the biggest sweetheart in the world — bald, thin, sporting coke bottle glasses and a long white beard. He looked like Santa in need of lasik and a sandwich.

The trees were coming in a few days and yes, he'll need guys to hump 'em. That previous summer's drywall and lumber dust up my nose was replaced by pine needles and spiders down my thermal. Unloading the flatbeds from Oregon packed with the bound and snow-crusted trees was a terrific ass-kicker. I had a blast drilling, standing and caring for the trees under the massive tent on one of the busiest intersections in Hollywood. Helping couples, families and celebs pick out their trees and securing them to car roofs felt festive, and proved lucrative.

I took few days off that December and would return nearly every season for the next five years, hanging with our quirky Mr. Greentrees family. The Highland lot, fragrant with Douglas Firs and eucalyptus chips, served as a sensory reminder that it was indeed the holidays, even amid Southern California temps in the 70's. Homeless guys would wander through the lot. Sometimes just to smell something nice, I think. Something nostalgic and happy.

Arriving in a long Mercedes caravan, yet haggling us down to our last nerve, were the regular gypsy families. Lyons always raced to put LAPD Hollywood Division on speed dial when these folks pulled up. They'd be shooed away after a few minutes of incessant haggling, piling in their luxury cars, and heading up Highland Avenue toward other, more gullible tree vendors.

Peter Frampton stopped by for his tree. Tim Roth and Noah Wyle, Richard Marx (Vixen fans, represent… both of you) and Marilu Henner. *Nardo.*

I would also go on the occasional delivery. CNN Entertainment anchor Bella Shaw ordered a 10 ft. grand fir up to her place behind the Hollywood Bowl, a few blocks away. She was extremely nice and signed me an 8x10, although I was secretly hoping for a plug on her show. And after all, a plug for what? *I'm green as hell, I don't even have a band at present, but I can sing my ass off…* Who gives a shit! I was twenty years old and didn't yet grasp that real success doesn't come from what you *can* do, but from what you *do.*

Nicolas Cage lost his wallet and I really think he suspected me of taking it. He'd bought his tree, left, and returned a few minutes later. "Did you find a wallet on the ground?" I told him I hadn't. But he was giving me the stink eye. You dick! Thus began my ban on Nicolas Cage films. Ok, I'll still watch *Raising Arizona*, but mostly for John Goodman.

Karla was my girl and my best friend through much of my time in LA, and she inexplicably remains a supporter of my various escapades. One December day, she dropped me off at the lot for my last day of the season. She then headed up to the Valley for a holiday party, which would run late into the evening. At the end of my shift I thought: it's an awesome night and I have The Police's *Ghost in the Machine* on my Walkman — I'm just going to hoof the four miles back home to Los Feliz. With visions of sugarplums and pockets full of cash, I walked past my first few Hollyweird neighborhoods. The Capitol Building and Beachwood Drive. Mayfair Market, kitty-corner from the big, spooky and high-security Scientology compound. I turned left and walked up Western Ave toward Griffith Park and my home stretch on Los Feliz Boulevard. Over my shoulder, the lights of LA glistened in the smog: "Shaky Town."

I was restless and not exceptionally happy in Los Angeles. But on this night it was beautiful. I sang to myself and was hopeful, for those reasons that are illogical and random — hopeful that good change happens. That work is rewarded. That dreams are occasionally realized, even if it's a long and slow process, even if goals aren't attained in black and white moments of clarity. And that... *ahh, dickcheese.* That *I don't have my house keys.*

I had made it to within a block of our place and remembered Karla had dropped me off. I was in my mud-splashed overalls and sweatshirt. We didn't do the hide-a-key thing and I wasn't about to climb through a window looking like Ted Kaczynski on a bender. We didn't have cell phones. Damn. There was a local bar a few blocks down. I'd call Karla from there. I began heading down Hillhurst Avenue, the city's lights strewn before me.

Ye Rustic Inn was a dark, quirky neighborhood bar. A bit Bukowski and not yet *Swingers.* I walked my grimy lumberjack ass right in and grabbed an empty booth. With my wad of tree lot money I ordered a vodka-something and checked out the regulars. A group of teamsters, apparently driving for ABC, had some tables in the far corner. There were fragments of conversations in my periphery, which are exclusive to LA: auditions, callbacks, and the lack thereof. Relationship dramas further convoluted by professional aspiration in an amorphous and malign industry that exists nowhere else on the planet in such concentration.

This bar was a few blocks from where I'd lived for over a year, but like many so-called neighborhoods in Los Angeles, you can go months or years without noticing the guy next door has grown a second head. My server came over, an older, cougar-ish veteran. She placed a little bottle of wine on the table in front of me, complete with a red bow and ribbon. "What's this?" I asked her.

"Tonight's our annual Christmas party," she smiled.

I told her it was my first time venturing into her fine establishment and apologized for crashing. "That's ok. Welcome! Merry Christmas," and she bounced back to the bar. That night began a holiday tradition of cocktails at Ye Rustic Inn. Karla and I hit it once a Holiday season, for several years.

- - - - - - - - - - -

Musicians Institute's Class of 1989 held our ceremony at the Henry Fonda Amphitheatre. Lew's brothers and my Great Aunts attended the ceremony and took me to dinner at entertainment history-rich Musso and Frank's afterwards. While I had been asked to audition for a post-Paul Gilbert lineup of guitar-fixated Racer X, no glamorous or lucrative gigs awaited me upon graduation. I followed an industrious buddy Rog over a few city blocks to a smelly old building near Hollywood and LaBrea Boulevards, which housed a market research company. They did phone surveys for the movie industry.

We weren't selling anything, mind you. It was strictly, "How likely would you be to see a movie about such-and-such, starring this bimbo and that stiff," etc. We sat in old, musty phone banks and were assigned area codes. Calling semi-screened residential numbers, we'd try to avoid dinner times and worked hard not to piss people off. But several times a week you'd hear the SLAM of a receiver and a stream of top-volume profanities from a co-worker across the room.

Turnover was quick. Many people on the other end of the line were dubious, which I understood. But the people that blew my mind were the ones who repeatedly answered, "I don't know." *What do you mean, you don't know?* I'm only asking you for your opinion. *Are you interested in this fucking movie?* This wasn't *Jeopardy* for Christ's sake. And you people vote? Astounding.

We'd cold call all around the country. I learned much about stereotypes, educational and economic disparities, and regional dialects. One afternoon I had completed a survey with a woman in Georgia. As often happened with our more willing participants, we got chatty. She was a native Georgian, having never left. I asked why she had no Southern accent. She told me, "Because a long time ago I realized it makes you sound stupid."

Some exchanges were points of light in my day, but most were just a drag, and I would eventually burn out like my predecessors.

The next Day Job came upon my move over the hill to Burbank, of *Tonight Show* fame. I pulled the inevitable shifts at Music Plus, a chain of record stores back when there were record stores. A hipper manager named Ty was my initial boss. I overestimated his knowledge of our VHS selection trivia when I quoted *Caddyshack*: "You wanna tie me up with some of your ties, Ty?" He wasn't amused. But rather a bit creeped out, I think.

Note to self: *Stop assuming everyone knows your obtuse comedy references.*

For a while, we set up an Employee Picks kiosk next to checkout. One day a short, balding middle-aged guy came in asking for something new. Something he hadn't heard. I was doing back flips over the new King's X cassette. I popped on a track and watched his nose wrinkle. He was a *no-buy* from the first note. But… "We Were Born To Be Loved!" I just couldn't understand it. The bluesy yet shredding guitar of Ty Tabor! The soulful lead pipes of Dug Pinnick, the Beatle-esque harmonies?

"Aw that's kid's stuff," I think he said.

No. Wait… that was Cheap Trick. Anyway.

This was the age of the cassette single and the hottest seller in my tenure at Music Plus, Burbank was "Ice Ice Baby." High school kids, completely ignorant of Freddie Mercury, would stream in looking for that piece of tripe. We'd just grimace and point them to the life-sized Vanilla Ice display, our heads bowed in defeat.

DA... BEARSSS

When I was a kid I spent fall and winter afternoons watching Pops scream at Chicago Bears games. It wasn't quite *Buffalo 66*-level domestic drama, but some weeks after a Sunday loss, he'd be pissy clear up through Thursday. I swore I'd grow up and never do the same, but godammit it's a hereditary affliction and I'm doomed.

Walter Payton and Dan Hampton preceded John, Paul, George and Ringo on my walls by a few years. I had closets full of burnt orange and navy. Later, in my 20's, Sunday mornings with fellow transplants at Tarzana, California's Corbin Bowl and Tin Horn Flats in Burbank throughout the woeful Wannstedt Years, with Brett Favre regularly crushing us on national television. I can sing you the fight song if you need it.

In 1999 I wrote to the Chicago Bears headquarters at Halas Hall. Not to gripe about a recent draft pick, but rather to volunteer my vocal services for the National Anthem. Wanting new professional challenges, I'd just dipped my toe in that performance water at an IHL hockey game in Long Beach for their Ice Dogs. But singing "The Star Spangled Banner" at Soldier Field, right before a DOD run through Bosnia, would bring some of my paths full circle. I have a tendency to create dramatic scenarios for myself, and that day provided in spades.

They had an opening for a pre-season game that August. It was unpaid, but they did send a stretch limo to bring me from Kingsway Drive. Lew dug that.

Anthem day at Soldier Field. Bears vs. Colts! Karla and family as my entourage under a humid late-summer mist on Lake Michigan. Childhood heroes and many ghosts, all in that house. We were told Jesse Jackson would be in the press box with recently freed Bosnian war hero and fallen pilot Scott O'Grady. And hell, when you get to meet Michael McCaskey, that's a moment, son. Throw in an extremely shaky soundcheck and it was a heavy day on just about every front.

All right, soundcheck was bad on my end. The soundguy John warned me alright — walking out towards the center hash that morning, he turned to me with the wireless mic and said, "Soldier Field has notoriously the worst slapback in the NFL." *Gulp!*

I'd been practicing in LA with headphones and a reverb unit to replicate a potentially awful "slapback" delay in the stadium. But my first two soundcheck run-throughs were indeed a train wreck, as I cracked high notes while t-shirt clad players paused their passing drills to turn skeptically in my direction.

Shit. That's Cade McNown!

Ok, so I was easily impressed.

John radioed up to the booth to ask the front of house tech: "Did you get it?" The voice crackled back with a laugh that yes, he received the signal, and that it was peaking. In other words, I was singing too loud. Sure, I didn't have shit for volume control back then. It was balls out and rock, "Like it should be sung," sound tech John said. Which was flattering, but did little to quell my anxiety following a really unnerving trial run through.

I walked alone through the passages beneath the historic and then-crumbling stadium. I kept my pipes warm for a tense seventy-five minutes, while the concessionaires passed me with quizzical expressions.

When game time finally arrived, I excused myself from my family and made my way to the turf's hash mark. Longtime Bears PA announcer Jim Riebandt has a peculiar delivery of the play-by-play at the pre-renovated Soldier Field:

"There is a time out (*long pause*)... on the field."

Following the much-maligned stadium renovation of 2004 (few American cities can rock the architectural snobbery like Chicago) Bear fans began embellishing on the mid-game fun with their own interjections:

PA: "There is a time out..."
CROWD: "WHERE?"
PA: "On the field."
CROWD: "Ohhhh!"

Riebant announced the lineup for "YOUR 1999 Chicago Bears!" The players streamed onto the field a short distance from my jittery ass, dressed in black and gripping a wireless mic. Bears and Colts arranged themselves on the sidelines; Offensive Tackle James "Big Cat" Williams was kneeling next to his helmet and still taller than Karla. If you've never been close to NFL players, you can't fathom what sheer machines these people are.

Riebant introduced me, and the stadium fell silent. The performance itself was a surreal time warp, where concentration and visceral emotion met. By the time we reached *"Rockets' red glare"* the hometown crowd of 38,000 was whooping; there is a clip of Colts fullback Dominick Rhodes fist-pumping to the vocal peak, and Peyton Manning with hand on heart.

I limped off the field to warm applause and was awarded with a rare and precious sideline view of an NFL game. Admittedly, I can recall more details from games I saw on TV as a pre-teen than I remember of that night's matchup. A huge task had just been completed and I was soaking in the lakefront ambiance, getting my tummy ready for some pie. It was to be Due's on Waa-bash Ave with my people. Deep dish! Bear Down, my frients.

ILLI-NOISE, REVISITED

One recent fall, I booked a working weekend back in my little brother's town of Dixon, Illinois. I needed some quality time with my tiny niece and nephew. In preparation for future ski trips out to Uncle T's, I taught them how to properly face-plant into the sofa cushions.

Dixon is the birthplace of Ronald Reagan, a prairie town of 15,000. I was curious to bring my solo act to his somewhat conservative neighbors. "Do you want The Show, like I do it in Park City?" I asked my cop bro. "Or am I toning it down for the NRA crowd?"

"No, do your thing. We need it here."

My little brother's daily existence as a law officer is beyond my comprehension. You'd never guess we're related unless you saw us planted in front of a Bears game or sitting in front of Fox News, bitching in perfect harmony.

A club called Tipsy's was on the corner of Reagan Way, spitting distance from a big statue of Ronnie on a horse. Right next door to the county Democratic Party Headquarters with a big poster of Barack Obama in the window. They sneered at each other from across the street.

I had garnered some local pre-show press and a good chunk of the town made it out for my first night in Dixon. A bunch of my high school and even junior high friends made the hour drive out from the far 'burbs to catch up and shout nostalgic requests my way. The MILF-factor was high. Mingling before my first set, one semi-attractive cougar nearly threw me off my work game when she listed her last three concerts: Kid Rock, Jessica Simpson and Bon Jovi. I was out at "Kid" and told her so. To her credit, she looked up at me and said, "This isn't going to work out, is it?"

I began the evening with singable stuff, classic rock and a couple of newer hits: Eagles, Floyd, Killers, Kings of Leon. In between, it was observe and report. Having split the Midwest straight out of high school, I suppose I'd forgotten aspects of the culture I had grown up in. I was at a Bears game once and some guy turned slowly from the beer kiosk and said to no one, dreamily, "God I love Miller Lite." I never knew those words had ever intentionally been spoken in that sequence.

With folks filing in Tipsy's front door at stage left, I introduced myself again:

"Hey all, my name's Tony and I'm from Park City, Utah — a town for the thinkers and the drinkers. You guys look like the latter."

Asshole!

"I shall be your request whore for the night. Take care of our lovely servers here tonight. Give 'em an Andrew Jackson right between the boobs, willya? Hey, who does a sailor gotta blow to get a Lowenbrau in this place?"

Lowenbrau. Man, they just straight out told you that you were drinking crap. In reality, Dixon was rocking the Old Style. You can't get it west of the Mississippi, went the legend back in the day. Back in the age of Hamm's (the beer refreshing).

"No, sorry, I have no Stevie Ray Vaughan. Listen, that guy was a mutant. I'm a singer that plays *at* guitar. You don't want me butchering SRV the way you don't want a crappy singer attempting Journey."

"Some Journey then!" shouts a girl.

"Nope. I'm not getting paid enough to sing that high."

Dick!

A bundled couple walks in, looks up and smiles.

"Oh good, my heroin dealer's here!" I shot, to much giggles. My two comedic sacrificial lambs blushed and joined the crowd.

"Alright what was that? 'Jane Says' — perfect choice, young lady!"

Our set ended with my brother and sister in law slow dancing to "Purple

Rain" and I believed in love for six or seven minutes.

Later that night in his kitchen, Andy and I are recapping. He asks me, "You remember I said for a while I was having some issues with the new police chief? That couple that came in, the *heroin dealer*? That was him."

Oh shit.

"And we've had a big heroin problem here this year."

Homer says D'OH!

"It's alright. He thought you were really funny and he enjoyed it," Andy said.

- - - - - - - - - - -

A word of warning, then, to any potential opiate distributors in the Northwestern Illinois Tri-County area: the local authorities are not only extremely vigilant in regards to drug trafficking, but also quite enlightened regarding their taste in live acoustic entertainment.

THE THINGS WE DO FOR LOVE AND THE THINGS WE SHAVE FOR BONO

While most of humanity looks forward to New Year's Eve as a night of friends, parties and libations, for us working musicians December 31 is a happily anticipated cash cow. It's the one night a year we can charge what we wish, and most years, hold out for the best offer (for players in Utah that means which gig requires the least humping of equipment through the snow).

I received a call from the organizers of a new, three-day New Year's celebration in downtown Salt Lake that they were calling EVE. On a snowy, outdoor stage they had scheduled a Battle of the Tribute Bands, which I naturally thought was a brilliant idea. However, I hadn't competed in a "battle of the bands" since my last summer in Illinois in 1988, with Higgie and Hatz. That contest's winner was to be allowed an extra two songs after the judging. We walked off stage and I told the rural crowd "We'll be right back."

Ah, the hubris of youth.

By late 2009 our U2 tribute Rattle & Hum had garnered a small but tenacious following in Utah and promoter Chris was inquiring into our availability for EVE's contest. Tuesday the 29th would be the first round of three acts, with three more on Wednesday the 30th. The finals would be held on New Year's Eve with the winner taking $2000 in prize money. We had an offer pending for a Coverdogs NYE in Teton Village, Wyoming so committing to two shows — potentially gratis — was not really an option at that juncture. Factor in also that the nightly victors would be determined strictly by audience vote. This is usually what our circles refer to as a no-buy. One of my motivations in becoming a working cover musician was the happy objectivity in simply getting paid for performing. Being a "starving artist" ain't my bag. Fuck starving. So the arbitrary nature of the scenario being presented to me was rather unappealing. Besides, I was rocking some fantastic mutton shops at the time. A U2 tribute gig means a boy's gotta shave. *Damn you, Hewson!*

"Listen, Chris, thanks for the offer," I told EVE's organizer, "but I have to take the bird in the hand. But if you have a band cancel, and my private in Wyoming falls through? Sure, we'd love to do the U2 tribute downtown. Your event sounds like a blast."

Well sure enough, fast forward a month to Christmas week and Teton Coverdogs wasn't happening after all. EVE's Santana tribute had cancelled and Chris called me back. I pondered it for a few hours, seeing two nice silver linings to a potentially unpaid gig: Park City Productions (PCP) had just locked a Friday venue where we planned a rotation of shows, so our involvement would provide a simultaneous band-scouting session. Also we were a few months past our first outdoor festival, Utahpalooza, that September and the more I could glean from different events, the more PCP could streamline.

I checked the band's schedules, Cam moved around a date with the in-laws (because his hottie Puerto Rican wife ROCKS) and we set about the daunting task of choosing only five or six U2 songs from their thirty-year catalogue. I was disheartened to learn that we had the first slot, on the first night...

Oh, we get to play for a crowd that would be gradually arriving, through a sound system and crew likely still getting bugs out. Then, all bands are to gather on stage after the third group's set, and hope the audience that heard us is there to cheer when we're announced? *Yeesh.* I had better shift to booking mode and get to the talent-scouting duties. I'll start weeding out potential co-workers; I'd brought my digital camera and was ready to muti-task.

Our future co-worker options (and lack thereof) revealed themselves immediately as we set up backlines on a snowy and bitter downtown stage that Tuesday afternoon. Our U2 guys, a Stevie Ray Vaughan cover band, and a Beatle trib were trying to determine logistics: where are we striking the drum kit? Can the other bands just use our kit? Why don't the drum risers have wheels? All shit that had been prepared via email was now in disarray. The whole day was already behind schedule, certainly exacerbated by our wintry conditions. The quickest time-fix would have been to allow all three bands to just switch out cymbals and use Cameron's drums, which were already set up and mic'd...

But still fresh in my head was one July day when Rattle & Hum drove down to Vegas for a show at a Station Casino. We were booked north of The Strip, in a rougher part of town. It's one in the afternoon and Cam pulls his Saturn

SUV into the covered, video monitored parking garage. He locks up and heads in to find the showroom. Cam comes back ten minutes later to his windows smashed and his drum kit stolen. $3k plus, gone. I cringe to this day. The Stations' crew guys were pros as always, and had a house kit for Cam to use, but with EVE organizers glancing at Cam for a little help on this day, I wasn't about to press him for it.

The Beatle tribute's "Ringo" had just arrived with his drums and joined in the discussion while loading his kit on a second drum riser. "I don't know," I was telling the stage manager. "We'd like to get his kit, especially the drum heads, out of the snow after our set if possible." Ringo-guy had walked in pissy, and in want of direction, looks at me and starts barking, "What snow? There's no snow on the stage! What are you talking about? What are we doing here?"

Wait a second. I wasn't getting paid to sing, but I was also taking shit for free? Fuck it. That guy ain't using Cam's kit, I know that. And I won't be booking Angry Ringo at any *PCP Tribute Fridays*, either. I walked off stage and it began snowing again.

From across the parking lot I hear "Tony!" and I squint through the snow. Up walks the night's emcee, which as fate would have it, was Park City Television's afternoon host Ori Hoffer. We shook hands and I quoted him some Elbow lyrics:

> *"The fix is IN! The odds that I got were delicious!"*

Back in 2005 Ori and his PCTV crew spent a couple of weeks following me around to various gigs documenting many a costume change, and assembled a tasty little expose on my various alter egos. Only a few weeks before I'd been plugging some PCP shows on his *Mountain Views* show and chose the aforementioned Elbow tune for my live performance segment.

As EVE's speed bumps would dictate, there would be no soundcheck for Rattle & Hum. With a curious or viral media savvy few gathering, there we stood on stage doing a line check and pre-show logistical stuff in our U2 costumes. Chris gave the go and Ori warmed up a shivering audience, introduced us:

"Throughout history, man has paid tribute to their gods. Tonight, tomorrow and New Years Eve, we will pay tribute to the gods of ROCK! We start off today with Park City's own, Rattle & Hum!"

(cue respectable smattering)

Donned in leather with hair slicked back, I counted us off in Gaelic and it was "Vertigo" to start. "Elevation" had people pogo-hopping in place to the beat — if only to keep warm. Out of the corner of my eye, I nervously watched water and ice dripping onto electronics and sound gear while my Bono boots slid around the wet stage in a tenuous Peggy Fleming impression. Our twenty-five minutes were gone in no time, an orgy of hit singles which none of our tributing competition had to cherry-pick from, Beatle band obviously excepted.

In the early days of Rattle & Hum, playing street festivals around Los Angeles, the wide appeal of U2's catalogue made itself evident. I was initially surprised at the number of Hispanic families who clung to the front row, singing every lyric by heart. But Bono spent much of his career being vociferous about his Christianity. Therefore, in both Alhambra and Utah, I suppose I have Jesus to thank for much of our applause. We closed with "Where the Streets Have No Name," apropos to Salt Lake City where numbered avenues mark one's vicinity to God.

Then it was out into the gathering crowd to watch the SRV trio, whose Stevie Ray looked more like Geddy Lee (but Rush trib Roll the Bones plays tomorrow!) and then to geek out over Imagine from the front row. The latter Beatle tribute went mop-top era attire and after early hits surprised me with a Paul-vocal fave of mine, "She's a Woman." Apparently the audience was caught off guard as well. As I sang along with their NorCal-imported McCartney, everyone around me bopped politely but most were unfamiliar with that fantastic B-side to "I Feel Fine." Perhaps that momentum loss pushed our group over the Edge *(groan)* but while standing there to comparable U2 and Beatle applause, the judges conferred and called R&H the winner that day.

Perhaps the event organizers factored in my media whoring abilities, because not an hour after heading back up the hill I got a call from Chris: "Congrats! So, there's an opportunity that just came up for you guys."

Great! I thought. A corporate gig? A private party? What did Cuba say?

> *"Show me the money!"*

But no.

"Hey, we're going to do the KUTV morning show on Thursday, want to go on?"

Oh boy. Morning shows and live remotes. Warming up the vocals before dawn is zero fun, people. I had an acoustic gig with JB on Wednesday night, so it would be to bed at 2 AM and up three hours later.

"Let me check with the guys, Chris, but at the very least I can come on as Bono to help promote."

Well, The Kids and their bottomless well of enthusiasm were in. So NYE morning after a brief post-gig nap it was back into the Bono gear and down a snowy I-80 freeway to the TV station.

"What's your New Year's resolution, Bono?" morning anchor Ron asked me.

"To save the planet, of course."

Slugging down lattes, we hopped on bar stools and did a few commercial break lead-outs with unplugged U2 set: "I Still Haven't Found What I'm Looking For," "Desire," and "Angel of Harlem."

"Salt Lake like a Christmas tree, tonight this city belongs to me."

EVE's media rep Danica asked Cam and Phledge on a break, "So how long have you guys been together?"

"Oh, over two years or so." I giggled off camera behind him. Phledge is a lawyer and he's smart as hell, but his math was off by about seven years…

- - - - - - - - - - -

The seeds of Rattle & Hum came over sushi at Seoul International Airport in 2002. The Coverdogs had just completed another slot-machine funded weekend in Kunsan; it was incongruous to know our travel and pay was being covered by the little old Korean locals feeding their Won into video poker machines. U2 was close enough to my heart to be initially hesitant in embarking upon a Bono impression. Back in junior high, two clever girl friends of mine paid for a birthday message in the classified section of the Aurora Beacon News (the "Be-Confused"). It was a cute little poem which read, "You listen to your U2 tunes, but if you ask us, we think they're goons." If I recall correctly, these chicks were really into the Thompson Twins.

A few years later when the popularity of *The Joshua Tree* album was peaking, I noticed girls around my high school sporting U2 concert shirts. "You dig U2, really? Weren't you just wearing a Def Leppard shirt yesterday?" I asked.

"Oh I love U2! Well, except for their political stuff."

Grrrrr. I was incensed at their fleeting fancies.

However, the Gig Gods work in mysterious ways. My bandmates that day in Korea were also huge fans, and damned if two of the guys sitting across from me weren't spitting images of U2's Edge and Adam.

Full time, working tribute bands were just catching steam in Southern California, with the likes of Led Zepagain, Sticky Fingers and The Fab Four beginning to pack LA clubs and outdoor festivals. So we dove in, bringing in Egodog's producer Matt Chidgey for a two-camera video shoot. Street fairs in Tujunga soon became casinos in Vegas.

Fast forward three years to winter 2005, when a Park City restaurant manager, employing me solo every Friday, mentioned his younger brother having a Salt Lake-based U2 tribute band. The same way I blew off Higgie through years of my family's prodding, it took me several months to get in touch with Phledge and assemble our Rattle-Utah lineup.

"My drummer Cam is the kind of guy that can hear something once and nail it," Phledge bragged to me on the phone.

"Phledge, I don't need those guys. I need the guy that's gonna study his ass off." As it happens, Cam was both guys. He would later become not only a Coverdog, but a fellow Southern rocker, joining Mullet Hatchet as "In-Brad" and sporting a really creepy white trash moustache which his wife makes him shave before sex.

New Years Eve 2009: For the final round, R&H was up against a KISS and a Nirvana tribute, although I personally thought the Beatle band was our tightest competition. But full KISS makeup? Shit! Instant crowd pleaser! And the crowd was already dwarfing Tuesday night's. Our opening slot two days before had likely factored in our closing slot on New Year's Eve. The KISS band played first, then a four-piece Nirvana group — *no buy* on that front — hey if yesterday's Rush band can go it as a trio, so can these guys with Cobain's three-chord material.

Rattle was keeping warm in the backstage tent, and respectable contingents of our fans were outside, singing along to "Smells Like Teen Spirit." With Ori announcing us as the last band of the three-day series we hit the stage — now fortunately carpeted this night.

On this night "Streets" was our opener. We had discussed backstage our desire to focus less on the contest factor, and to enjoy being on a great stage in front of our hometown peeps. A holiday crowd, a beautifully organized event, downtown in a media glare — "City of Blinding Lights." These are the moments that counter all angst. That said, the Midwestern athlete in me has a very Michael Jordan-like competitive streak, and with my pipes warmed up I probably hit stage with a little extra give-a-shit. We sang "Mysterious Ways" to that evening's blue moon. I schmoozed the crowd:

"On June 5th, 1983 it was 38 degrees for U2 at Red Rocks in Colorado. But who's tougher? Those people or the people of UTAH?"

Sychophant!

"Beautiful Day" was next, into "Sunday Bloody Sunday," as anthemic a song as they come. Mid-guitar solo, I snuck behind the amps and grabbed our white "Sunday" flag which that night was signifying anything but a "Surrender."

> *"This is not a rebel song..."*

We waved our flags high and downtown Salt Lake wailed our disdain for 2009, for "Politicians!" If you are angry at your parents, scream "No more!" All was decidedly not quiet; we launched into "New Year's Day."

THANK YOU SALT LAKE CITY!

A few announcements by PCTV's Ori, and it was back on stage for the judging. Twelve costumed musicians, whooping up a happy crowd. The Nirvana band got some love. KISS guys got more. And in those boots? They're all a foot taller than us! Oh crap! Ori turned to Rattle on stage right, and I had ducked back to grab our white flag.

"And finally, from Park City, Rattle and HUM!"

I hoisted the flag and whipped it through the air while Phledge, Cam and Ty hammered it up. "And the winner is..."

Ok, maybe the flag sealed it for us. Or maybe our victory was preordained on live TV between 6 and 8 AM that morning. No matter, I went into the process with full knowledge of its ambiguity. But yes we'll take it, and to my band and I? *Gloria.*

That next week I'm behind the piano bar and the table to my left is asking for Beatles. They were from New Jersey and had just taken their two pre-teens to see a Beatle tribute up the street at Park City's Egyptian Theater. Yes, it was our friends Imagine. Their weekend's cut of a $20 ticket price quelled any angst I might have had about besting them at EVE.

"Oh they are great! I just shared a bill with them down in Salt Lake last week," I told the Jersey family. The nutty uncle lights up and says, "Hey are you in a U2 tribute? I just saw you guys on the news that morning!" And he began singing "Desire" at top volume.

Morning shows require *uber* effort but are usually worth their weight in promo. Back the previous St. Patrick's week R&H had an intense three-day run on the Vegas Strip, which included a morning live-remote on Las Vegas' NBC affiliate. The New York New York Hotel & Casino had set up a stage out on their Brooklyn Bridge, where the days would be filled with Irish clog dancers, tunes about beer and every Irish cliché imaginable (if I hear that Flogging Molly "Kiss Me" song one more time I'm going postal).

Rattle & Hum would close all three nights, Sunday, Monday and Tuesday (St. Patrick's Day) with three 1-hour sets. We'd also booked a 90-minute show down the Strip at Mandalay Bay for Tuesday afternoon, bringing our Irish New Years schedule over seven hours of performance time. I utilized every bit of my bel canto training, but by Wednesday morning, "Tono" had but a squeak left.

Sundance Film Festival 2008: If you've ever thought: Hey, let's drive up to Park City during Sundance and stargaze? Um... *don't.* For ten days each January, we live in Nowhere-To-Park City. Locals pay $75 for a ten day parking pass that doesn't guarantee you a spot, it just keeps you from being towed if you happen to find one. Just watch the highlights on E! from your couch in West Jordan. The Rattle & Hum crew and I circled the China Bridge garage for a good hour before finding spots and humping our gear through the snowy alleys to load in to The Sidecar Bar, located upstairs in the architecturally incongruous Main Street Mall.

As we approached the building, loaded down with amps, drums, and a big white flag, the local police was buzzing about, lights flashing. Some kid had broken into a second story business and stolen a big screen TV. I suppose he figured, in all the insanity of the festival, he could pull it off. His planning ostensibly went no deeper than that. He had jumped some ten feet, from the roof to the angled glass beneath, while lugging the big screen. He hit the glass, dropped the TV, bouncing another twelve feet to the ground below. And died.

Natural selection, baby.

The band set up on The Sidecar stage, located within arms reach of the crime scene outside. Main Street was slammed, and The Sidecar was wall to wall with visiting actresses, agents, aspiring filmmakers, and a healthy smattering of local U2 fans.

We changed into our Irish duds, hitting the stage with 80's and 90's sing-alongs. A few songs into the set, we were halfway through "Angel of Harlem" with the crowd in full sing-along crescendo.

At that very moment, BLACK.

And SILENCE... The power had gone.

We peered out the huge windows, and we weren't alone. All of Main Street was dark. The crowd upstairs with us groaned for a second, then exploded in childlike glee. *Hey, our parents aren't watching!*

Phledge and I stepped out from behind our impotent microphones and continued the song acoustically then continued in the darkness with "I Still Haven't Found What I'm Looking For" and the room sang along at top volume.

When the lights came back up, everyone moaned in surprise. I heaved a sigh of relief for our beloved Mayor/musician Dana Williams, who along with Summit Country officials would doubtlessly be taking a ton of shit for the shortcomings of our humble infrastructure. Hey, give us a break. CNN is on the corner satellite-feeding and sucking all our juice!

"Desert T's Island" CDS

The Beatles - Abbey Road

The last pre-breakup Beatle release was actually
Let It Be in May of 1970, but Abbey Road
was recorded after those cold and miserable
Twickenham Get Back sessions. Abbey Road was
last time the post-Fab Four behaved and played
nice together. George Harrison and Martin were
at their creative peak. Frank Sinatra, however,
wrongly credited John and Paul for composing
"The greatest love song ever written" - "Something."
Aww, George always got the shaft! And just when
Paul's side two medley couldn't get any cooler?
Ringo solo!

U2 - The Unforgettable Fire

"Pride" was this album's hit, but its title track
and "Wire" are just silly-good. A youthful Bono just
wailed his ass off. The Brian Eno production
dripped of melancholy.

Altered State - DOS

"I walked a mile with pleasure and she left me none
the wiser, I walked a mile with sorrow, and oh the
things I learned from her."

The music, produced by Ben Grosse, is equally
brilliant. They lost their collective minds on this
unappreciated masterpiece. Also worth investigating,
their erstwhile guitarist Christian Nesmith -
another brilliant cat hearing crazy shit in his head

T's "Desert Island" CDS

Catherine Wheel - Chrome

Unconventional arrangements go from whispers to roars, and this album absolutely flowers after a few listens, a sensory onslaught, perhaps my favorite album to ski to. Just mountaintop EPIC. Chrome is also a fave of prodigy/local artist Lionel (vinyl) williams, son of Mark (Air Supply, CSNeY), nephew of Joe (Toto), and grandson of John (Star Wars, Close Encounters, Indiana Jones, Jaws...)

I beseech my readers - if you seek out one artist in this book previously unknown to you, make it vinyl williams.

Radiohead - In Rainbows

As with most Radiohead records, the opening track is perhaps the least orthodox, then "Bodysnatchers" pushes rock to a new place entirely.

The Best Band on the Planet, if there is one. Rock as art, truly. Yes, I paid them £10 for the "free" download.

COVER-ING LOS ANGELES

I wasn't a gun guy when I lived in LA. But there was one week when I really wished I had more gangsta in me.

Spring 1992: I was living in Los Feliz, just east of Hollywood. Pretty Spanish style mini-castles nestled at the woody feet of Griffith Park. Dinner at Louies', where Big Bad Voodoo Daddy was making a scene at The Derby next door. Then down to The Dresden for drinks and snarky observations above the musical stylings of Marty and Elayne, exactly as they would appear in *Swingers*.

I was at the tail end of a few years working for a battery store out in the dreaded West Valley, selling computer backup systems over the phone and installing car batteries out in the beaten-up parking lot. I'd been somewhat stranded out in Canoga Park as penance from The Universe following a nasty breakup that required trips up to Ventura County and back on my red Nighthawk 650. The commute was always a drag because in Los Angeles no time or place is immune from congestion. Many years in LA saw a motorcycle as my sole means of transportation. This made for more enjoyable scenery, especially when skirting Mulholland Drive on a crystal perfect California morning. However, dodging old Armenian women lost in their cell phone conversations often proved hairy (no pun intended) and one winter saw me strapping paper shopping bags to my tennis shoes for the ride through many an El Nino downpour. Good times.

But 29 April was bright and sunny — until Los Angeles was set literally on fire. The Rodney King verdict had been handed out to my west in Simi Valley, and LA violently exploded in both civil indignation and petty opportunism. Reginald Denny's brutal beating and his attackers' subsequent celebration put a big ugly dagger in those idealistic "people are generally good" platitudes. Long-victimized business owners had their stores set ablaze for no reason. Looters loaded themselves down with TV sets, microwave ovens and diapers. But by and large, this was not a socio-economically oppressed populous exacting revenge or expressing frustration. It was a pack of scurrying rats, grabbing cheese from an unguarded ship's hold.

The centers of the rioting were primarily to my south, in the basin over the Hollywood Hills. But out in Canoga Park looters and dirtbags were seizing the day, and when a liquor store two blocks down Sherman Way was robbed at gunpoint, my manic French boss Didier pulled me aside. Dee rode my ass pretty steadily around Battery Specialists, but he generally had my back. He handed me a tiny .22 and shooed me off home back to Los Feliz across The Valley. It was usually about an hour on the motorcycle and I packed away my little girly gun, making a run to the hills. I decided to take Mulholland, conjecturing that I'd encounter the least resistance on that route, be it traffic or thug-related.

What I hadn't counted on, however was the view. When I got atop Coldwater Canyon and peered over into Los Angeles a thick gray ceiling of smoke met me at eye level as far as I could see. Columns of flame and smoke stretched upward forming a huge ominous temple across the skyline while helicopters would periodically dart in and out of the hellish clouds.

I really could have used some water or a Gatorade but I thought twice about stopping into any convenience stores — it's always convenience stores hosting drama on the evening news, even on non-riot days. Who knew what flock of losers would be lurking today. I rode under the 101 Freeway at Gower and in thick, black spray paint someone had written: "LAPD — GUILTY!" That very next day, with many buildings and businesses still ablaze, that sentiment had been painted right over in white. Quickly and quietly.

- - - - - - - - - - -

On 12 May 1997 I composed a letter for the head of City National Bank's Human Resources Department, informing them of my departure and giving my two weeks' notice. Following the battery gig, I had worked at CNB for over four years, donning a necktie and pulling back my ponytail. I worked in the file room and ran the place efficiently as hell if I do say so myself. Being a bank catering to the entertainment industry, they allowed my rotation of varied late-90's goatees and supported fully my musical endeavors. But my live and session work around LA was rapidly increasing and I needed more time to focus on what I'd been trained to do.

At some point, you've gotta make that leap.

My co-workers were great people and I remained friends with a handful of the crew from the Beverly Hills Head Office. In time I would grow to miss the parade of celebrity drop-bys, including Little Richard's Friday visits to the safe deposit vault, heavy in makeup with a posse of boy-toys in tow. "Tutti Fruitti!" His role in rock and roll history is monumental and his guest rap on Living Colour's second album is just perfect. "Elvis is dead!"

On one of my daily file runs I pushed my cart onto the elevator and turned in awed respect to the older Brit standing next to me.

"You're Chris Squier from Yes," I said. He looked to be surprised by this recognition whilst running his errands but I kept my exchange at a short props. His reaction was genuine and stately in that first generation English Rock Star way.

Doing the 9 to 5 at California's largest independent bank — a financier of many a lucrative movie and album — provides many opportunities for schmoozing. Most of those opportunities should not be taken, mind you, as one former loan officer will attest. He fancied himself a songwriter and while working peripherally on a loan for a film in pre-production he obtained some personal information for high-powered music exec David Geffen. This moronic co-worker of mine proceeds to write a long, creepy letter describing a dream he had in which he was directed to get his music to Mr. Geffen, and get it to him immediately. He was just as immediately fired from City National Bank.

Living and networking in Los Angeles requires a precarious balance of letting people around you know what you do, opening possible doors, but conversely never pushing too hard when meeting people you admire. Karla was working at Castle Rock Entertainment during the early seasons of *Seinfeld* and we attended many functions with big hitters like founders Rob Reiner and Alan Horn, the latter of which held a Castle Rock anniversary party one evening at his Brentwood home. We were introduced briefly in the foyer upon our arrival, and I was impressed when he remembered my name much later in the night. The *Seinfeld* cast, Elaine-hubby Christopher Guest, and an amazing circle of comedians mingled around the pool. Between *Saturday Night Live* and *Spinal Tap* circles, my head was swimming with my immediacy to the people who have influenced me so. Karla and I had a brief hello with Jerry Seinfeld, but you don't go hawking off a fucking demo tape to the reigning King of Comedy at a backyard industry party.

City National Bank, its Head Office smack in the middle of Beverly Hills, held a hodgepodge of employees from all around Los Angeles: beach bums from The South Bay and Santa Monica, nouveau riche housewives from Glendale, rock musicians from The Valley, and Bruthas from Inglewood.

Big John worked with us down in the Credit Dept., interned in the basement of the eight-story headquarters. We were somewhat autonomous down there and often served as an unofficial break area for the loan officers upstairs who would hang for some bank gossip with us while they ran down to pick up a file or two. John's desk positioned by the door served as the most gregarious welcoming committee to our guests. It was always, "Hi, sweetheart! How you doin' today darlin'?" Always sincere, even to our most dreaded of office-world enemies. Enter: Loan Officer Amy. Strutting in and plopping herself down next to a smiling and accommodating John. It was Superbowl Week, and she extolled the virtues of her favorite team, the San Francisco 49ers. Hmm. Last season Dallas was in the Superbowl and I explicitly recall the Cowboys being "her" team. She gets up and says goodbye to John, and I pull up her still warm chair at John's desk.

"How do you do that?"

"Do what?" John asked.

"You just let her spew that bullshit, when you see it just as well as I do."

"Well bra," he broke it down for me. "Everybody in my world has a file. Shit they've said, shit they do. When Amy comes in and sits down, I just open up her file. I remember what she's about, I close the file, and then there she is and it's all good." John looked like The Buddah. His advice was sage.

Big John taught me much about his culture that Aurora, Illinois couldn't. He also tried to teach me how to play basketball. That didn't work out. One Monday morning he bounced in — which at his girth was amusing — and I asked him how his weekend went.

"Aw bra, it was great! Had me a colonic!"

A WHAT?

"A colonic. Yeah they just clean you right out, you gotta try it some time." He explained the process. *Yikes*. How 'bout I just shine the daily barbecue and skip the middleman? I'll stick to my trail mix, thanks!

It was my birthday and John planned a treat for me at lunchtime. Big John never called out my Caucasian-ness but on that afternoon we ran to the liquor store and he bought me my first malt liquor. Woah, baby! We retreated up to the upper lever of our parking garage and on a hot August LA day I popped me a Colt 45. *Jesus, Johnny! Where's the fucking pancakes?* It was a fine and thick introduction to stimuli I hadn't yet known and by the time we headed back down to the basement I was a wee bit sloppy. Our cute little supervisor Cheryl wandered down to our department just as I was departing for my 1 PM file run and I wobbled in front of her trying to make small talk. Delivering files while intoxicated: a possible misdemeanor?

Lucy was an older Black woman, a little grumpy but all right to work with in our little file room. She was sitting next to me one morning, cross-legged, and I found myself studying the curious patterns of her stockings. She was wearing a skirt and the patterns on her hose were rather haphazard and... *oh.* That's not a fashion design. Lucy just didn't dig on the razor.

Craig was a tall and athletic colleague. We discussed Marvel comics and weightlifting. Craig was deeply and sadly in The Closet and our office danced lightly around his attempts to throw us off the scent. We didn't give a shit, really. We liked him, but it's difficult to become friends with someone who's so busy keeping up a façade. Perhaps, had he more real friends in whom to confide, Craig would have been less reckless in his personal life. Shortly after I left the bank in April of 1999 Craig died of AIDS complications, aged only 30 years.

- - - - - - - - - - -

My last years at CNB saw me dipping my toes in local San Fernando Valley-based cover bands. Most were competent, consisting of fantastic players like Jason Hook, later of AM Radio with Higgie, and ex-Dio axe-man Rowan Robertson. Rowan is a sweet, diminutive Irishman with humility incongruous to his heavy metal resume. One Friday night we had a little bar gig up in Ventura. After a drag of a drive, Row arrived late from his recording session. The band was on the makeshift stage assuaging the nervous club owner when Rowan raced through the door and plugged in. We had been starting our Friday night sets with Stevie Ray Vaughan's "Pride and Joy." But when Rowan turned up we all realized that although we'd been gigging with our guitars tuned down 1/2 step (a common trade trick amongst vocalists), Row's session had been in standard tuning, one half-step up from us. "Just go,"

Rowan said, aware of a waiting dance floor and bar management. We did GO, and I cannot explain to non string-instrumentalists how difficult a task it is, transposing that guitar voicing on the spot. But had I closed my eyes, I never would have known the gymnastics that cat was pulling off.

My SoCal cover band histories had less glorious stints, with less gifted players. I hacked away weeknights in a garage studio in Reseda with a band that found me through mutual circles. They were already named The Milk Crate Thieves and I was thus, fucked. Apparently there was a clever anecdote regarding their moniker — which couldn't have been that clever or I'd have remembered it. What I do remember is learning a very crucial musician equation: the rehearsal-to-gig ratio. For the number of shows the bassist/garage owner lined us up, there were far too many post-day shift rehearsals for my liking. Take also into account my inability to dig the material. The Thieves were all about Seattle and its numerous remora rip-off acts. A few of those vocalists were challenging for me to imitate, but generally the arrangements were meandering and the hooks were non-existent. "Cumbersome?" Indeed.

En route across Los Angeles in my beat-to-hell Subaru, I studied bands I didn't give a shit about. From a 6 AM workout with lifting partner Jorge at Gold's North Hollywood to my eight hour shift at the bank over Coldwater Canyon, then straight to rehearsals smack in the middle of The Valley. One evening, with my schedule in dire need of some fat trimming, I arrived at their garage studio and the bassist pulled me aside. "Can I ask you something?" he said.

Oh GOOD, I thought. Now I'm going to get the bandleader's "We're not seeing a lot of enthusiasm from you" speech. And I was indeed re-focusing priorities in my head.

"Sure, what's up?" I said, probably with an annoyed sigh.

"Well, um… can you tell I wear a wig?"

My eyes darted undiplomatically yet inevitably upward at his head. Which I'd always thought was just covered by bleached out ex-80's rocker hair. But… now that I think about it. And look at it. Well…

"No. No I couldn't," I told him.

Sometimes you have to cut a cat a break.

Soon it was *kaput* for The Milk Crate Thieves and all that grunge tripe. A few years later while stuffing bubblemailers at Polygram Publishing I had the chance to meet Kevin Martin, the singer of Candlebox. Although I couldn't sing you one of his songs if you put a gun to my head, mimicking his vocal performance had gained my respect and I told him so. Candlebox would play Salt Lake City's Gallivan Center in 2008 and although mine was one of their opening acts for a radio-sponsored event called Viva SLC, I didn't bother saying hello backstage. Perhaps because I was wearing snakeskin spandex and leather chaps?

- - - - - - - - - - -

Burbank Bar and Grille in my waning SoCal years was a little hub of musician circles, despite most players' animosity toward management. The pay at BBG was weak and the manager could be abrasive. Then again, he did have an intolerance of bands starting late, finishing early, and taking 45-minute breaks. You know, the little things.

BBG was my first steady solo acoustic gig and helped sustain me between overseas tours. There's a lovely little patio out back of the club with a tiny stage in the corner. I hung out between sets with local guitarist Doug Aldrich who would soon land the slot with Whitesnake and hit the road blazing for David Coverdale.

"I don't know where I'm goin', but I sure know where I've been..."

My solo set would finish up right before the guys in the production show hit the inside stage, clad in wigs and polyester.

I was shaking off the taste of the semi-competent cover and original hard rock bands I'd been "working" with. I planted myself on a bar stool, delving deep into The Beatles' catalogue, chatting with customers a few feet away and sprinkling in a stupid joke or two. In the long entertainment shadows of NBC, Warner Brothers and Walt Disney, I began dipping my toes into the "AcouSchtick."

Ok so at this point many of my readers are growing impatient. You know these people. They can tell the Kardashians apart. Right now they're going, *"Hey man, we're at chapter 11. We were expecting a tawdry rock and roll tell-all and what are you giving us — Beatle songs and BOSNIA? Even the 'Joan' story had ZERO details! Give us something, man!"*

Well firstly they probably wouldn't use "tawdry" and secondly, if I correctly recall that night in Champaign, I was a bad lay. So joke 'em if they can't take a screw.

Anyway here you go, folks. If you're under 18 or a blood-relative of mine, kindly skip ahead a few chapters…

UFO PABLUM AND GLOVE THE ONE YOU'RE WITH

FM Station on Lankershim Boulevard was, for a while, *the* club for Sunset Strip refugees in the San Fernando Valley. There, local rock legends like the Bang Tango and Atomic Punks cut their teeth. Very accessible to those of us living in Burbank. You can still get ripped on for claiming the 818, you know. Christ, LA. Really. Get over yourselves.

SOMA, a side project of then-Uberdeath drummer Rick Renza was "showcasing" at Filthy McNasty's place up in North Hollywood. Yes, the club's owner's name was Filthy McNasty. Showcasing essentially means playing a weeknight slot to nobody. We invited as many industry people as we knew (which weren't many) and the ones that wouldn't piss off Rick's lead singer (even less) and the next day apparently our set was all the buzz around the Capitol Records building. Which gives my career, to the best of my knowledge, exactly one day of "Major Label Interest."

Whether Uberdeath's drummer was genuinely invested in SOMA those few months or whether he was just trying to rattle his capricious boss, I'm still unsure. He did hook us up a recording session with their producer who had a respectable 80's metal resume. I thought we would record a proper demo, laying down the songs (see rather: riffs with singing on top) that we had accumulated. But instead, it was techno-playtime for our producer and his still new and exciting cut-and-paste digital recording software. Indeed, the final mix sounded nothing like the tune we walked in with. The pre-chorus was trimmed and put here, the verses became choruses there. Call me old school, but the best songs are usually the ones that are written long before you hit the *record* button. The Beatles "played around" in the studio only after they knew how to write a fucking hook.

Also adding to my angst was the fact that these guys were obsessed with aliens. They had replaced the lyrics I'd prepared, forcing me to sing about Area 51 and faces on Mars, through gritted teeth.

So Producer Man is about two or three takes into our vocal track, and he's just not digging it in the least. I was countering the array of distorted guitar and washy drum tracks with my best hard rock wailing at top volume.

"Right. But can you go lighter? Nobody wants to hear singers like you right now," he tells me from the control room.

Wait. This guy has to listen to Uberdeath's "singer" caterwauling for hours at a time, and he's telling me what *the kids today* want to hear? Fine. He's got the resume.

"Ok. What are you thinking, I'll give it a shot."

"I'm thinking more like John Anderson from YES," he instructs.

YES???

You're kidding me, right? No one has gotten laid to a YES song in decades!

Nevertheless I gave the man what he wanted. Which was incongruous as hell. But that day I also realized SOMA wasn't for me. In fact, I soon took the master 2-inch tape of an original song I'd brought to the band, and with the help of guitar wiz Christian Nesmith I went back in studio to re-record everything but the rhythm section. The old guitar track was self-indulgent to the point of nausea. When there's a faded-in guitar trill before the drums even count in, well then I'm OUT! Christian heard this too, and just crinkled his nose and nodded at me. "I gotcha. No problem. Hit *record* and I'll do a few runs, tell me what you like."

Good players just *know*. The song didn't call for John Sykes or Steve Vai. It screamed for Stevie Ray Vaughan. Christian provided. Surely being the son of a respected and brilliant artist (certainly no mere dancing Monkee) provided a young Christian with a vast array of musical influence. Recently he even took a stint with soft-rock veterans Air Supply. You can't do that kind of gig without the ability to play "for the song." On the other hand, SOMA's guitarist apparently listened to nothing that didn't go *biddly biddly biddly* really fast. Rock guitarists, like too many female pop/R&B singers often miss the fact that busier isn't always better. Shut the fuck up sometimes.

Rick had invited some call girls to the FM Station show. Sometimes we have classy circles. One girl in particular wasn't atrocious to look at, and she asked me for a motorcycle ride back to the after party at Rick's Valley Village house. I should've asked her more about being a true working girl. But then again, who wants the ghost of that conversation mid-erection? We drank and briefly mingled then snuck upstairs. She was far from Tori Amos (a longtime crush of mine) but sometimes when life hands you lemons? There's just gonna be some suckin'. Besides, the idea of getting head from someone who literally gets paid for it was frankly enticing. Finding a bedroom, playtime went straight to the floor — I do have respect for a guy's linens after all. I'll skip the Penthouse Forum-isms and keep this allegorical for the kiddies. But let us say only — *this poor woman was drowning and my personal snorkel was her only means of survival.* We're all lucky I was there.

At one point the guitarist — who had already failed to endear himself to me musically — decides it'd be a hoot to bust in and snap a photo. That pic is probably out there somewhere. Just give me my residuals, pal. If you're gonna do porn, a muthafucka's gotta get REAL PAID!

For the record, I have discovered there's actually a gay Latin porn star named Tony Oros. I found him on YouTube while Googling myself, as all entertainers occasionally do (not as an "exercise in narcissism," as many an ex-girlfriend has accused). But, anyway, that other guy is out there. Oh he's *out there*.

Incidentally, Uberdeath drummer Rick apparently did meet Tori Amos at some event or show once. I expressed my admiration for her work to Rick while he feigned indifference to the meeting. As I imagined a short, one-sided exchange between them I thought: This is exactly the kind of guy Tori Amos would absolutely *destroy*.

Rick always had pistachios in bulk. The band mingled in his kitchen, sucking down Coronas. Once I asked him where his recycling bin was located. He scoffed, "Ppft! YOU save the planet."

Charming.

Besides, dipshit — if you're right and I'm wrong and there *are* little grey men running around down here, shouldn't you tidy up for 'em a bit?

Idiots.

HAIR BAND ERSATZ AND THE BEST LINE HEARD MID-COITUS

The BongBoys gig came to me via player circles in the San Fernando Valley. Their debut album was one of my few pop-metal guilty pleasures way back in my Musicians Institute days. Late 80's *testostro-rock*. The lead singer's pipes were bluesy and fantastic. Produced by a respected hard rock veteran (not SOMA's), there was melody and groove all over that record.

One autumn about a decade after their peak, BongBoys' drummer *du jour* Paulie asked if I knew of anyone who might be interested in their recently re-vacated bass guitar slot. "Maybe," I told him. I did know one or two possibilities, and I made the calls. "But if you need a third option, I could always do it." Sure enough? No one else was available. I would soon discover why. Thus began my brief yet colorful tenure as bassist for The BongBoys.

· · · · · · · · · · ·

Chris Rock once said, "You can 'asshole' your way out of show business."

The first BongBoys single had been a huge MTV hit in the 80's, and the whole West Coast scene was blowing smoke up their ass. But when their second record was released, its first video wasn't getting many spins. One night at an industry event, lead singer Marky was skulking around the party, livid. Furious about some vague and perceived "disrespect," he approached an MTV executive — a big one. As Marky launched into a finger pointing and expletive-ridden assault on the stoic exec, the other BongBoys raced over with mouths agape in horror, "Like we were underwater in slow motion watching our careers ending right before our eyes!" When their vocalist had finished his tirade he was calmly informed: "As long as I work here, MTV will never play another one of your videos again."

BongBoys were booked as one of three co-headliners at a retro show at The Galaxy Theatre in Santa Ana, California. A night of three buttrock B-lister bands doing their hit. Or two. We were still a few years away from full-blown 80's nostalgia, but the room was capacity with Orange County mullets and bang-claws. Cheese never dies — a fact I would embrace and exploit in Salt Lake City a few years later.

That Galaxy gig was a blast. After years of lead singer/MC duties, I was pleased to find how enjoyable it is simply being the bassist — no addressing the crowd, no dealing with promoters, press, or stage managers. Prior to soundcheck I got my first taste of my frontman Marky's particular strain of LSD — Lead Singer Disease — when he discovered we only had time for a line check and not a proper, putz-through-a-few-songs soundcheck.

"That's bullshit bro!"

Pissed or happy, everything from this guy was "bro," I soon came to find. Many a rock musician will address you as "bro" — right before they stab you unceremoniously in the back.

"We get a full soundcheck, bro!"

Ever see a grown man pout? Good times. My initial political instincts tempted me to approach our just-blindsided stage manager and try to smooth things over but I quickly came to my senses in a liberating jolt of revelation: *Not my problem!* So I watched Marky burn yet another in a succession of countless bridges while I fell contentedly into my role as the new and anonymous bassist for The BongBoys.

"Wow, what happened to Lenny?" the kid from the local opening band asked me after soundcheck. From the outset, I knew that playing stupid was the smartest modus operandi. Yet Marky was so vociferous in his denunciation of former band members that I quickly became privy to more band history than I wanted or needed.

"I dunno man," I answered the kid politely as I could muster. "I'm just happy to be playing bass."

Backstage after the show people were eating and hanging about while I was mingling with the more interesting people in my head.

One rather dweeby guy was on a couch, regaling stories about his recent birthday party/debacle: "Man it was crazy. I'd invited two of my chicks by mistake." He had two young long-hairs completely rapped. "They ended up fighting over who was gonna take me home that night!"

I'm over in the corner thinking who IS this schmuck? I won't give you his name, but it does rhyme with Rokken. People that really dig on his band are by and large guitar players. Or people who think it's brilliant to rhyme *fire* with *desire*.

Meanwhile Marky was jumping around in the band room.

"Fuck yeah! Wooo!" Marky hoots in post-gig euphoria. "That was the best set in years!" He started in about announcing the "new lineup" and issuing press releases and such. I was silently inventing possible pseudonyms so as to distance myself from the dark karma politics of the BongBoy circles.

"And they didn't expect me to whip my shirt off, huh hon?" His wife nodded in rote agreement. Apparently Marky had spent a few recent years battling a little weight issue and worked hard to take it back off. Props on him, truly. Only problem was, unless you really followed the band closely through the underground 80's metal press you wouldn't have known the lead singer of The BongBoys had gone through a *fat phase*. All we saw was a guy taking his shirt off who shouldn't have. After my fill of cheap pretzels, Bud Light cans and banalities, I began wandering the theatre.

There was a burgeoning circle of us working players back in the mid-90's filling in with hair bands whose original members just couldn't play nice anymore. We were in tight spots — a hot girl says "Oh I LOVE that song!" and what's a boy to do? We can't accept the credit. But we can accept the blowjob.

So I found myself with one of the two or three Black girls in the room. Long hair, beautiful face, rail-thin — ok sue me, I know what I dig. We drank and attempted what some people might call conversation. Then *fuckit,* it was out to her car — a tiny little Mazda or some logistically impossible piece of shit. Apparently at some juncture my physical discomfort showed, or perhaps I was working things too Caucasianally. But she throws her pretty head back and groans, "Fuck me. Fuck me like you're never gonna see me again!"

And some eight-to-ten seconds later? *So it was.*

The BongBoys and I did some one-off shows in LA and road tripped to places like Bakersfield and Fresno, passing billboards warning of God's imminent wrath. The scene at one desert roadhouse was decidedly *basura blanca*. You could almost smell the crank in the air as I navigated my way back to the makeshift dressing area. Sprawling between two dirty back rooms, the band spread out and tried to kill time before downbeat. Having invited a girl from Las Vegas to attend, I was the lone soldier out amongst the crowd, attentively watching the entrance in a growing hope that she had *not* made the trip. In our backstage area the local rabble, pseudo bouncers and hangers-on coaxed road stories and dirt out of frontman Marky.

Jay was on guitar and one-liners. Some kid was bouncing around backstage, grilling him about what brands and models of gear he uses. "I don't care, man. All I want to know is who's blowing me and where's my vodka tonic?"

Short of chairs, Jay and a few local mullets sat on the filthy all-weather carpeting, leaning against the storage room wall. When a club employee came back bearing a request by a local girl to come backstage, Jay immediately piped up his approval.

"I gotta warn you man," Jay is admonished by the clearly grimacing messenger.

"Sure, why not?" he answers as I turn to make my escape. *Why not, Jay?* Because you weren't out there scouting the room.

"Alright. But I did warn you!" The kid was smiling now, anticipating the impending horror show. When I stuck my head back in the room not five minutes later, there she was — speeded up and overweight, skin pasty to the point of varicosity — squatting over an appalled Jay with her skirt hiked up and her goodies but inches from his face. Be careful what you ask for. Be terrified of what you agree to.

In naive enthusiasm I had agreed to a week-long jaunt through the Midwest with Marky and his BongBoys. The brief tour went badly by any standards. I immediately knew it would be a rough week when the drama ensued upon landing at Chicago O'Hare. Someone at the car rental counter had again "disrespected" singer Marky. This was a repeating theme. In the weeks prior to departure I had volunteered to swap flights and utilize my own ticket to return to Los Angeles after my visit, thereby saving everyone a few bucks. It was agreed that would put a little more cash in the band's pockets. But at a diner in Parma, Ohio I was foolish enough to mention the aforementioned exchange and ask Marky what the current pay figure was at. Paulie later said he "Saw it coming and waited for the shit to hit."

"I'm not screwing you, BRO!" our singer screams, as horrified Buckeye diners look on.

Eeeeasy, punchy! I'm only going by what I was told. Note to self: no more verbal agreements in these circles. And needless to say, no leftover travel monies ever came. I was zen with it all, even despite getting hammered for a $90 speeding ticket racing through upper Michigan the day before (also never recouped). We were trying to get from the Upper Peninsula down to Cleveland for that night's show. Note to tour booker: Any reason we didn't do the gig in Lansing first? Then head down to Ohio? I had just experienced similar logistic stupidity through Norway with my band, Egodog.

I really didn't mind driving that morning. Northern Michigan is beautiful in the fall and I hadn't been back in the Midwest during autumn since I'd moved to LA more than a decade before. On the Walkman I had The Beatles' *Rubber Soul* and Hall & Oates' *Voices* (awesome album — *awesomely gay* album cover!) and the band was sleeping quietly behind me. I saw the cherries behind us and our fearless leader begins mumbling, "Fucking cops. I hate fucking cops. Fuck this, fucking that..."

Oh GOOD. But that was Marky. "The Man is always fucking keeping me down cause I have brown skin." *Lighten up, Francis.* You're a Puerto Rican rock singer. You just look well tanned.

Our venues were small clubs, which do little to sooth an already long-wounded, arena-sized ego. The club owners are treated with disdain and bad vibes were never far from surfacing. From unsuccessfully chasing down non-existent strippers that he knew from *back in the day* to being left out of some Lansing after party, myriad situations gave rise to rock star-sized shit-fits.

A few days into the week I decided I'd be done at tour's end. Our last gig was out in suburban Chicago, one town away from my family in Aurora. Marky and I had butted heads from day one but on the final drive from Akron, Ohio I was piloting the rented AstroVan and Marky was spewing orders to the effect of *get me to the next hotel NOW!* Informing him I would be staying with my peeps following that evening's show and seeing them all beforehand, he countered firmly that it was to be hotel first. *Do not pass GO. Do not collect*

$100.

"But Elgin is way out of our way," I argued. "My family is about 10 minutes off I-88." As we approached the Aurora and Elgin off ramps I was getting the distinct feeling my plan was meeting resistance. Half-drifting off in the passenger seat, Marky would curtly counter any mention of a pit stop with his absolute need to reach the hotel room post-haste. At present, however, I was driving.

"Is this the way to Elgin?" He asked as I exited Orchard Road.

"Yeah. This is the off ramp." That seemed to mollify him and he leaned back against the window, closing his eyes again. Some three minutes later Marky voiced more doubts about our direction, caught my intentions, and went off:

"Bro, we are NOT going to your family's. Stop the car!"

So I did. Right in Lew and Hesh's driveway.

Putting the truck in park, I headed inside for a quick hug or two, then back outside carrying a map. My poor unsuspecting Grandfather, while knowing I was coming, had no idea of the politics currently a brew in his driveway. He had gotten used to the Four Musketeer dynamics of my previous bands, all of whom at one point or another had been over for Hesh's cooking and hospitality (Egodog's McLefty still raves about beefsteak tomatoes from their garden). Lew wanted to come out to the truck, say hi to "the guys" and give directions to nearby Elgin. I stopped him short and promised to explain later. I returned to the truck, found a disgruntled Marky in the driver's seat, and handed the map over. "Here ya go, pal! We went about a mile and a half out of the way. And in the end, you got a smaller room and saved a few bucks."

Marky was back in the driver's seat. I was planning my impending desertion.

That night about half a dozen friends and family came out for the show, which was as usual, tons of fun. On stage, the four of us just grooved. It was really enjoyable. And ultimately, a shame.

Afterwards, amidst the post-gig back-patting, Marky and I had the little pow-wow he'd obviously been scripting since that afternoon. He was aware of my growing Defense Department touring resume and began with: "Hey bro. In this situation there's one person calling the shots. So you'll just have to see me as your superior officer and not question my orders. Or else we can't work together."

"Yeah. I guess we can't," I countered. I had figured as much in Parma.

Fuck you very much... *Sir!*

For the record, my bass playing on that tour was largely for shite. Then again, so were the drama and the pay. The universe balances itself.

THE GODFATHER

Late 1990's: I was recording in Simi Valley, California with Disco Show bassist Matt Chidgey. Matt's recent brainchild was the 80's Geek Show — four grown men in pocket protectors and golf pants playing Cyndi Lauper and Duran Duran tunes. An absolute riot. Chidgey was also a brilliant engineer with one of the best ears I've ever known.

People will tell you, "Oh I listen to everything."

No you don't. Matt did.

In his chaotic strip-mall recording studio, Chidgey let me and my guitarist/co-songwriter McLefty take the reigns while indulging our musical whims and anticipating our every request. His production skills and objectivity made Egodog a much better band than it deserved to be. It took many of us years to discover Matt had a physics degree from California State University, Northridge.

Matt was always busy as hell. McLefty and I squeezed in recording time when Matt was able. He would arrive late and stumble through the studio door in unmatched stocking feet. On the mixing console there were un-cashed checks for, at times, thousands of dollars. They were from playing in polyester-and-platform disco shows. We were intrigued.

McLefty and I weren't alone in our curiosity and admiration. Chidgey presided as a guru to many a musician/entertainer. He was the hub of many circles. He was The Godfather. He taught us how to be clowns and could drink anyone in any band under the table. My first "Irish Car Bomb" came courtesy of The Chidg. He cut his production-show teeth playing disco gigs around LA when few of us had the balls to put on a wig.

When I'd had enough of my Metal Show bassist six years into our Thursday Salt Lake stint (2008) my first call was to Matt. He was doing a Vegas weekly and was unavailable for the Utah gig but he recommended a young player named Dave who brought sorely needed good vibes up to Utah. For all our recording history, I had only performed live with Matt Chidgey once, at McLefty's wedding. Matt brought the Disco Show. I joined in on Kool and the Gang's "Celebration," happily channeling my Pops' old wedding band gigs.

- - - - - - - - - - -

January 2010 saw nasty rains and mudslides in Los Angeles. On Wednesday the 20th, Matt was hiking near his home in Thousand Oaks. He was caught in a flash flood and died. He was 40 years old.

Phone calls and correspondences flowed in earnest that week; there were many large souls in a lot of pain. Matt's family and longtime band mates assembled a tribute show for that upcoming Wednesday at The Canyon Club in Agoura Hills, California where Matt had performed hundreds of times. For the second consecutive Sundance Festival, I was booking a flight for an absolutely un-missable event far from Utah.

It felt like half of the working players in Los Angeles had subbed out gigs and turned out that night, as well as several hundred fans and admirers. Karla and I hung before the show at McLeftys' place and were joined by drummer Paulie (BongBoys, Metal Show, Queen Nation) and his wife, who had just arrived from Matt's church service.

This was to be a night of concentric circles; while Matt Chidgey's influence on me was deep there was a large group of people — mostly based in LA and Vegas — who enjoyed his company for much longer and more intensely than I. McLefty and I were content to hang back in the audience, connecting social and professional dots with those who were already deeply missing Matt.

**Commemorate Matt Chidgey World Tour t-shirts
are available in the lobby, with the following quotes —**

I'M BLOWIN' IT?
YOU'RE
BLOWIN' IT!

ANY STATEMENT CAN BE MADE CREEPY
BY ENDING IT WITH "LADIES"

WHY DOES IT SMELL LIKE BLEACH
UP HERE ALL OF THE SUDDEN?

ARE YOU IN SHOW BUSINESS? NO?
THEN GET THE FUCK OFF THE STAGE!

AIRPORT SECURITY?
YEAH THOSE ARE MY TOILETRIES,
THAT'S MY GUITAR CABLE
AND THAT'S MY GIANT BABY BONNET!

WHAT ARE YOU DOIN' LATER?
I DON'T KNOW, BUT THIS DICK
AIN'T GONNA SUCK
ITSELF!

HEY, CAN YOU HELP ME?
I'M JUST TWO GIRLS SHORT OF A THREESOME

SO, DO YOU HAVE A SISTER ON THE PILL?

SHOT? NO THANKS,
I GOTTA SLOW DOWN.
I GOTTA DRIVE A SCHOOL BUS
IN A COUPLE OF HOURS.

HOW'S IT GOIN'...
LADIES?

They ran out of the XL shirts by 10 PM and the printer ran another stack over to the club around 10:30.

I watched a fantastic parade of Chidgey-proteges and bandmates grace the Canyon Club stage. Matt's life-long friend and bandmate Mike read an eloquent and humorous eulogy which kept the audience rapt. McLefty and I caught up backstage with old friends and met cats whose names we'd heard forever, yet had never met or worked with.

Brilliant performers were raising the joy level steadily throughout the evening. By the last few 80's cover jams the stage was elbow-to-elbow, much to the chagrin of the jaded stagehands. The crowd was ecstatic. No costumes on stage, no politics off stage, just much love for a cat who never should have left us.

THAT
JUST HAPPENED.
YOU'RE WELCOME, AGOURA HILLS!

THE BLACK MARLIN
AND MONKFISH NIGHTMARES

Imagine Soundgarden and Foo Fighters had a baby. In a nutshell there was Egodog, my last "original band." For our band name I took some liberty with an Ayn Rand concept. In Objectivist-speak, "Ego" is not at all a derogatory term. It's synonymous with individualism, with a sense of self. Unlike, for instance, a "collective soul."

McLefty was on Ego-guitar. He is a self-styled Mass-hole and remains forever a brother. McLefty and I unknowingly crossed paths in the mid-90's, while our respective projects shared the bill at The Palace on Hollywood and Vine. It was a tribute show to departed Thin Lizzy singer/poet Phil Lynnot. Lynnot's mother flew in from Ireland for the occasion. I sang a short set with SOMA and jammed a few Lizzy tunes with Carmine Appice and Billy Sheehan while McLefty fronted his supporting act.

I ran into McLefty months later at a King's X concert. In Los Angeles this essentially means a room full of musicians and their girlfriends. Late in my Musicians Institute days I had wandered into Lip Service on Hollywood and Vine shopping for stretch jeans — *yes, you may cringe now.* On the store stereo was Pure Rock KNAC spinning a band called King's X. It was a moody and bluesy song about home — "Summerland."

Halloween 1989: I read that King's X would be playing The Greek Theater with my childhood fave Billy Squier. I hopped on my bike and rode up to the Greek's box office. Also on that night's bill was late-metal "super group" Blue Murder featuring the aforementioned Appice on drums, looking pretty much as he did in Rod Stewart's "Do Ya Think I'm Sexy?" video. It was show day and I approached the woman behind the glass rather pessimistically: "I'm hoping you have anything left for tonight's show?"

She punched her keys and grinned wide. "How about 1st row, center?" I shit myself on the spot, purchased one ticket and hummed the *Don't Say No* album all the way home.

The next few years saw Higgie and I in a pseudo-prog outfit with Bass Institute grad Rog. Rog pulled shifts at a local record store and when L.A. Guns did an in-store signing. Rog was complimentary of their demeanor. "They really are nice guys," he told us at a rehearsal. As I winced at the banality of that band's material I remember telling Rog, "I would rather hang out with assholes that play like King's X than nice guys who play like L.A. Guns." Higgie thought my comment so ridiculous that he printed it out and hung it in our North Hollywood rehearsal studio, where it remained for two years. I still generally hold to that assertion, although by all accounts, the guys in King's X actually are "nice guys" as well. King's X would play Salt Lake in the spring of 2004 and I stood in front of Dug Pinnick, geeking out all night — as I had done 15 years before at The Greek.

· · · · · · · · · · ·

Late 1990's: Egodog's founding bassist was the tall and very blonde Norwegian Lars. His big and smelly Irish wolfhound skulked around when we rehearsed at his Woodland Hills home. Both Lars and his dog had colitis. The stank of ass is not very conducive to creativity. But I put my vocals on the Chidgey-produced Egodog tracks that Lefty, drummer Mitch and Lars had previously laid down and we made a record.

And the planet yawned.

Egodog played the obligatory club shows around LA, steadily — and to no one. A few years into our run of obscurity we were days fresh from our first DOD tour of The Balkans. We booked a slot at Santa Monica's West End Club. Prior to soundcheck, Lefty unfurled our black vinyl Egodog banner. It was splattered with mud from the previous week. Instinct found me reaching for a rag but McLefty stopped me short:

"Hell no! That's mud from KOSOVO, we leave it!"

The eventual crowd was but a smattering of friends and girlfriends. A few days ago we were playing in front of twice as many people at a dining facility in Bosnia. *Ugh!*

Egodog had a few media and record label allies, but as with bands far more brilliant than we (see also: The Szuters, United State, Gingersol, etc etc) McLefty and I were met largely with indifference. It was years past the late 80's deal-signing frenzy that sustained LA musicians' hopes for so long. The whole music scene had shot up the coast and was laughing over chai lattes in

Seattle.

Through an acquaintance back in Norway, Lars began selling us on the feasibility of a small club tour through Norway with a probable opening slot in Oslo with Deep Purple.

"Probable" was a key word here. Months and years have been pissed away chasing record industry promises and ambiguities. Skim through a *Music Connection* classified and count how many times you read the words "major label interest." Young musicians are now finally grasping the quick death the music industry, as we knew it in the 20th Century, is currently experiencing. Yet many aspiring bands are still out trying to find some record company pot of gold that just doesn't exist. At least not the way it used to. The A&R guys these kids are racing to blow are the last dicks on the Titanic, clawing for the life rafts. Listen some time to the lyrics of Boston's "Rock and Roll Band," with its tale of the cigar-smoking record executive, discovering the band in a club and making them famous — just like that! It's fucking comedy!

The early rock and roll payola scandals of the 1950's have been replaced by "Radio Promoters" (Egodog certainly did cut a check or two) as The Telecommunications Act of 1996 allowed media conglomerates founded by used car dealers to buy up significantly larger percentages of radio stations in any given market (thanks, Slick Willie) thereby assuring you, the listener, a slim chance of ever hearing anything interesting. Or local. If it got more difficult for listeners to find non-corporate music, it became an even harder row for musicians to get it found.

So Egodog went to Norway.

Our first drummer Mitch balked at the three-week Norway run. He had a "solid" day job. He was working at Countrywide doing home mortgages way before the bubble burst, so there you go. But... "The Road." It screamed to me. I wanted shitty motel rooms and Jackson Browne on the Walkman. I was festering in LA and I wanted to get our music out — angst-ridden artist and all that horseshit. Time to audition drummers!

Egodog, Mach II: Drummer Klaven finds us, or we find him. Klaven grooves like hell, and crams tunes. He had toured with early 80's Euro-Metal also-rans, Krokus. Yet we forgave him. Also on his recent resume was a fantastically funky Island Records band called Royal Jelly with a mutual friend of mine and Hatz's (of the old Illinois barn days). Klaven laid the tastiest organic drum loops on those Jelly tracks. His grace notes were just floaty. That band consisted of Hatz's buddy Dave Seaton on bass, Daniel Steigerwald of Kingdom Come on guitar and Johnny Edwards of Foreigner. Johnny had been Lou Gramm's first replacement, and his vocals on Jelly's eponymous release were pristine. Egodog later did a demo at Johnny's studio and I picked his brain about working with renowned rock vocal producer Mick Jones. Also Foreigner's guitarist, Jones was largely responsible for a clean, strong signature vocal sound that carried Foreigner's hits. Jones went on to tweak Sammy Hagar's pipes on his debut with Van Halen, 5150. I asked Johnny about recording with Jones: "What is that guy's secret?"

"He just kicks your ass," Johnny told me.

- - - - - - - - - - -

My first attempt at playing booking agent sent Egodog through Northern Illinois on a warm-up run for Norway. I did some local print press and got CDs in independent record stores. College radio WONC in Naperville kicked us some airtime and kid-jocks asked edgy interview questions like: "If you were a Muppet, which Muppet would you be?"

"Oh that's easy. I'm the two grumpy old guys in the balcony."

Now play my fucking single, boy!

My Uncle Action loaned us a van and the band crashed free of charge with my accommodating family. We opened our mini-tour out in the farmland…

Elburn Days! Nothing but miles of corn all around. People wearing bibs as fashion default. The big, pro stage had been set up within a horseshoe throw from the livestock barn and you could smell the pig shit. It was beautiful. In my homecoming and nostalgia euphoria, I completely tanked a song arrangement and fucked up our first tune. Yes — our first song, first show, first tour. We re-grouped and recovered, blasting our original / cover tune mix to a medium sized but engaged crowd.

We had that Monday off so we day tripped into Chicago and took the "L" to a Cubs game. I also introduced Lars to a Chicago culinary necessity, deep-dish pizza. We hung out on Navy Pier and took in a Ferris wheel ride. It was all very romantic. I had a little hang time with the family, but spent much of my days running to Kinko's, faxing documents to Norway, renting and borrowing gear, and popping into the radio station to promote. I was working every angle I could, both on the ground in Illinois and with our people back in Los Angeles: internet radio, record labels (of course) and multiple press outlets, trying to create that ever-illusive "buzz." Being mid-gym rat phase at the time I even landed an article in *Natural Muscle Magazine* and shamelessly plugged the band there. I had accrued a little endorsement deal with Sportpharma, which made nutritional supplements. Oh, the WHORE! Anything for press! McLefty even appeared on VH1's short-lived game show, *Rock and Roll Jeopardy*. His internal classic rock hard drive garnered him the second highest score in the history of the program. Unfortunately, the top scorer was his competition that very day and *you get nothing!*

For the most part, Egodog's run in suburban Chicago saw low attendance at the clubs and weak CD sales. The band was getting tighter, but pissier. I asked Klaven to blow off a friend's wedding — for a gig that fell through at the last second. I lost much sleep that night. Home cooked meals at Kingsway smoothed over much but not all angst. Around Lew and Hesh's kitchen table McLefty gobbled down late-summer sweet corn. I took consolation in my Tour Manager and Booker learning curve, knowing it would soon be Lars' turn to take the Ego-reins. When we hit the ground in Norway, I had learned three new and magic words: *not my problem.* Of course McLefty and I angsted about the speed bumps that would ensue overseas. But I was learning to delegate.

Egodog closed our Illinois run with a terrific mid-day show at Naperville's Last Fling festival. It was classic late summer Midwest misery at 95 degrees and 90% humidity. The pictures look like we were dipped in baby oil. *Enjoy the heat,* I thought. Autumn in Norway would surely give us the other extreme.

- - - - - - - - - - -

Wednesday, September 16 1998 was my ten-year anniversary of arriving in Los Angeles. I sat next to my guitarist aboard a Scandinavian Air flight, bound for my first overseas tour. In my bags I'd packed a shiny new passport, round trip plane tickets, a Eurail pass, and three decades of anticipation. Twenty hours later we were on the ground in Bergen, Norway, meeting our local manager Kjartan and hopping a ferry out to an island called Stord.

We tooled around the fjords of western Norway in a converted milk truck spray-painted black and adorned with the name of roadie Jonas' last band: the BLACK MARLIN. In retrospect, we could have boosted the attendance of our shows in Norway by just changing the band name to Black Marlin. That thing was impossible to ignore — an eyesore even before Asle had years prior applied its huge obnoxious white stenciling. It was straight out of a *Young Ones* episode. Lars, being the native, shared driving duties with his old mates-cum-sound crew Asle and Jonas during those three weeks. Although somehow at one point no Norwegians were available to drive so I took the wheel through some very dicey mountain roads, sometimes a single lane with long, sheer drops to the ocean below. Every few turns there was some knob in a Saab screeching around the bend. The Marlin handled like a crippled elephant and we screamed like girls the whole way.

Lars had friends on Stord. Our first of a dozen shows was booked there. Klaven, Jonas and I went fishing and all jaws dropped when Klaven returned with an actual fish. "Livin' off the land, boys," Klaven beamed, holding up our dinner on a hook. "Livin' off the land!" He made us a killer spread with the cod, which we all devoured immediately. Drummers with talents other than drumming are just adorable. While old Norwegian buddies caught up on our night off I retired upstairs to follow a Bears game online * and stare at the Euro-shower controls like a retard.

The Stord show the next night was sloppy, and it all had to do with a guy named Jack. I left it to our new boss Lars to council the drummer he'd commiserated with back in DeKalb and Naperville.

The Marlin hit the road: Stavanger and Egesund. A pit stop for a night at Jonas' family cabin in the middle of nothing. Cold, foggy ferry crossings and moonrises on the fjords. We did a radio show in Bergen and first experienced hearing, "Blah blah blah, yadda yadda yadda, EGODOG!" in a foreign tongue. Few of the shows were satisfactorily attended but McLefty, Lars, Klaven and I kept our chins up. The scenery alone quelled much discontent on the worst days.

* *Loss @ Tampa Bay, 27-15*

My pre-gig ritual often consists of some yoga and at the time I was fairly psychotic about it, establishing a routine that would keep me sane over the next decade of international touring. Mike and I were sharing a room above a non-descript roadside restaurant where Asle and Jonas had dutifully set up our PA for a gig that evening. I was in the room sporting only some tiny undies and nose-breathing into a prayer side-twist when Mike opens the door and takes one step in holding a bag of groceries. I looked up and Lefty deadpanned, "It's a good thing I get you." And probably a good thing we were still pre-camera phones.

The band headed downstairs to the restaurant after my vocal warm ups (which incensed many a sleep-deprived Norwegian hotel guest that Fall). The restaurant was empty at thirty minutes from downbeat. The owner opted to cancel the show. He comped our rooms and meals but we collected no cash that night. No CD or t-shirt sales, either. And I had warmed up my pipes for nothing. And we had driven all day for this one. How do you say *ugh* in Norwegian?

But just when the fuel is lowest, you pull up to a gig and there are teenage kids in the parking lot that start inexplicably chanting "Ego-DOG!" Now, had they been shouting "Black Marlin!" that would have made sense, but we'll certainly take it and *tusen tak.* *

One show in Kristensand was on a weeknight, located at an amusement park called Folken. It was cold and wet, the place was dead — you could say it was Folken *sad!* Yet the stage was huge and we had a blast playing to a few dozen kids. Some were in fact children; the venue served no alcohol and bored locals just wandered into the cavernous room despite minimal advance advertising. Shows like that hone your between-song banter skills in a hurry. Unless the band's going to segue cleanly from song to song the whole night, you have to address those people. Some of which in this case spoke mostly Norwegian.

* *from the Norwegian: "A thousand thanks"*

But generally, even in the rural fjord areas on the West Coast where our three weeks began, we had no trouble getting by in English. There was a promoter in a village out in the middle of the woods who invited the band back to his home after soundcheck. For dinner! Don't hold your breath for those invites from booking agents in Vegas, oh my droogies. When we arrived his wife was in the kitchen and their two pre-teen daughters were helping. The girls broke their Norwegian conversation to turn to us in perfect English, "So you guys are from LA, huh? What's that like?" Mike and I shot each other shameful glances. We're idiots!

Mike did eventually learn how to order a hot dog with mustard. *Un polse mer senep!*

And thanks for the soup, our random family in the forest. That promoter's wife. Don't mean to be a pig but she was quite attractive. Norwegian MILFs? Who'd have thunk it! During our first week on Stord I jogged one morning through misty and sleepy roads to the one gym in town. I gave them some info and a few bucks and headed towards the weight room. There was a cardio area where an aerobics class was in session, with baby strollers lining the room. Being mid-week in a remote Scandinavian town, I peered in expecting a room full of enormous, frumpy housewives. But there they were: a room full of hot, multi-lingual European women. What is keeping them so svelte and sexy? Is it the snowshoeing? The igloo building? Perhaps just their cultural ability to avoid eating crap.

There are, at any given Norwegian convenience or grocery store, only two kinds of mustard: the yellow and the brown. *That's all you get, now deal with it!* Upon returning to The States, McLefty found himself standing in an aisle of a Ralph's super-mega-market, transfixed by the 35 types of mustard he could purchase.

"And another thing," I thought aloud on Stord: "Where's the litter in this country?" I was starting to feel self-conscious — this place is immaculate! And how come we can't get day old bread in Norway? You people need fresh-baked bread, even from the petrol station? The band would walk back out to the Marlin, and there'd be a goat herder with his flock, grazing around the pumps. Our heads were spinning.

And trolls.

Trolls! These people are obsessed with them. It's like the Japanese with anime. It's in their advertising, as home décor — trolls are ubiquitous. In the promoter's bathroom there was a ceramic troll next to the toilet. An indoor garden gnome. This little guy was grimacing with eyes locked shut and fists clenched. I finished up my business and washing my hands, I studied the base he was planted on. I bent over and spun it around... Sure enough:

A tiny, perfect, ceramic turd. Genius.

Towards the end of our run we crashed a few nights in Bergen with Trond, a friend of our "manager" Kjartan, who kept talking about regional label deals that — *let's face it* — were never gonna happen. I had a few good lifts, one show in a big empty room (shocker), and a stroll through Bergen's fish market on the pier.

At most of our stops the night's venue would cover our meals and we'd repeatedly been given the choice: meat or fish. The meat was most often reindeer, which was fantastic. We said grace to Santa and chowed down. I'd usually order the fish, watching my girlish figure as I was wont do. We soon learned it was monkfish, a crustacean — "poor man's lobster" we were told. It was delicious. And what is every musician's favorite kind of meal? *Free.*

That morning in Bergen's fish market I happened upon a booth that was displaying whole monkfish for sale. Nasty, bottom feeding, beady-eyed things. That night I had a most unnerving nightmare starring that very goddamn monkfish. Only now he bared big sharp teeth, out to exact revenge on his friends whom I'd been gobbling up since Stord.

Drummer Klaven, however, emerged from the fish market that day not with a new phobia but with a nice fresh cut of whale steak. He fried it up in Trond's kitchen. I know whales are smart and cute and all, but *damn* that was yummy. Norway only hunts grey whales in season. They aren't endangered, folks, and again — they really are yummy.

With disappointing money and low band morale, a pow wow was convened. Lars and Trond and our Euro-Manager began the meeting in Norwegian... Man, you don't see McLefty get pissed often, but try to hold a business meeting about his band in a foreign language, and look out!

Our fearless leader Kjartan had booked us at a pizza place the night before the Deep Purple gig — a logistically hellish nine-hour dive away in Oslo. Standing onstage seconds before our downbeat an old Norwegian man shuffled his way to the stage. He was sporting a Gandolf beard and minimal English. He approached us and quietly asked, "Can you play maybe… some traditional Norwegian folk songs?" McLefty and I, wearing electric guitars and with hair halfway to our ass, stared blankly at each other. Egodog was a decidedly electric band. Thirty minutes later the owner pulled the plug on us. Apparently we were drowning out the pizza orders.

"Good evening (insert semi-pronounceable Norwegian town name)! Are you ready to ROCK?"

Three weeks prior, we had departed Los Angeles, at long last confirmed to open for Deep Purple at the 7,000-seat Spektrum in Oslo. Our primary motivation on this tour was to play our first Arena Gig but we were dubious up until the moment we were actually soundchecking at The Oslo Spektrum. Already cynical into my late 20's, and I was indeed wondering if Kjartan's promises were really going to materialize on this day. McLefty told me once: "When I meet people I give them an 'A' and they work down. You give them an 'F' and make them work up."

Deep Purple are musical deities in Norway. By 9 AM that morning, after a slick and cold mountain drive through the night, we arrived to find the Norwegian papers trumpeting the concert. At the arena Purple's crew was polite and accommodating to our obscure indie band. I was warming up in the backstage bathroom — warming up to some Ray Gillen. If you appreciate any Zeppelin-esque bluesy metal or want a late 80's gem, go get you some Badlands. Deep Purple's legendary vocalist Ian Gillan (no relation) walked past my vocalizing — yes, the door was closed — and shot dirty looks toward McLefty in the next room. Yeah. I used to warm up loud. I'm not proud of it.

Mike and I hugged and geeked out in the dressing room before hitting the stage to a capacity arena. These people didn't know us from dick. But we hit the climax of our opener, "Shade of Green" and at its crescendo the crowd responded with a beautiful roar that almost caught us off guard. I shot them a *Tak!* and we ripped through the set on jet-fueled adrenaline.

Predictably, the minimal video that Kjartan shot was worthless. But that didn't stop our "manager" from reciting a to-do list immediately in the dressing room as we were bopping off stage, ecstatic. It was: *We need this, you guys need to do that.* I broke from our back-patting euphoria to shout back at him, "You know what we need to do Kjartan? THAT! What we just did out there. We need to do THAT — every night!" And alas, we never did again.

At least, not in another big arena. And never again with Deep Purple. I do hope it wasn't the post-show, dressing room excitement that nixed us from additional dates, potentially out Space Truckin' with the Highway Stars. Egodog's Norway tour was about to end with a wince…

Bassist Roger Glover and guitarist Steve Morse were gracious and complimentary, posing with us for the Norwegian papers.

"Man, are all you Norwegians so damn tall?" Purple guitarist Morse asked McLefty.

"Hey, I'm from Boston!" Lefty pointed to me, "He's from Chicago."

Morse added, "Hmm... I thought it was a Viking thing. Maybe I'm just really short!" Then he shook our hands and told McLefty, "It's really cool to see a band that bucks the trend of sounding shitty." This was, remember, the era of forgettable cacophonic bands like Seven Mary Three and Bush. To which Mike replied, "Thanks man. That's good enough for me to call all my friends from Berklee and tell them Steve Morse said I don't suck!"

Meanwhile behind us our drummer had a drink in his hand and was apparently conducting an interview with a reporter from a national paper. A shiver shot down my back as I recalled the brief chat Klaven and I just had, from the rafters above Deep Purple's set, a mere hour before:

"These guys? Fuck these guys." Yes, he was referring to Deep Purple, on the stage below us.

"We had twice the energy, they should open for *us*!" He was holding a drink at that moment as well, come to think of it.

Now backstage he was across the room with the Dagbladet reporter and getting louder. Shit, where was our "manager?" We have something that most definitely needs to be managed. As I broke off from a conversation and turned in their direction, our drummer stumbles forward and — like the town rummy in a Western flick — falls into the reporter.

Yeah. I think our work here is done.

The following day Egodog was gig-less and taking a train into Oslo from Lars' sister's place in the country, where I would stay and rest for 48 hours as the guys returned to The States. One dapper passenger was reading that day's Dagbladet, the country's second largest newspaper. And there was Egodog on the back page, mugging with Purple's Glover and Morse. That photo was probably snapped pre-backstage alcho-drama, as I was not visibly cringing.

EURO, SOLO

Autumn, 1986: In the dying days of the Cold War, my grandparents Lew and Hesh organized a homecoming tour of Eastern Europe, inviting Lew's two brothers and their wives. These three septuagenarian couples took a rented mini-van to Normandy then through Berlin's Checkpoint Charlie and then east to Poland, where Hesh found her cousins literally picking potatoes in babushkas. Lew and my great uncles drove south to our native Romania, where the aged Popp brothers saw for the first time the bleak poverty and tyrannical repression their parents' move to America had spared them, and us. It would be three dark years before thirty-year dictator Nicolae Ceausescu and his wack-job of a wife would be overthrown and executed on Romanian national television — a big Christmas present for a long-suffering people. While visiting their roots, Lew, Gus and Jim Popp and their wives witnessed the final moments of a nightmare.

My family sat around the sturdy maple kitchen table at Kingsway Drive and passed around maps and pictures. Lew went over every detail of their three weeks through Europe. Hesh (maiden name, Krzeminski) would nod in agreement while occasionally slipping in and out of her now-refreshed Polish. I soaked in their travel tales and silently vowed to have my own.

OSLO, BERLIN, ARNSTADT, MUNICH, BUDAPEST, VIENNA, SALZBURG, FRANKFURT, COCHEM, AMSTERDAM, COPENHAGEN, LOS ANGELES.

October 1998: My three Egodog mates had just departed Oslo for Los Angeles, carting with them my guitar and gear. I hung back in Norway, having purchased a ten-stamp Eurail pass.

My Walkman, packed deep in my gear bag, was flying back to LA with McLefty. I had decided to do three weeks backpacking through central

Europe without music. This was a deliberate decision, as my head is deluged by music, constantly, incessantly, whether or not I'm actually *listening* to anything. There's always a soundtrack running through my skull. So I gave my music-head a break while opening my ears, schlepping through six countries in three weeks.

Ego-bassist Lars' sister saved me the time and energy I didn't have, taking me in and feeding me for a few days. After a second brisk October night with every window inexplicably thrown WIDE OPEN (a habit I would eventually adopt in Utah) I grabbed my Eurail pass and rode straight to the Continent on an overnight train. My backpack Ol' Blue was loaded with only the bare necessities, including one of my first in a long succession of travel journals…

13 Oct, train:
Ferries to Denmark, then Germany… felt good in
Hamburg, singing Beatle songs…

It was raining like hell and I found the tourist bureau. I rifled thru brochures and picked a nearby youth hostel. Exhausted and seeking my bed for the night, I passed an imbiss and bought myself a deliciously greasy falafel. My ad-libbed destination was in the former East Berlin's Mitte district and a short ride on the U-Bahn — a hostel not overly friendly and not overly hip…

14 Oct, Berlin:
OK today kicked some ass… just genuinely digging
where I am…

I did the bus tour: Potsdamer Platz, Brandenburg Gate, The Reichtag and Berlin Wall, followed by a hard-boiled egg for lunch on my Henry Miller Diet Plan. It hit me that I'd been around too many people, too closely and for too long. I threw a mental dart at my map of Northern Europe and I was off again.

15 October 1998, Thursday: Arnstadt is a tiny town in the Thuringian Forest, central Germany. There's a church at the town center where two generations of Bachs bashed away for the congregation. I strolled in and stood among the construction dust and musical history. The people in the tourism office didn't speak a bit of English! I managed to tell three giggling ladies that I wanted a bed and breakfast in town. They sent me to their neighbor Ilse who had a lovely little home with four comfy rooms around a foyer area upstairs. In the morning I woke to a pot of coffee on a tea burner and a perfect *frühstück* of meats, cheeses and breads. It was mid-October — rural Germany's "shoulder season" — so I had the place to myself.

I wandered Arnstadt and crunched leaves under my sneakers. I found a pizza place open in an otherwise sleepy village. Walking home through unlit streets and cobblestone alleys I stopped in my tracks when I thought I heard singing. I turned a corner and there was a church. Not the aforementioned Bach Kirche, but a different church, nestled up on a hillside en route back to my room. I stopped and listened for a while. It was only practice. Just Wednesday night choir practice…

> So beautiful… it almost wasn't real… really enjoying myself, may stay one more night then hit Munich… money OK…

Hitting the gym was a more challenging task than I had anticipated. My English/German dictionary was lacking. I now understand the funny looks I received that day in Arnstadt, as *gymnasium* in German means "high school." Here's this American longhair looking for the high school. *Oh GOOD.* The kid working at the village's only *Sportstudio* (that's what I was looking for!) didn't comprehend that I wanted to work out, not apply to work there. Was that a language thing or was that kid not all that bright? Come on Gunther, I was holding my workout bag after all.

17-18 October, Saturday: Eurail to Munich where I hit a *Waschsalon* (laundrette) and lunched at Marienplatz…

> Cold rain, checkout… fruhstuck and museum - nice… then S-Bahn out to Dachau.

When I asked the local driver if I was on the correct bus to "the camp," her face turned dour. The townsfolk were obviously *over it*. And I didn't need dark weather to accentuate the mood of walking around that place. Back in a corner of the compound the concentration camp had prison barracks. Behind those, through the iron bars were the gallows.

19 October, Monday: Budapest was rainy and miserable and the limit on my secured credit card was ominously approaching. My left foot was killing me. My shoes sucked. I kept repeating a quote I'd read…

*"Travel is only glamorous in retrospect." ***

I felt vindicated, knowing I wasn't obligated to enjoy my daily battles with phone cards and international country codes. I walked from the train station across town to a bridge over the Danube with a nice older couple who spoke only Norwegian, tempting me to ask them for a hot dog with mustard. We trekked together up to the castles overlooking the *Duna* before my evening train into Vienna…

> 20 Oct, Vienna:
> Early walk, bought opera tix… everything's breathtaking… out of food stash and $ starting to concern me for the 1st time - moments of bliss to get me home - it's been a long trip.

I wandered through the Austrian capitol and hacked away in the Steinway store, feeling timidly ashamed to be a mere rock musician, lowest on the artistic totem pole as far as Europe was concerned. Unless of course you were Deep Purple in Norway.

After *Wien*, a day trip to Mozart's hometown. Salzburg is Candy Land come to life. Strolling under the town center's sheer cliff faces, I passed a little old man wearing lederhosen and a little black feather hat. I wondered if there was a holiday or a parade or something. Nah. It was just Thursday. He was out shopping.

I indulged in an all-Mozart day at Wolfie's home and museum. I don't claim any depth of appreciation for classical. Or jazz, for that matter — my profession is unapologetically Rock. But being in the presence of greatness of that degree, greatness and genius I'll never understand, made for a splendid day.

* *Paul Theraux*

From Austria, north back into Germany for a timely pit-stop with Karla's sister and Air Force Major brother in law. I did a load of laundry, caught a Bears game on AFN and one evening joined them on a USO excursion to a haunted house at Burg Frankenstein (!) far up into the foggy woods above Darmstadt.

Outside of my respite at Rhein-Mein, those were lonely weeks — no cell phones, no emails, traveling solo. It was a happy loneliness, though — no one with whom to debate my destination.

The Ugly American default: getting way too stoned in Amsterdam. All alone in a hotel room with sound all around. My eyes are locked on some anonymous Dutch ceiling. At midnight all I wanted to do was sleep but there's these guys in the room next to me shouting in Farsi... and either they're too loud then they start whispering... and I'm sure they know I'm stoned... and I have a train to catch tomorrow, and...

And the rest is mystery.

31 October, 1998: Northeast to Copenhagen and I sure as shit wasn't about to miss that train! From Denmark I was scheduled to catch the flight back home after a month and a half on the road. Three weeks by foot and Eurail turned out to be more an endurance test than anything resembling a vacation. Cash poor and nursing a broken filling dangling from my wisdom tooth, I nonetheless squeezed all I could from my first trip abroad, not knowing I would return to Europe several times in the next few years...

I didn't dig this turning into a 'survival' thing...

SAVING FACE AND
THE SEAT OF SHAME

December 1999:

HAWAII, KWAJELEIN, POHNPEI, GUAM, OKINAWA.

January 2000:

REPUBLIC OF KOREA.

My second Department of Defense tour began painlessly, with Coverdogs snorkeling the bathwater shores of Kwajalein, skydiving in Guam, and enjoying a relatively easy gig and travel schedule. The Tour Gods' payback for that admitted cakewalk came during our second three weeks, in the fashion of a brutally frigid and logistically rough Korean January.

Ross was again on drums. Due to a scheduling glitch, my new buddy Fab was signed on, not as bassist, but as Tour Manager and soundman. I'd scoured my black book of musicians, but all my known guitar and bass commodities were unavailable. Thus, two of the guys on *Coverdogs' Asia Y2K Tour* came as blind recommendations. Pressed for time, the four of us had a couple acoustic run-throughs and I mistakenly assumed their competence was at levels to which I'd grown accustomed. Gigging around Los Angeles countless times, you just shake hands with a new player in the parking lot of a $75 sports bar gig, run down the set list, decide on song keys, then BAM, you're off. Only occasionally would a train wreck ensue. But on this run, a DOD tour of the Pacific Rim and South Korea, Fab, Ross and I were stuck with?

Lumpy and Shuff.

"Shuffle-fuck" was an old Higgie term, short for Shuffle-uffagus. There's always one: the last guy in the hotel lobby for checkout, the last guy sauntering into soundcheck. When the designated departure meeting time at LAX had come and gone and we did eventually find Shuff, waiting atop his gear — in the wrong terminal — I knew it was going to be a long tour. And his musical skills didn't make up for his tardiness, either. "Where's Shuff?" someone would ask. "Looking for the One," we'd reply.

Guitarist Lumpy wasn't a huge step up. A solid jazz and big-band player, but Lumpy was ignorant of the key licks and hooks in our classic rock setlist and proved incapable of watching the players around him. Shoe-gazing is inexcusable as a Coverdog, where solos, song endings and breaks come largely from visual cues... *I know I'm sneering at you, but watch me for the changes!*

That first Asia tour began with a layover in Hawaii. We putzed around Hickam Air Force Base, spent a day visiting the U.S.S. Arizona at Pearl Harbor — its oil still seeping to the surface — and had a few room rehearsals in preparation for that week's only flight to the Marshall Islands, about halfway to Australia out in the South Pacific. During our first few days we were unsure if Kwajalein would even happen. Our booker Dwayne was telling Fab it might be an extended stay for The Coverdogs in Oahu then straight to Guam. Powerless, I still hoped we could keep our initial itinerary. I was curious to see Kwaj, knowing how rare the opportunity would be. Commercial seats run pretty pricey — *if* someone living and working on the atoll sponsors you, that is. Kwajalein is an island a half-mile wide by 3 miles long and part of the world's largest lagoon at some 1,100 square miles. It serves as a target for unarmed ICBMs launched from Vandenburg Air Force Base in California. Most of the island's 1000 or so American residents were DOD personnel or employees of Raytheon Corporation, which runs the atoll's huge satellite dishes. We landed just in time for a tropical cloudburst as I scrambled for my Anarak at the bottom of my backpack. We were driven in a golf cart to an interview on the island's sole radio station then off to comfy lodgings, settling in for three shows over five days on the atoll.

A redheaded girl I saw at the airfield intrigued me from across the little terminal. I learned she works for MIT, tracking rogue Chinese satellite launches. I did my best to talk her into attending the next night's gig at a thatched-roofed building called the Yuk Club but I never saw her again. *Let's face it, she ain't comin'.* My social consolation prize that night was a Shirley Manson look-alike with a choking fetish and a room full of empties who was cute enough, but comparatively opposite in the stability and conversation arenas. For the record, Your Honor, no choking actually occurred, as I had no liability releases handy.

Our third show saw the band setting up on the outdoor basketball court during a BBQ that was interrupted by the occasional violent downpour. I caught myself fantasizing about a lightning strike taking out Shuff, forcing Fab to step in and bring us up to ¾ musical competence, but no bolt from the blue came. The lineup remained intact and we pressed on over the next weeks getting only marginally tighter despite cheat sheets, rehearsals and eventually scoldings, dirty looks and chalkboard tic systems.

After a few days in travel purgatory we got our marching orders. We were to overnight on the tiny Micronesian island of Pohnpei as a stopover before Guam. Our flight from Kwajalein was in its descent but all I saw below me was water. *Water, water, water,* then BAM! There's a runway and we were taxiing. The jungle hugged the perimeter of the airport in a thick foggy wall. It was a scene reminiscent of *King Kong* and I kept an eye out for Pterodactyls. No gigs were scheduled at Pohnpei, just a jeep ride up winding mountain roads to a jungle hotel, its walls climbing with geckos. Our civilian guide Zeder detoured us first to a local "bar" before checking us in. Its open-air, bamboo construction was straight out of a bad Elvis film. Families were eating and talking outside on picnic tables in the steamy foliage.

People have shown us the truest hospitality over the years. Who were we anyway? Some nameless musicians lugging guitars through their country! Zeder and his crew showed us how to cop a tiny buzz by chewing beetle nut leaves, and shared with us a local beverage called sakao, which looked like YooHoo and tasted like chalk.

The Coverdogs had only one show on Guam for our naval contingent there. Tamara, our POC, had the band over to her home for Christmas dinner in the 80-degree sunshine. Her family served up many Guam delicacies including octopus salad and coconut wrapped in palm leaves. *Nummers!*

Coverdogs would be on Guam for a few additional days past show night, so we had a choice: with a few bucks to kill we could hop a flight to overnight in Australia or we could skydive in Guam. I had picked up a flyer at the airport and none of us had ever jumped. We opted for the slightly more frugal choice, trusting we'd get to Australia someday and the next morning I called the number for the jump school. A Japanese girl answered whose English was extremely limited.

"So is there a class, what do we need?" I asked her via phone from the base.

"No class. You come. You jump!"

Hoping our tandem partners would be slightly more detailed in their instructions, I locked up my room and headed down the hall to knock on Fab's door. He was awake and pumped and we headed over to get Ross. Lumpy and Shuff had already decided against leaping out of a plane, doubtlessly still shaken from their high-tide dog paddle and near drowning in Kwajalein... *Hey guys! Wait up!*

Ross answered his door. "Yeah buddy, it's on! Are you ready to hit it?" I asked him.

"Man, I don't know. That's a lot of bread..."

"Alright put your shit on, Ross, you know damn well you're going."

Driving out to the airport I was trying to relate the directions the girl had given me: "Airport! You drive around back. You come, you jump!" It was our three stooges and one tiny Japanese tourist skydiving that day. Our instructors were Aussies. In no time we were packing into the Cessna, roughly by weight: Japanese girl, Fab, me, then Ross, all attached to our instructors. The pilot was dropping us over the ocean and the wind would blow us back onshore.

Our tiny tourist and her teacher went first, and the whoosh and suction when they leapt through the door made our jaws drop. Fab scooted up to the door and turning to the camera on my instructor's helmet gave a Led Zeppelin "Immigrant Song" yelp —*"Aaah-Ahhhhhh!"* and he was gone. I leapt out next, to a blue and perfect ocean below through a smattering of puffy, postcard clouds. My legs dangled uselessly beneath me and I wished it could have lasted forever. We hit the ground hooting and vowing we'd do that as often as we could.

From Guam we flew via C-130 cargo transport to Okinawa where Lew had gotten his battle star after serving aboard the U.S.S. Trousdale in World War II. I snuck away after a soundcheck and walked down to the beach at Camp Shield where I scooped sand into a jar to bring back to him. The Marines that night were out of their minds with beer and homesick holiday angst. Much moshing ensued. Someone barfed. We stayed at Kadena Air Base and emailed holiday wishes to our families.

31 December 1999: Of all my New Years Eve gigs, my lamest remains the one that landed pathetically on the Millennium in Okinawa. Booked arbitrarily in an officer's club at Camp Schwab our set began at 6 PM and much to our horror, dinner was still being served to the clientele — many of advanced age. Seeing even our mellowest selections of the "Hey Joe" and "With Or Without You" ilk going over like proverbial lead zeppelins we convened during our first break and assembled a makeshift list of pseudo-jazzy Beatle and Lyle Lovett songs. Fortunately these choices were more up Lumpy's alley and no serious Amtrak moments ensued.

During that first set Fab had seen me move my mic stand a few feet to the side as I was stationary — doubling on barely competent rhythm guitar — directly underneath an air conditioning vent. When I returned to the stage after set break, the vent had been taped over. I pride myself in being a hands-on, low maintenance performer, but the deference Fab showed me here on our second tour together was testimony to his professionalism. I soon found in him a kindred soul and confidant — one I would sorely need when we hit Korea a few weeks later.

Our show at Schwab, Okinawa concluded before 10 PM and we tore down our gear to make way for some anonymous local band to whom we happily gave the honor of ringing in a geriatric New Year. We grabbed styrofoamed to-go dinners and high-tailed it back to Kadena Base. We weaseled our way into the base's biggest club despite no reservations or tickets. *"We're the band, we just want to check out the stage for tomorrow night!"* The Coverdogs rang in the Millennium anonymously drinking cheap champagne among a hip-hop crowd.

- - - - - - - - - - -

In prepping for tours through new places I did my best to read into local customs, occasionally trying on a local phrase or two. The second three weeks of this tour would be my first trip to Korea. I was curious to try kimchi (that enthusiasm faded after a few bites) and soju — a clear, thick, nasty liquor and perpetrator of many a GI hangover. I also read about a big Korean cultural faux pas. "Saving Face" is important in personal and business exchanges — you never want to put someone in a position where they feel slighted or disadvantaged. It sounds universal, but *Go Korea* told me it was an issue to be cognizant of while traveling, so I made a mental note.

5 January 2000: The Coverdogs arrived in Seoul and were put up in the dreaded Rainbow Inn, a few blocks off base. Fab and I shared a tiny room that had a miniature tub/shower (one of many hose jobs to come) and little Billy Barty beds — which we intentionally *never* looked underneath. We performed at nearby Yongsan Base but used Seoul as our central point for long drives to Osan, Inchon, Itaewon, even a show at the "Bridge to Nowhere" on the Han River. The GIs in Korea were happy and surprised that their presence was being acknowledged by a humble MWR band. Some of their facilities it seemed hadn't been updated in ages. One Officer's Club had vinyl album jackets on the walls as decoration... *Yes folks, 33's.*

It must be hard to feel appreciated by your countrymen when you've got Foghat's Afros staring down into your beer.

Another gauge of your place on the Pentagon priority totem pole is the state of your base's workout facilities. The equipment at Yongsan was antiquated and located in a musty basement gym. After a deployment in The Balkans or Middle East — with their meatier MWR budgets — I could easily envision soldiers in Korea feeling extremely neglected.

We were scheduled for one show in Panmunjom, a civilian-less village straddling the border with North Korea. I was familiar with the city as the site of peace negotiations during the last years of the Korean conflict from watching many a *MASH* rerun with Lew. The no man's land here between the two Koreas is one of the most heavily mined areas on the planet and was a major American argument against Princess Diana and her attempts to globally ban land mines. Idealism is all well and good, until your neighbors are trying to kill you. Every spring thaw both sides ramp up their military readiness. Each expects the other to launch a full armor and troop barrage when the snows begin melting. The communist North has periodically constructed a series of tunnels underneath the DMZ wide enough to allow tanks and whole infantry divisions, and their soldiers attempt minor incursions every few years.

It was a clear, windy, frigid afternoon when we toured the Joint Security Area (JSA), a series of trailers where the armistice had been signed in 1953. When we approached the Peace Village for a security-heavy tour, you could see over in the North the empty town of Kijong Dong. Like many of the modern, well-lit structures we'd seen along the Han River nights before, these buildings were unoccupied and serving solely as displays of opulence that everyone knew didn't exist. We could hear the distant loudspeakers pumping

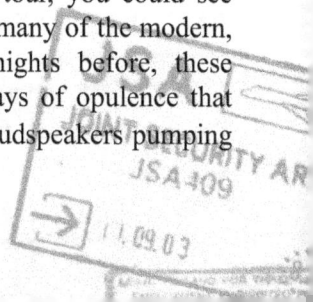

communist propaganda over to us in the South. An enormous North Korean flag flapped in the January air, high atop the world's largest flagpole. The tallest pole was once here on the South side of the demilitarized zone, but the North would have none of that and quickly constructed a taller flagpole.

Saving face.

Our MWR guide took us out to the small, rectangular buildings in the middle of the JSA. There was a North Korean guard a hundred yards away pacing back and forth atop freezing concrete steps in front of their structure. Meanwhile, we were walking by Republican (ROK) soldiers standing rigid in Tae Kwon Do stance, facing their Northern counterparts. The wind chill was near zero that afternoon and those ROK soldiers didn't as much as twitch. Bad asses. We entered a trailer where the cease-fire was actually signed. Our guide instructed us over to his end of a long conference table that took up the entire trailer. "On this end of the table? Step over here. Now we're in North Korea." I suddenly felt *so rone-ree.*

Many stops were "wet" (allowing alcohol) and at those bases naturally came the wildest shows. The mosh pits were always intense but brief, as inevitably someone of rank would wag a finger or hop out onto the floor, assuring there wasn't *too much* aggression being released. Although on an occasion or two we have had Commanding Officers let down what hair they had, joining in the ad-libbed rugby scrum as we egged them on from the stage.

Show by show, the band was improving — somewhat. Fab spent most of this tour singing backing vocals from the soundboard, covering for Lumpy and Shuff's inability to multi-task. There were a dozen or so transgressions that Fab, Ross and I had grown weary of. The three of us devised a seating system for the van rides back to the Rainbow Inn: our MWR mini-bus only had seats for four passengers but it did have a little metal kiddie chair that folded out from the bucket seats. Whoever fucked up most obviously on stage that night would be relegated to the Seat of Shame on the return trip.

Late in our sixth week, we were setting up the PA around pool tables when Ross spotted the dart game's chalkboard behind his drum stool. We devilishly developed a silent tic system, counting the evening's musical mistakes behind Ross' drum kit. From wrong notes to missed accents to blown cues, the chalkboard made tour qualms tangible and added some much needed levity after a month and a half of frustration. However, soon a few of the soldiers in the crowd caught what we were doing and we decided to cease our game despite the chuckle it was giving everyone except Lumpy and Shuff.

The Coverdogs played the Mustang Club, on the air base in that shopping mecca of Osan. As with most clubs on military bases, the crowd was extremely dude-heavy. But at least they had booze. We did manage to get a dance floor going, even luring one of their three women on stage.

Our local civilian driver was Mr Yi, assigned to us by MWR. He was soft-spoken and professional. After the Mustang show we were tearing down PA and rolling gear out towards the back door. Mr Yi pulled the van around as the band assembled our speakers, amps and travel cases at the loading dock. With pieces being shuffled from the stage we began loading our enormous speakers in the truck. Mr. Yi grabbed one of the heavier amps and started hoisting it toward me. Being a smaller guy well into his fifties, I cringed as I watched him hump that hefty amplifier. I hopped down and took one of the handles. "It's ok thanks, I have it Mr. Yi, you're good." Then I grabbed the other handle from him. He huffed for a moment, then stormed off and sat in the driver's seat, his pride obviously wounded. I realized right away what I'd done. And what I'd forgotten.

Saving face.

Nice one, T.

I had one long, quiet ride up in the cab with Mr. Yi before relegating *myself* to the Seat of Shame for a few days. I swear the guy didn't speak to me for a week.

On my Walkman spun a cassette soundtrack of travel tunes:

Wings — "Band on the Run"

XTC — "Senses Working Overtime"

Hendrix — "Highway Chile" and "Stone Free Again"

The latter of which was hilarious, as DOD entertainers are anything but "free" while they're on tour. Downtime is rare and precious and time is the master. Guys like Shuff learned eventually: when the military says the convoy leaves base at 0700, *it fucking leaves at 0700* — whether or not your chubby civilian ass is on it.

We had a run of eighteen shows in twenty-one days in Korea. All five of us were beat to hell the day we rode through the snow to Pusan. When we arrived, the base hadn't advertised the show and few troops were around. The MWR representative and Fab and I debated the merits of doing a show to no one, in the dim hope that word would spread and guys would break their schedules at short notice. Fab let the decision come down to me. We knew the next night's show would be a big one and The Coverdogs were fighting a late tour burnout.

Regretfully, I let my exhaustion make the call for me and I nixed the show. We turned around and went back to the Rainbow, my heart heavy with the decision I almost immediately regretted. Surely we would have sung to a few guys there. A few guys that needed the distraction. Many tours have at least one *blow it* moment. This one would stick with me.

*Korean culinary tip: Street vendors barbeque little squid called yujingo that are delicious whilst fresh, NOT to be kept in your hotel fridge overnight!

SENT BY WASHINGTON: COVERDOGS, MIDDLE EAST SUMMER 2000

LOS ANGELES, BAHRAIN, SAUDI ARABIA, UNITED ARAB EMIRATES, QATAR, OMAN, KUWAIT, JORDAN, EGYPT, ISRAEL, LOS ANGELES.

The flight attendants on Gulf Air were beautiful. Fortunately their faces remained uncovered, although to maintain a degree of modesty, their hats did have these cute little veils in back. In mid-air, the plane's video screen displays an arrow. *Which way to Mecca?*

It was our third flight in 24 hours, coming from LA to Frankfurt, now on our final leg into Bahrain where we will be eased into the Arab world. Fab had been through The Persian Gulf before and had briefed us on the significant cultural differences we would encounter. I had packed and dressed accordingly — collared shirts with my long hair in a ponytail — having no desire to be the ugly American in a region where standing out can place Westerners in actual physical danger. I nibbled a couscous and chicken salad and allowed myself to daydream of lying prone in a hotel room.

JAY LAWSON
"MOOSE"
DRUMS
COVERDOGS

"YOUNG BEN"
ADAMSON
TOUR MANAGER
TRUMPET
COVERDOGS

We arrived in Manama, Bahrain but unfortunately our thirty-two pieces of gear did not. As Fab painstakingly described every container to an airport employee with marginal English skills, I waited with drummer Moose, guitarist Spark Myth and sound guy Young Ben as locals kneeled on the prayer rug in the corner of the baggage claim area.

Later that afternoon from my seventh

floor hotel room window I watched an older woman in a black abaya cross one of the countless open stretches of sand that separate Manama's hotels, restaurants, and apartment high rises. I wandered up to the roof pool just in time for one of the five daily calls to prayer. The chanting soon surrounded me from all sides, creating a haunting cacophony. For the next six weeks it would serve as a beautiful reminder of how far we were from home.

6 June 2000: The first full day in the Middle East found me traversing the quarter mile from our off-base hotel to the naval base, sending emails and hitting the base gym — standard DOD tour routine. After a quick and rough soundcheck though a PA on loan from a local Filipino band I sprinted back to my room for something decent to wear on stage. Much to my horror I found myself in a white wife-beater at the time and got a few disapproving catcalls from the local cabbies for exposing too much skin. I felt quite the knob.

The Coverdogs borrowed two guitars (Fab played basslines on the low strings — *yikes*) and gave the sailors as solid a performance as logistically possible: Zeppelin, Hendrix, Free??? — all of our solid one-guitar rockers. We distracted some sailors for a few hours, sold a handful of CDs and prayed to the Baggage Gods for our remaining gear, which fortunately showed up the next afternoon in time for our second show in Bahrain.

We were out hitting the streets and dirt alleys of Manama, borrowing mountain bikes from the MWR department. We rode up to the Grand Mosque, surrounded by kids playing football (the round kind). We correctly assumed it wasn't a holy day and wandered inside hoping to see the inside of the largest place of worship in the island kingdom. Ahmed was a gregarious, bearded cleric in his early forties. A member of the mosque's staff, his English was excellent and he happily volunteered a tour for the five shaggy Americans. Having driven across The States once, he was vastly more familiar with our culture than we were with his. It was evident that he relished every opportunity to debunk ignorant Western myths about his religion: *Yes, men and women worship separately.* He pointed to the balcony of the beautiful and vast main chamber of marble and limestone, ordained with Italian wood crafted locally in Bahrain: "If you are kneeling and praying next to a pretty girl, is your mind completely focused on God?" Ahmed explained. As I harkened back to my endless Sunday mornings scanning the crowd for teenage hotties at Our Lady of Good Council, I also noticed the lack of paintings or statues. "No idols or pictures," he explained. "That is designed to eliminate impediments between God and man."

As I meditated on the concept a cell phone went off. I glared at my colleagues, wondering who was enough of a dope to bring his cell into a mosque. When Ahmed said, "Excuse me one second," and reached under his white dishdasha to take the call, I felt the planet shrink around me.

The band said our goodbyes to Ahmed, extended our gratitude for the tour, and grabbed our bikes, which were still leaning against the mosque wall not far from the impromptu football match. Using one's hands isn't allowed in football and these kids had no desire to lose theirs for the sake of our mountain bikes. They probably hadn't even glanced at them.

Shari'a law in most Gulf States was explained to us this way: first time you're caught stealing, you lose a hand. Second time, lose a foot. On the third fuckup you lose the other hand and on the fourth off comes your head, which you obviously weren't using anyway.

Heading a few city blocks over to the coast, we passed wooden fishing boats half-beached in the low tide. They could have been either antiquated relics, left for gawking Western tourists like us, or completely functional vessels, we had no idea. My eyes caught a stable down the beach where a sign advertised camel rides at half a Dinar a pop.

Camel rides! What's half a Dinar? Three bucks? We're IN!

We interrupted the owners' lunch but they happily took our money and roused their livestock for us. Camels make the most ungodly noises when they'd rather just lie in the sand and spit. That June afternoon was hot and these animals were certainly not into the idea. But I climbed aboard for my five-minute ride — much smoother than I'd anticipated, even when it took off into a slow sprint. Fab is about my height and weight and he was up next. Spark and Moose, however have done a few extra rounds at the dessert table and when struck by the owner to stand, their camels bleated an unnerving howl of displeasure.

The day was capped by a delicious late lunch of hummus, tabouli and shish tawook. The pita bread came hot from the oven and we burned our fingers from the steam trapped inside. The gorgeous waitresses, adorned in headdresses, giggled at us as we argued about UFOs. There's always one Coverdog ready to play devil's advocate in any given discussion and that day it was Moose, "just leaving the possibility open" of spaceships and Greys and all that silly shit. In my skeptical leanings I appreciated his points, but after a year or so of DOD tour experience I was dubious of my government's ability to coordinate a global cover-up of that scope. Not if they can't always keep track of four knucklehead musicians.

In addition to our normal array of paperwork for the Pentagon we had signed "Death Certificates" in order to gain entry into Saudi Arabia. These documents stated that we were not, under any circumstances, to bring certain items into The Kingdom: narcotics, alcohol, tobacco, pornography, religious propaganda... The penalty was death by beheading. There aren't a ton of Jehovah's Witnesses knocking on doors in Jeddah.

In a big rubber bin, The Coverdogs brought with us some 400 units of our recently pressed CD, titled *Sent By Washington* — a reference to DOD touring that only a solitary Colonel caught, much to my disappointment. Promptly upon arriving at Riyadh's King Khalid Airport, our entire tub was immediately confiscated by Saudi customs and taken to a back room "to be checked for anti-Islamic content." *Sent* was just a compilation CD featuring tracks from band members' various solo projects. Army Joes dig buying CDs as an option so we sank some bread into a run of 500 discs. The sole Coverdog release opened with the Egodog song "Bad Guy," a very heavy piece with hopefully enough innuendo to throw off the average Arabic-speaking Mutawah stooge. Had I been allegorical enough? My head scrolled through the first English words the religious police would be hearing:

> *"Don't tell me it's too soon for you, don't give me 'give me time'*
> *Once I'd say that it's alright, but tonight I'll make up your mind*
>
> *Black hat, dead eyes, and secrets to hide*
> *I'll be the sin, I'll be the crime, I'll be the lie*
> *and I'll be playing the Bad Guy*
>
> *If conversation was your true intent,*
> *you should've thought twice to wear that dress*
>
> *How could I face myself without your notch on my belt?*
> *Mean streak, cold stare, and darkness to spare.*
>
> *I'll be obscene, I'll be the swine and I'll be playing the Bad Guy"*

Swine! No pork allowed, I know that much. The admittedly edgy lyrical content I had penned raced through my head: *"I'll be the sin, I'll be the crime!"* — and my heart sank when Fab described the back room full of CD players, with uniformed agents in headphones, and stacks of confiscated CDs. The Mutawa also had a healthy collection of Maxim and Joe Weider fitness magazines. I wondered if these dudes are allowed to take them to the can. With no choice but to let the Muslim branch of the PMRC do their thing, we exited the terminal to meet our American escorts.

We knew we weren't imagining the dirty looks from the locals. Our military escorts began immediately warning us of interactions with the Mutawa. Saudi Arabia's notorious religious police roam the streets looking for unveiled women or, in our case, longhaired Americans. Wielding canes, they will in fact use these sticks to express their displeasure at unsavory influences. One Point of Contact (POC) turned to us, straight faced and said, "If the Mutawa comes up and starts hitting you in the leg with a stick, just run back to the van, lock the doors and we'll diffuse the situation." All heresy resides in the calf muscle, apparently.

There was currently one American soldier serving a year sentence for consuming alcohol in public. Not being intoxicated, mind you, just drinking. Likely a beer. The Gulf States had an unorthodox arrangement with the U.S. military. Whereas most nations hosting U.S. troops sign Status of Forces (SOFA) agreements with America, some GCC States had not. Therefore, service people accused of crimes in Saudi, Qatar, etc are subject not to American military law, as in Germany or Korea, but rather to ancient and draconian Sharia Law. It's a tenuous balance, an arrangement based on both mutual necessity and mutual disdain.

Ok hell, it's based on oil.

We were told of one servicewoman caught smoking a cigarette on a Riyadh street. A Black woman mind you, so imagine this scene: a Mutawa began striking her leg with his cane, and she promptly reared back and laid him out. Quickly snatched by her American comrades, she was driven at top speed, not back to her barracks on the base, but directly to the flight line where she was hurried onto — literally — the next plane out.

We did a bus tour through Riyadh on our second day in Saudi. It basically consisted of the driver pointing and saying, "That's Prince So-n-So's Palace. But you can't see it behind that wall." Moose opted out of sightseeing in the Kingdom and then later in Kuwait. Moose was hesitant to mingle with the

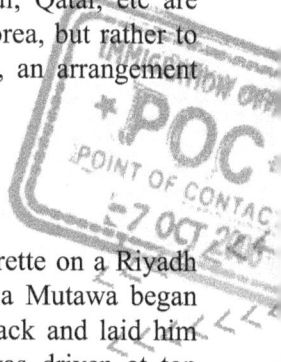

locals, being of Jewish ancestry. I wasn't sure how exactly that would make itself evident on the streets of Riyadh, unless he suddenly lost it and started screaming for matza balls.

Fab and I had the opportunity to shop the gold souk (market) downtown one Sunday night, and traversed infamous Chop Chop Square. A non-descript football field sized area located next to City Hall, the square serves as the weekly location for corporal punishment in Riyadh. Fitted with small metal grates where the blood is washed away, on this particular night it was serving as a football pitch for several pre-teens culturally numb to the square's alternate purpose. Depending on who you ask, Westerners are either discouraged from attending the Friday festivities or they are pushed to the front of the crowd, ostensibly as a warning and shot of Sharia reality. Rapists, adulterers, and the occasional murderer are (mercifully) sedated and led out to the block. A broadsword is heated in order to cauterize the wound and minimize the gore. Most offenders tend to be TCNs, or Third Country Nationals — laborers from poorer nations like Bangladesh, Pakistan, and Sudan. Americans weren't the only guys contracting out their physical labor.

Our first friend in Saudi was our Palestinian liaison Fadwa, who tirelessly worked the phones back to the censorship clowns at the airport and somehow secured the release of our tub of CDs. Fab and I borrowed a car from the base and nervously raced out to the airport to retrieve our booty. I waited outside security and paced anxiously until Fab emerged humping that beautiful rubber bin — the whole tour was still ahead of us. I grabbed the other end of the tub and Fab and I double-timed it back to the SUV, looking over our shoulders, half-expecting someone would change their mind and chase us down like infidel dogs.

The shows in Saudi were all outdoor and all energetic. Fortunately the first gig was at Eskan Village, the base where we were billeted for a few days. We arrived just as the DFAC was serving steak and gigantic king crab legs.

There are two very distinct reactions DOD entertainers get from troops as we wander their bases: the pre show and the post-show vibe. Playing a gig early in your stay reduces the dirty looks at the dining facility, while in the days after a performance, soldiers are engaging and warm. A common third we get from soldiers pondering our non-regulation haircuts is the tentative, "Are you Special Ops?" I once momentarily considered letting that assumption slide as an affirmative, until I envisioned coming across actual Special Ops guys, who would be doubtlessly un-amused.

Per the "bunny" scene in *Apocolypse Now* we would often open with "Suzie Q" by Creedence Clearwater Revival (as opposed to Creedence Clearwater *Revisited* — minus John Fogerty and coming to a State Fair near you!). The Eskan show consisted of the C-Dog no-brainers: Stones, Floyd, Weezer, Bad Company's "Rock and Roll Fantasy." At show's end the band was hot, sweaty and drained. But these are by no means USO luxury tours, and we proceeded to tear the gear and PA down, to store until the next day's trip out to Prince Sultan Air Base.

Occasionally we run across young musicians, eager to talk shop at inevitably the most inopportune times. Ok, let's face it: I never like talking shop. But Spark, Fab and Moose were more entertained by such exchanges, and we were tearing down gear, exhausted as this over-exuberant kid bounced between us like a gnat.

"What kind of strings do you use? I saw Pantera live last year, man they fucking rocked... How long have you guys been together?"

The guys were placating him the best they could, but I'd about had it as he went on and on and fucking on.

"I used to have an amp just like that one! My brother has a band... why don't you guys do any Korn?"

"Because they SUCK!" I shot back, over my shoulder. Man, you could see the poor kid deflate right there. I pictured him heading back to his bunk, surrounded by Jonathon Davis posters, shaken and disillusioned. My band has never forgiven me.

Guitarists, it seems, always enjoy shoptalk. Following dinner one evening during that tour, Spark got into an animated debate over the merits of some music versus others. We are on a Middle-Eastern street corner, arguing loudly over the musical relevance of grunge bands.

I pressed Spark, "So you're telling me Nirvana has the same musical validity as Cole Porter?"

"Yes. It's all subjective. All music has value."

I knew he detested the British Nirvana rip-offs, Bush. I took my argument further: "And by that measure, Cole Porter has the same value as Bush."

"No. They don't have the originality of a Nirvana," Spark countered.

"There it is, then. Not that there is one all encompassing objective guide to follow, but you definitely *have* an opinion. An opinion that certain music is in fact better than another. That is your right and your duty as one who creates music. Be picky as hell!"

That said…

I recall standing in a Music Plus store in 1991, and seeing some band making the most horrific cacophony on the video monitor. "That's awful," I said aloud to no one. It was Nirvana's "Smells Like Teen Spirit." So as far as my finger on America's music pulse, Bob's your uncle. Maybe one day I'll learn to dig Cobain. But probably not. What, he lived in a city with the nation's highest suicide rate, did heroin *and* was married to Courtney Love? That suicide wasn't a tragedy, that was inevitability.

After the Eskan Village show came a two-day trip to Prince Sultan Air Base (PSAB), at that time the largest air base on the planet. Both bases were closed quietly after September 2001 when Al Queda convinced us that they were in fact, very, *very* unhappy about American troops chillin' on sacred soil. Given a tour of the expansive area we took photo ops amongst a sea of Patriot missiles, lying dormant in the desert sun awaiting their reactivation. An up-close tour of the F-15s was insightful but Fab's long-term goal of riding in a fighter jet remained sadly unachieved. We did stop at the end of a runway just in time to see the blind landing of a U2 spy plane, returning from a mission at 75,000 feet. Our tour guide said we should give a shout out to their unit, the "Fighting Cocks" at that evening's show. I gladly did so between songs, early in our first set. Unfortunately, it seemed absolutely NONE of the pilots or ground crew was in attendance, and my evening's first attempt at banter went something like this:

"Hey, we got any fighting cocks out there?"

Cricket… cricket…

Nothing. The guys love it when I eat shit.

14 June 2000: MTV India is available on cable systems throughout The Gulf, and I watched as often as I could. Between traditional belly-dancing shows (the authenticity of which were marred only by names like *Boogie Woogie*) I caught videos from artists like Canadian Punjab rapper Jazzy B, whose disc I ran out to purchase immediately. While chatting up an Emirati shop owner I learned of Om Kalthum, "The Diva of Arab Music" and bought one of her haunting and majestic CDs as well.

Lazy hotel afternoons and long flights were accompanied by loops of Catherine Wheel on my Sony Walkman (yes kids, cassettes). After much prodding in LA from Higgie, I was delving into their *Adam & Eve* and *Chrome* albums. The latter opened itself to me gradually, and became both this tour's soundtrack and narcotic. *Adam & Eve* was co-produced by *The Wall's* Bob Ezrin, and the whole record beautifully channels The Floyd and late-era Talk Talk.

The Coverdogs performed small, indoor shows at embassy compounds in Abu Dhabi and Dubai before packing up for Qatar.

16 June 2000: As with our gigs in United Arab Emirates, our stop in Qatar (pronounced "cutter or gutter," we were admonished) was intended to entertain the few American Marines there. With single rooms reserved in another beautiful hotel, we realized we were blessed with a dream scenario for the touring musician — an in-house gig! On both nights our show would be held at the Ramada's club downstairs, a short elevator ride from our comfy lodging. We counted our blessings while frequenting the swimming pool and gym often. I wandered across the street to a Qatari TCBY and stirred protein powder into my yogurt.

Setting up for soundcheck the afternoon of the first show, we were surrounded by drunk Englishmen loudly following the World Cup on the telly. We kept our amp volumes low and went about our business. A few of the Brits were already hammered on Harp and warm Guinness, and they engaged us in conversation. They were foreign contractors working in Qatar, telling us about a neighbor's seventeen year old who had tried to smuggle hash into the country while visiting his parents. He'd just completed two long months in a very nasty Qatari prison and was expelled from the country for life. He was very fortunate. A local woman convicted of adultery was just executed that week we were in Qatar. She was stoned to death.

One swaggering and stumbling Englishman was far more interested in the band of longhaired musicians than in the football match in progress. He followed me around as I hooked up mics and unwrapped cables.

"You've got a bottom like Doris Day," he stammered.

Yeeeeeeesh.

21 June 2000: The Grand Hyatt Muscat in the Omani capital is an enormous castle, a semi-circle facing the beach, ornate and absolutely gorgeous. Our stay there balanced out the drama of dealing with our Point Of Contact. We'll call him Dick.

"You guys tour a lot, eh? Yeah. Been there, done that, bought the t-shirt, wore it out," Dick told us at baggage claim, having known us all of five minutes. It's amazing how many people given the entertainer liaison position have *zero* social skills. POC Dick continued, "I play guitar. Think I could sit in with you guys?" Our bassist was diplomatic as always. "Uh, yeah sure," Fab sputtered, caught off guard — words he would later regret.

We learned of a schedule change. Our day off had been nixed at the request of the Ambassador who was throwing a dinner party and wanted The Coverdogs as the evening's entertainment. Yes, he knew we weren't a lounge act. He wanted to impress the invited Omani Royalty with an actual American live rock and roll band in his home. When we arrived at the Ambassador's residence, there were a few adjustments. "Can you guys do something nice and jazzy for background? Just while the guests are arriving."

Heeere we go.

Spark bit the bullet and set up his amp in the foyer, dialed in a clean tone and proceeded to play a few jazz standards. In a back room, Dick went to fetch drinks as the rest of us listened in to Spark in the entryway. After a few minutes I turned to Fab. "What am I hearing? Is that... "Enter Sandman?"

"Yep," said Fab. "Bossonova Metallica."

The itinerary was as follows: Spark's entry music, sit quietly through dinner in the anteroom, then on a servant's cue begin setting up a scaled-down PA in the main hall where the attendees would be gathering. Dick returned with five clear glasses and one dark. He offered the tray first to Fab who naturally reached for the cola. "Hey, hey! Not that one. That's for me," Dick smirked. "It's got a little something special in it, to help get me through the night." So he was rude and also an idiot. Stupid people tend to assume you're their buddy. They often reveal information that can harm them later. This guy was on our *no-buy* list right from the "been there done that" quip and now he was telling us he drinks on the job. In Oman? These are the penis-pumps my government gives security clearances to.

Just as we couldn't take any more of this guy's butchering of Rush tunes on Fab's Fender bass, we were instructed to begin setting up. Chairs were brought out as American diplomats, their spouses, and members of the Omani royal family in stark white robes filed in and sat politely in front of us. Drinking in the surrealism of the whole scene, I found myself focused on the prettiest girl in the room, whom it turned out was an Omani Princess. She'd been quarreling all day with her father in an attempt to gain permission to attend school in the States. Surely the presence of an American rock band did significant damage to her case.

As we mellowed out polite versions of "Magaritaville" and "Sweet Home Alabama" I scoured my mind for appropriate between-song repartee, coming up with only tongue in cheek apologies for the lack of earplugs to go around. I felt like quoting Lennon: "Those of you in the cheap seats can clap your hands. The rest of you can just rattle your jewelry."

The set ended to polite applause and we mingled a while with the guests. An American Air Force general apologetically expressed his desire to hear the band at full volume, hinting at wilder days in his past. The Royal Family was charming and appreciated the show, which they were apparently unprepared for. I kept my interaction with the Princess at a diplomatic minimum.

With the PA torn down and the guests departed we were ready to load out when Ambassador Craig invited us to stay for coffee and cake. Adjourning to an elegant but comfortable living room we immediately began picking his brain: "What is the current state of relations with Oman? Why do we capitulate on SOFA agreements with GCC States?"

I hope the good Ambassador wasn't expecting to discuss bar chords and delay pedals.

An appointee of President Clinton, Ambassador John Craig was kind enough to explain the tenuous relationship between the State Department and our Middle East partners, but that Oman is one of the friendlier nations in the region. There was a great deal of ambivalence on both sides regarding American servicewomen being obligated to wear traditional Islamic headscarves that cover all but the eyes. Clearly the entire arrangement was touchy, even pre-September 11, and unorthodox by U.S. foreign policy standards. We left that night a little more knowledgeable and grateful for Ambassador Craig's hospitality, yet certain that our evening was, and may remain, the strangest gig of our lives.

Masirah is a tiny island off Oman's East Coast. It serves as an unloading point for C-141 and C-5 cargo aircraft supplying Naval battle groups in the Arabian Sea, a spot of sand serving as a temporary home for a handful of hard-working Yanks. Arriving mid-morning aboard a C-130 we set up our gear for a lunchtime show in their small recreation center. What that afternoon set lacked in ambiance, it made up for in enthusiasm. The more remote a location, the more appreciative an audience, as the good people on Masirah proved. Oblivious to bright fluorescent lighting, low ceilings and ping-pong acoustics, The Coverdogs jammed an intimate set of Doobie Brothers, Beatles and Iron Maiden. Snapping some great runway shots on our way out, we were airborne again by 4 PM on our way back to the Hyatt and a hang at poolside.

The next afternoon, we were loading gear for our final show there in the Omani Sultanate, an outdoor gig in sweltering heat and unusual humidity on the Embassy grounds. I was admonished at soundcheck not to take any pictures of the stage; we were to perform smack dab in front of the embassy entrance and photos would be a security breach. Even going inside to piss was an ordeal. POC Dick growled at Moose: "Here," handing him an acoustic guitar case to load on the truck. Moose just looked at me with that *whatthefuck* glare. Some guys never quite understand that if players don't like hanging out with you, they likely don't want to jam with you. Dick apparently thought he would be included in a jam session that day. He would be mistaken.

"So, you think I can get up and jam one or two with you guys tonight?" He asked a blindsided Fab, who hesitated. Even had it been a stranger — who hadn't vibed us out every second he was around — I'd be wary of having Dick on stage sans-rehearsal. The Ambassador would be attending this night, as well as several other diplomats and military brass, and such "jam sessions" are professionally risky. Nine out of ten guest appearances turn into sonic disasters that make everyone look and sound like ass.

"Man, uh, I don't know," Fab shook his head.

"Hey man, you said we would play something! The day we met at the airport."

I couldn't believe Dick was pushing the issue and I lost it. "What? Are you actually vibing us? This is our *job*. Maybe Fab was being polite, but this one is my call. We don't have people up on stage that we've never played with. Besides, it's your job to facilitate us putting on the best show possible."

POC Dick scurried off, acoustic in hand. We'd be parting ways the next day and good riddance. I later struck up a conversation with a woman officer under whom Dick works. "He wigs me out," she told me. "I don't like being in the office alone with him." She'd come close to filing some harassment charges against him but knew that with government positions getting even the most incompetent people fired is a monumental task. I empathized with her and took quiet consolation in the accuracy of my initial assessment, which had little to do with his sub-par bass noodling.

Ambassador Craig did attend that second show, actually breaking a meeting and arriving in time to introduce us before the crowd of a few dozen embassy employees enjoying the BBQ atmosphere on the lawn. Our mission in Oman completed, we soaked in the last night of our Grand Hyatt single rooms and prepared for rougher logistics that undoubtedly lay ahead.

24 June 2000: There were nasty sandstorms the afternoon The Coverdogs arrived in Kuwait City. These *shamals* color the sky like heavy LA August smog and sometimes last for days. We were met by our Kuwait-based POC (yes a different guy, Allah be praised), a Toughskin-wearing good ol' boy named Ron. Pot faced and chain-smoking, Ron had that affliction so unfortunately prominent in civilian contractors overseas: the gabbies. Oh! New ears! "Let me tell you about my Filipino wife..." Ron had no qualms about sharing the most personal details of his relationship with five guys two decades his junior whom he'd only met that morning. "It's the best," Ron told us in the MWR truck one afternoon. "I get home, she has dinner ready and then afterwards she rubs my feet." *Oof.* We didn't need that visual, buddy.

Ron proudly informed us that we'd be staying at the Marble Palace, a structure across the highway from Camp Doha. While getting our IDs on base we received several envious comments regarding our accommodations, which we were disappointed to find consisted of unflushable (yet still *full*) urinals and gigantic Arab cockroaches. But when we arrived a few days later at The Kabal we understood The Marble Palace's reputation for luxury.

Being the center of American Forces Operations inside Kuwait, Camp Doha also served as the central meeting point of the region's MWR politics — a big bullshit blender. We walked into the middle of a big ongoing drama as to where shows on Doha should be held. Ron wanted everything at the huge field house, which was a cavernous acoustic nightmare but conveniently only a few feet from a majority of the living quarters. His superiors, however, insisted on using the Marble Palace's dining room for concerts, which while aesthetically pleasing, was off the main base a ten minute bus ride away and ergo a logistical pain in the ass. Especially considering the long security lines in and out of Doha: Mirrors under the chassis. Bomb-sniffing dogs. All with good reason — a few years later in 2003 a nearby stretch of highway was to be the scene of an ambush shooting as two Department of Defense contractors were killed amidst the anti-American sentiment of the pre-Iraqi invasion. So, powerless to sway the MWR decision-making machine, The Coverdogs played the Palace — to about a dozen people, tops. Your tax dollars at work, folks.

A long bus ride to Kuwait's main air base, Al Jaber was made longer by our young GI drivers. If you ever find yourself in a position of transporting musicians around, here's a tip: never assume musicians want to listen to music. And especially not at TOP FUCKING VOLUME!!! Kid Rock albums cranked to eleven when you only want to sleep are fingernails on a chalkboard in the 9th ring of hell. Our strongest requests for silence went unheeded and I arrived at Al Jaber groggy and grumpy, yet now privy to perhaps the worst music ever made.

Yes, good reader, this assessment warrants clarification: Kid Rock *is* the Antichrist.

While certainly boasting a resume replete with troop-supporting USO performances, Bobby Richie (real name, too funny) makes a living perpetuating the cliché that everything good emanating from The United States of America derives from either machismo-rap or hillbilly culture. Fuck that guy. "Fuck him in the asshole with a big rubber dick," as George Carlin once said. Ok, so Carlin was referring to Mickey Mouse. But the late Bill Hicks might have also concurred, had he survived to witness this Billy Ray Cyrus on crank, flexing his pasty biceps in front of my flag.

There. I feel better now.

Immediately upon arrival at Al Jaber we were met by the most cordial of greeting parties. Al Jaber was home to the 332nd Air Expeditionary Wing: The Tuskegee Airmen, America's first Black pilots. Showing us around were two young girls from Alabama who had set a comfortable little dressing room aside for us, complete with a huge basket of fresh fruit. *Unnecessary but appreciated!* Once the PA was set up, the band and soundguy Ben were walked over to the base DFAC where a table was made for ourselves and the base commanders, name cards and all. Instead of the usual chow line, servers were coming around the table with each course. Although grateful and hungry, it was approaching show time so I excused myself and retreated to our room to begin my pre-show vocal warm-ups. My Coverdogs played the show on full stomachs but our sandpit/dance floor was fun and full by night's end. We enjoyed all the 332nd's amenities, as the next day's show would give us all a large dose of perspective...

"It's about twenty minutes out now," Ron told us from behind the wheel. We'd already been driving for a few hours, and had parted ways with the pavement some time ago. Our last bit of road had been a stretch of the infamous "Highway of Death" immortalized on CNN during the Gulf War, although we saw none of the roasted remnants of Iraqi vehicles that served as a shooting gallery for American pilots some ten years prior.

We were heading out to The Kabal, a remote base void of solid structures or running water some 15 kilometers from the Iraqi border. Through the blowing sand, a slight rise in the terrain grew through our windshield and we could soon make out soldiers on guard duty, keeping vigil in the 110+ degree misery. We were driven to a flatbed trailer that would serve as our stage that evening. Straining to load our gear onto the trailer while shielding our eyes from a nasty late-afternoon sandstorm we hastily beat a retreat into the nearest tent once the last drum and speaker was chaotically piled up.

The tent door slammed shut behind us and a table full of weary and annoyed soldiers silently glared up at us from their card game. When they did warm to us we were half-jokingly offered green packets of MREs. Meals Ready to Eat — calorically dense and vacuum-sealed sustenance for soldiers out in the middle of sand and shit. We were treated to horror stories about patrolling during shamals even worse than that day's. Folks never really get clean out there — the moment you leave the shower building, the wind immediately re-coats you with microscopic sand and dust particles. *Dry heat, my ass.* Most of the soldiers had at least one encounter with the dreaded camel spider, a nightmarish creature that leaps onto animals (or people) and quickly injects a numbing agent into the victim before proceeding to gnaw entire chunks of flesh away. One day a group of guys on patrol spotted one on the sand between them, and they took turns trying to smash it with their rifle butts, while scampering backwards in terror (unauthorized discharge of a weapon is a major no-no, even in the face of a really big bug). Apparently some Riyadh museum features one specimen whose legs stretch out to nearly the circumference of a Humvee tire. There are JPEGs on the net, go creep yourself out.

We tried our best to kill a few hours before the sun, and thus, the winds died down. It's these long pauses, physically draining and void of any pleasant stimuli, which surely must be the most taxing on the deployed.

We wandered around, trying desperately to distract ourselves from the stinging awareness of how uncomfortable we were. I spent a while in the makeshift MWR tent consisting of a pool table, a ping-pong table, and a few VCR/TVs which were naturally hooked up to a video game system. The corners and one end of the tent were temporary housing, it seemed. Cots and shaving kits strewn about. I put my backpack Ol' Blue on the wood floor and proceeded to lie down in an attempt to squeeze in my sweet and precious pre-gig nappie. I hadn't been prone for two minutes when a soldier was hovering above me. "You might not wanna lie down on the floor," he suggested, continuing before I had a chance to ask why, "A lot of things live in the sand." I was on my feet too quick to maintain any trace of rock-singer cool.

The whole camp seemed to turn out for the show at dusk. The soldiers had parked their vehicles in a huge semi-circle facing our flatbed/stage forming an impromptu bleacher section; it was obvious they'd done this before. These are the guys that come back to their hometowns and organize those gargantuan concert-raves out in the middle of the country on someone's cousin's farm. American military ingenuity, applied directly to the Partying Arts.

The roars came up before we hit downbeat one and continued generously for three hours. Set two saw a soldier hop on stage to play guitar at the behest of his buds. Mind you, pursuant to ad-libbed jams with strangers — completely different situation than POC Dick in Oman: this guy had a gun. We tried a slow twelve bar blues and his boys yelped approval.

While tearing down, there were still a few soldiers lingering by the front of the stage. These guys often volunteer a hand with gear, which we generally try not to accept. But one kid, not even engaging the band in any conversation, was standing behind one of the yet un-gathered folding chairs and was pounding the shit out of it with an empty water bottle. He just had more to release.

The drive back from the Kabal that night provided some of our more uneasy travel moments. Ron had a rough time staying on the pseudo-road that afternoon, now staying on course was proving infinitely more difficult in the pitch black of the desert at 1 AM. We were all very cognizant of how many unexploded ordinances were undoubtedly still buried in the vast Kuwaiti sands. It was just endless black. Sleep was impossible, thrashing about, and we rode silent in the tension. Arriving finally back at the Marble Palace intact, Fab and I came to the mutual conclusion that The Kabal was the worst conditions we had yet seen in our history of military touring. They do 120 days out in that hell. In subsequent years Fab would see much worse in Iraq and Afghanistan...

No matter where you are, there's always somewhere shittier.

29 June 2000: A terrorist threat closed the borders of Jordan to American travelers, and The Coverdogs were almost stuck in Kuwait. Having spent nearly a week there, we were very ready to move on. When Ron suggested we could perform at the Marble Palace again that night, our angst to split hit urgent levels. Although there was no green light as we departed for the airport, there was no red light either. We crossed our fingers and with all 32 pieces of gear loaded we arrived curbside to begin again our chaotic ritual with airport security and local travelers. Attempting to efficiently move an entire PA system and five guys' baggage through Middle East security is one challenge (try explaining the function of a rack-mounted EQ unit to an Arabic-only speaking X-Ray machine technician — air-guitar skills come in handy) but the crowd was a different logistical hurdle entirely. One must let go any notions of courtesy and manners, lest he be squeezed out of the melee and run the risk of missing a flight. Sometimes in order to get the job done, to paraphrase Bono, you gotta take your "Bastard Pills."

Aboard the flight and oblivious to the other guys' near fisticuffs with another passenger, I was treated to an enlightening conversation with a Kuwaiti girl around my age who lived in Kuwait City during the Iraqi occupation. She recalled apartment-to-apartment searches and lootings by the invading force, and the daily fear she and her family lived with for some very long months. But she also related how the men guarding the banks went from young, uniformed soldiers at the beginning of the occupation, to old and crippled shabbily dressed men sent from Baghdad near the war's end. An ethnic Palestinian born and raised in Kuwait, she kindly warned us not to allow Israeli immigration officials to stamp our passports, lest Arab nations not allow us to re-enter their borders. Many people in the region own and use two passports.

Exhausted and happy to have departed Kuwait, the five of us arrived at the Amman, Jordan Marriott in late afternoon. After a brief argument in the lobby over the issue of single rooms versus saving cash, we agreed to touch base later in the event we were up to taking advantage of an off night in a modern and relatively Western-friendly city.

After sunset, we were back in the lobby, refreshed and hungry. I asked the bellhop in the carport to recommend some good local cuisine, as I had a taste for some baba ghanoush and the guys were feeling adventurous. Shouting Arabic into a taxi, the bellhop shuttles us into the cab, where we pile upon each other, half hanging out the back windows and the taxi races off into the night with the band realizing we have absolutely no idea where we're going.

Stopping outside a low stone structure with thatched roof, which we learned was formerly a horse stable, we fell out of the cab, making sure to kick the good driver a few extra dinar in an attempt to counter any pungent American dog-stink. Attempting to snap a shot of the restaurant entrance I found my flash wasn't working (old camera) and resigned myself to keeping the memories internally. Just then, one of the doormen rushed up, and seeing me jostling the AAs, volunteered to run across the street for a fresh pair. I thanked him and told him it wasn't necessary but he soon arrived at our table inside, batteries in hand. More tips for you, good sir!

Every employee that evening, upon learning it was our first night in Jordan, took extra care in making us comfortable. Our Egyptian-born server suggested an amazing combination dinner which allowed us to indulge in grape leaves, hummus, lamb lung and various other goodness. Fab and I split a half a carafe of red wine and just when the night couldn't get any better, the live entertainment arrived — local musicians playing traditional tunes on lutes accompanied by a terrific female vocalist. I wondered if shouting out for Om Kalthoum was akin to requesting "Free Bird" so I just shut up.

As a server in white dishdasha with a dagger on his belt brought us a strong mint tea for desert, we decided to treat ourselves to the region's after dinner practice of smoking a little hubbly bubbly. Shisha bars had yet to catch on in the States, and we were all game for this local indulgence. Two large water pipes were brought to our table, and plastic mouthpieces were given to each of us. A smoldering charcoal was placed upon the top of the shisha pipe (don't call it a bong, Spicoli!) which ignited a small block of flavored tobacco packed in molasses. Ours was flavored apple and strawberry, and we non-cigarette smokers caught a slight buzz and found the neighboring tables laughing at our lack of technique.

One of us might have even said it at the time: "Best dinner ever." Then Fab gets back to the hotel and promptly throws up. Well, hell! Lamb lung and shisha?

- - - - - - - - - - -

Often while touring for the Department of Defense you'll run across logistic snags and various ball-dropping by people up and down the chain of command. We don't delude ourselves. We're only the entertainment. But we like to assume that when it comes to the really important things — dropping bombs and such — that the military has its shit together. We had a very brief layover in Cairo, en route to Sharm el Sheik in Egypt's Sinai Peninsula, where we would be concluding the tour. We were told that an MWR representative would be at Cairo's international terminal to assist us in not only in navigating a chaotic Egyptian airport, but also in pushing our formidable array of cases and bags over to the domestic terminal where we'd catch the flight down to the Sinai Peninsula.

Let's face it...

Not having a contact name or number for this alleged Point of Contact and not wanting to risk missing our connection we sucked it up and organized our gear, pushing it towards the curb outside where hopefully our guy would be waiting... With half a dozen eager volunteers, maybe? Ah, no...

They ain't comin'...

Squishing through the crowd, we got our first whiff of summer in Egypt. We learned that the National Bird is the housefly, and that bathing is optional. Seeing no friendly American faces awaiting the arrival of the world famous Coverdogs, we spotted our destination: Cairo's domestic terminal. It was a couple hundred yards away across a very uneven blacktop parking lot or two. Stacking our PA pieces precariously upon the only six cases having wheels we decided upon the shuttle system whereas the five of us would painstakingly and gradually move the front stack forward while we rotated the rear position. Being one man short we rotated in and out of the caboose position, retrieving the last stack, all the while keeping every tower of gear within view of someone. The whole process took long enough for us to begin worrying about our check-in to Sharm el Sheikh.

When each gear pile reached the domestic terminal, a waiting Coverdog would clap and cheer enthusiastically as the weary bandmate crossed our imaginary finish line. Bracing against the afternoon heat, we smiled back at giggling locals and resumed the leap-frog of tiny wheels under precariously piled cases, across a parking lot far more moon-crater than pavement. *Young Ben to the back stack! Moose to the front! Did you almost eat it? We're almost there, woooo!*

Up ahead on an adjacent roof an Egyptian soldier shakes his head, machine gun in hand and laughs as we shout a play-by-play of each guy as they reach our finish line. Weren't we just smoking shisha and eating dolmas?

After the 1979 Camp David Accords, for which then-President Jimmy Carter received the Nobel Peace Prize, the Sinai Peninsula was to be a no-fly zone, off limits to both Israeli and Egyptian military aircraft. A multi-national coalition called the MFO (Multinational Force & Observers) was established to enforce the no-fly zone and strategic Bay of Sharm el Maya. American soldiers have been performing that duty, quietly, faithfully and effectively ever since.

Arriving late at night in the Sinai we were taken to our home base for the next week, South Camp. Also present at the base outside of Sharm el Sheikh were troops from Columbia, New Zealand, and Fiji. It took us a while to get used to large, buff Pacific Islanders standing in the dining facility line wearing flowery skirts.

Throughout the Sinai, there are several remote camps, consisting of around a half dozen soldiers each. Their job is to basically sit atop a tower and watch the sky. These are our Forward Operating Bases. If there's ever a bunch of guys that need some entertainment, it's FOB grunts. We packed up a couple borrowed acoustic guitars and Jay's snare drum and piled into a minivan for the day. To call those desert back roads "rough" would be a magnanimous compliment to Egyptian infrastructure. The Sinai topography is mountainous, being situated upon a major fault line, and the roads are barely sufficient for the herds of goats and camels we passed during our ten-hour day. We bounced and rocked and picked out pre-packaged foods from our dreaded box lunches, brought from the base DFAC. The sandwich choices were either a ham-like substance or beef tongue. Beef tongue in 115 degrees. Think I'll pass. I ate apples and chips.

The last few days at South Camp found most of the Coverdogs fighting the bane of the traveling musician — stomach virus. We blamed it on the raw fish platter, available daily in DFAC. We indulged often and we paid the price. It was only at that point of the tour that we all gave serious credence to the rumors of un-sanitized working conditions in Middle Eastern kitchens. However, we did leave with a "handy" regional colloquialism: *eat with the right, wipe with the left.*

Our trek out to the Forward Operating Bases that day was punctuated by a stop at Bedouin Bob's. There's a makeshift sign on that lonely structure that served as a restaurant/shisha bar/home. We hung around only long enough to hit the facilities (you gotta rock the hole in the floor) and be accosted by his kids circling us like hungry gnats, shrieking "Chips! Chips!" They were cute... for the first five minutes. Then it is pretty much GAQ! (Coverdog-speak for "go away quickly")

Our task at hand was saving the soldiers at these remote bases from another afternoon of abject boredom. Assembling a snap-together acoustic set list, we let drummer Moose take the lead vox on Marley's "Stir It Up." Moose had performed it a thousand times with his bread and butter State-side act, Panjive, a steel drum Caribbean act he steadily books for weddings and summer parties. Some CCR, Beatles or whatever sounded good without amps and drum kit rounded out a half hour set, hastily assembled in the FOB's central outdoor area. These invariably consisted of a few picnic tables and a crappy weight bench and rusted, dusty old barbells. The logistics of the day kept us from hanging too long, and we piled back into our minivan in silence. It always took a few miles until we got talkative again. Those conditions re-define "roughing it."

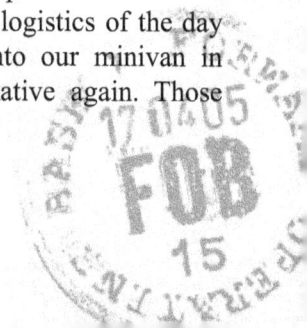

The following day saw us hit four more outposts, but they were relatively adjacent to South Camp and we were back by mid afternoon, in plenty of time to catch the inter-camp amateur boxing tournament! We mingled with the troops, parking ourselves on the bleachers and accepting cigars from an officer who quickly figured out who the longhairs were. We hooted and catcalled the first few rounds of fighters, who, with no formal training or experience, flailed their arms wildly. Annoyed by our vociferous critiques, one GI turned around and asked me point blank, "Have any of you guys ever gotten in the ring?"

"Oh hell no," I admitted. "We're just being smarmy. It's our job." The soldier was mollified and I dodged becoming an unofficial undercard. After the last of eleven bouts, the band was again sequestered for an acoustic performance, this time at the NCO (Non-Commissioned Officers) club. My voice was trashed from cheering but we pulled it off and all were happy singing along through slugs of near-beer.

4th of July, 2000: Unidentified insect bites and a rash accompanied my knotted stomach that morning but the excitement of performing that night at South Camp's mini-amphitheatre outweighed it all. Stationed right along the beach, the bench seating was cut into a small hill, giving the audience a view of the Gulf of Aqaba behind the stage. We also caught wind of the base's Ordinance Team being in charge of the evening's firework display and sure enough, as we were loading gear up that afternoon several troops were laying some kind of cable on the shore behind us. Our Independence Day show in Egypt was rowdy from note one, with a homesick and patriotic crowd screaming us on to louder and heavier songs. A final set of Foo Fighters, Ozzy, and Zep brought the show to a climax. Closing with Metallica's "Enter: Sandman" just put it over the top. The band had been asked to handle the National Anthem duties that holiday evening. The Hendrix version was begun as a 3-piece and I wandered off stage into the crowd with my camera to grab a few shots and drink the moment in. Sure enough, at the *"Land of the free"* coda, the ground shook and one by one, huge orange mushroom clouds of fire rose behind a startled band. The Ordinance Team sat somewhere nearby, smiling in deserved and patriotic satisfaction.

"The bombs bursting in air…"

Following the post-show ceremony of receiving plaques from the camp CO, we had more opportunity to meet some under appreciated American servicepeople. Ben tore down gear while the band hopped off stage. One soft-spoken soldier in his late 30's spoke of his family Stateside and how much an Independence Day night of American rock and roll lifted his spirits. I tried to deflect his compliments. What we do is trivial in comparison. "I don't know if I could grab a gun and defend my country at a second's notice," I told him. "You guys are the brave ones."

"Tell you what," he thought, and gave me one of the greatest compliments I've ever received: "I'd go into battle with you."

The bus ride up to North Camp, at the other end of the peninsula was a nasty one. Despite the enormity of the tour bus we were being jolted about pretty violently. My attempts at the bus' bathroom all proved futile, and I gave up and proceeded to scribble some thoughts to distract myself from my bladder. My musings were ultimately illegible and I was overjoyed to reach North Camp several long hours later.

The second of two North Camp shows was the last of the tour, and we invited Young Ben up to jam during B.B. King's "The Thrill Is Gone." Young Ben Adamson had recently been accepted to UCLA's Jazz Program and he had brought his trumpet and muzzle on tour to practice in off-hours, and his performance that evening was fantastic. Moose, Fab, Spark and I shot surprised glances across the stage at each other, as Ben became the first horn player to join the Coverdogs on stage.

The next day, all gear and baggage was packed into a large moving van and we were once again dressed down with the do's and don'ts of Middle Eastern security protocol. The long drive to the Israeli border wound through a few sparse and impoverished Egyptian villages. Passing an intersection, one of our escorts discarded a half-empty water bottle out the van window. A group of kids suddenly broke off their soccer game to dive towards the drinking water. *Water.*

Beaten down by the flies and the heat, we made ourselves as presentable as possible and began the process of exiting Egypt, accompanied by our MWR hosts. Grouchy immigration officers checked and double-checked our paperwork, put up minor resistance and eventually allowed us to bypass the crowds of disheveled locals back to our van. From there we made the several hundred yard drive to a second barbed wire gate. Passing through the final barricade, we caught a sight we suddenly realized we hadn't seen in perhaps weeks — grass. Green. I swear, the temperature dropped as we crossed the border into Israel. The first officials we met were smiling and cordial, sincerely welcoming us to a land in which they took obvious pride. Military service is mandatory for Israeli citizens, and more than a few of the soldiers that processed us in were young and beautiful women. We took care not to let our passports get stamped, and we were on our way to Ben Gurion Airport.

The topography of Southern Israel is rolling green hills and farmlands, healthy and vibrant. It made sense, after our five plus weeks in the sand, why the surrounding nations — religious differences not withstanding — have been historically poised to pounce on this small oasis of a country. An oasis built and supported, admittedly, by over half a century of American taxpayer support. Stopping at a restaurant along the highway we were reminded of the high price for Israel's survival as plain clothed soldiers strolled into the rest room with Uzi sub-machine guns slung casually over their shoulders. Violence could come at any time for these people. Kind of like Compton with plastique.

The airport in Tel Aviv was full of beautiful women. We drooled our way to the security lines where, lo and behold, all the security officials were gorgeous as well. Each traveler was taken aside by his own individual agent, and bags were all thoroughly searched while being questioned in great detail about our trip: *Where have you visited? With whom did you stay? What was the purpose of your trip?* We certainly didn't mind the interrogation, and I secretly hoped for a strip search. However, Tour Manager Fab jolted me back to the task at hand with a rushed and frantic order for Ben and I to take all the gear and run — not walk — to our terminal. It seemed Spark, Moose, and Fab wouldn't make the flight home, but Young Ben and I could, and we had to bring the equipment with us — all thirty-two enormous pieces of it. Doing our best OJ Simpsons (dashing through the airport I mean, not the double-homicide), we trusted our TM's wisdom and did make the Continental flight with no time at all to spare.

Trans-continental coach flights are never fun but after such a long and hectic run we found ourselves thankful and pitied the remaining Dogs, who, we would find out later, were forced to overnight in Tel Aviv. Fab had it even rougher as he attempted to visit a relative in New Jersey on his way back to Los Angeles. He found himself trapped on a runway in Denver for four hours, not arriving back in Cali until a travel time of some 36 hours had elapsed from Tel Aviv to LAX.

All hail Fab the Road Warrior, getting our cadre of knuckleheads back home.

With Pops and baby bro, 1976.
Some time after this photo was
taken, my right arm grew back

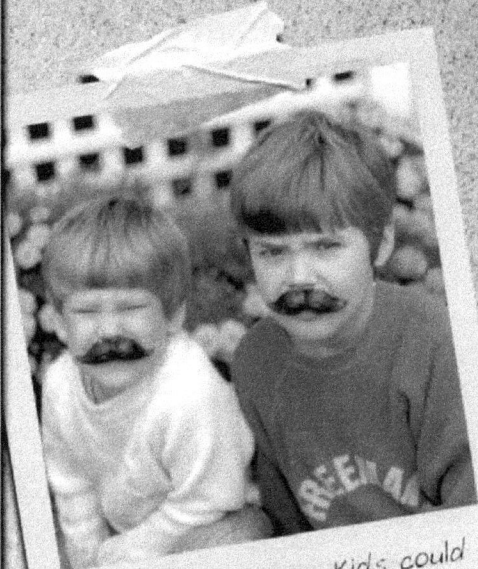

As happy as two kids could
be with those haircuts

oldier Field
hicago 1999

First garage band with Higgie
and Erhart - Illinois 1986.
Nice trousers, kid!

Olympic Torch Relay -
San Jose, California 2002

139

IMMIGRATION OFFICER
(10)8)
15 MAR 2002
HEATHROW (1)

Lewis Popp and Officer Andy -
Illinois 2002

With McLefty (far right)
and new friends -
Camp Bondsteel, KOSOVO 2001

Coverdogs and guide Ahmed
at Grand Mosque -
Manama, Bahrain 2000

Macedonia   United Arab Emir

Iraq   Qatar

Kosovo   Oman   Kor

Iceland   Kuwait

Norway   Jordan   Isre

Mexico   Japa

Canada   Egypt   Ger

Mic   Hunga

Mullet Hatchet's Tayler Parks
and DJ Marcine - Park City
2006

The future Prez - campaign
stop in Park City 2007. Who's
the clown in the shades?

On the road again -
colorado 2008

AUG02

STOR COOP

ID-CARD Z 081618

Z 081618

18 AUG 70

OROS, ANTHONY J.

CIV US

TONY OROS
NIGEL TONES
TONO
TAYLER PARKS

141

me and Higgie -
Bosnia 2001

metal Dogs, circa 2010 -
Nigel with Axl Grease
and Dave Granger!

muscat Island
Oman 2000

coverdogs with Higgie, Fab
and Spark myth - Santa
Barbara, California 2010

MAKEOUT IN A MINE FIELD:
COVERDOGS BALKANS II

September 2000: Fab was on bass, with Moose on drums. Bart — soon to be my Edge in our U2 tribute — handled classic rock guitar duties. Touring for the DOD requires infinite patience through capricious travel logistics. *Hurry up and wait.* We sat for three hours at Camp Bondsteel's helipad awaiting a shaky ride on another Boeing CH-47 chinook. Those workhorse cargo helicopters were notorious through MWR entertainer circles for their rough and sometimes harrowing flights through the SFOR and KFOR theaters. A few years before the Goo Goo Dolls were in a "shit-hook" over Bosnia when smoke filled the cargo area/passenger cabin. The pilots had to execute a "rapid descend," where they opened the back hatch and basically let the plane nose-dive a few seconds to — literally — clear the air.

Don't tell the Goo Goo Dolls your Jet Blue flight was rough. Eat your peanuts and shut the fuck up.

Drummer/backing vocalist *par excellence* Moose is easy to travel with — as long as you're not a semi-insomniac rooming with the guy. That big boy snores like a chainsaw, winning him a second moniker, "Buzz." MWR Balkan entertainers are jammed into the dreaded connexes — sometimes known as CHUs or Combat Housing Units. Just envision cargo freight containers stacked one atop another, poorly ventilated, rarely if ever cleaned, with absolutely no sound insulation. Now put four to eight guys in each CHU of about 8x20 ft. Just when you're drifting off, a bandmate starts sawing away. *"ZZZZZZZZZ!!!"* And why does it always seem to be the drummer?

There was a jogging path that snaked through Eagle Base. The woods were full of UXO signs: unexploded ordinances. So when I chatted up a female soldier after the show and we strolled together in the Bosnian moonlight, we

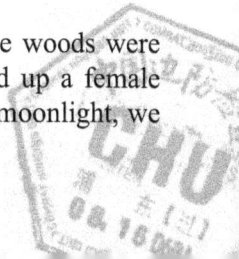

143

were careful not to stray too far from the trail. She was in Psychological Operations. Her job was to fuck with peoples' heads. So naturally, I was fascinated. Only rarely did my tour-mates or I stay in touch with the servicemen or -women we had met while flying through their lives in 24-hour increments. Mind you, our earlier tours happened before social networking took hold. A decade later we would find ourselves Instant Messaging with soldiers we'd met some 36 hours before, 7000 miles away.

I bought a sword at the Turkish Market on a day trip from Pristina in Skopjie on a sightseeing outing with POC Glenn, who pronounced the 'j' (Skope-GEE) and we wondered why no one corrected him. Glenn was tall and Baby-Huey-esque in appearance but man, that dude could ball. We do not suggest challenging that POC to a game of HORSE. We stopped at the marker where Mother Theresa was born. Saint or Catholic soldier fighting a lifelong war of futility, I wasn't sure. I've always thought she could've been handing out condoms and lightening her workload, but what do I know. I snapped pictures of the bronze plaque anyway.

Last show of our second Balkan run was at Camp Able Sentry in Macedonia. The MWR staff assembled their pre-fab stage on the basketball court right behind the espresso bar.

Our arbitrary and welcome gift from the Travel Gods: a stopover in Munich —during Oktoberfest! Our hotel was a few blocks' stumbling distance from the festivities. Bart, Fab, Moose and I cut the crowd of inebriated Euros and eventually chose the Hoffbrau tent, where we weaseled spots at one of the dozens of picnic tables — they won't let you order beer unless you're seated. Soon we were downing steins and hooting at the *oom-pah-pah* band stationed in the center of the tent. Ignorant American assumptions had me anticipating polkas and traditional German sing-alongs, yet what were the biggest songs of the night? ABBA and Beatles. "Let It Be" and "Hey Jude" had the whole tent screaming along, and German fascination with John Denver blew my mind.

> *"Country road, take me home?"*

Did these people even know where West Virginia was? Hilarious.

We drank with Austrians, Dutch, Belgians and Italians. When we finally had our fill of hefeweizen and with "Dancing Queen" stuck in our heads, we waddled back the two city blocks to our hotel. Moose was feeling frisky and in a spontaneous display of affection he leapt onto Fab's back, and Fab crumbled helplessly under the sudden addition of our drummer's girth. No one was seriously hurt that night, we all made our flight with time to spare and to my knowledge, no one blew chow.

THIS IS THE PLACE
AND POPCORN NIGHT

April Fool's Day 2003: I pulled my truck into the carport of a crappy apartment complex in Salt Lake City. I was weighed down with the last of my stuff, and gosh darn tuckered after the cross-country drive. I was armed with a copy of Krakauer's *Under the Banner of Heaven*. It was less than two weeks since Bush II had invaded Iraq, and rednecks everywhere were giddy.

I spent my first morning in the Beehive State absorbing war coverage on Mormon-owned KSL radio (listen for their anachronistic LDS mini-drama spots, they're a RIOT!) while staring at a fresh dusting of snow. My new buddy Hedley had promised me a ski lesson and I'd be damned if I was going to live in Utah and not dip my toes. Yet at that point, into my 30's, I had yet to ski. Thus, the late wintry scene out my window was more of a drag than anything. I was ready for spring, ready for change. I'd locked two weekly shows in Salt Lake and there was much additional untapped gig potential. Fifteen years in LA and six hard months in Illinois were behind me. All I wanted now was steady work and some autonomy. I had the Thursday 80's Metal Show as a solid anchor. I knew that gig would last as long as we busted ass at it (it would last seven years).

My first acoustic night in Utah was at the old Shaggy's Living Room on State Street. Our Wednesdays were a scene: The Erics, asking for Tenacious D. Lexi and Lori joining me for red wine, if only to perplex the Pabst Blue Ribbon crowd. The owner, Bones, paying me cash with a smile. I printed musical menus with possible selections for the evening. I burned Stereophonics and Travis CDs for my new friends. Wilson burned me Ben Harper and Jack Johnson.*

---

* I must say, that if I do have any guilty pleasure artists on my iPod, surfer/singer Jack Johnson certainly qualifies — fluffy, yes, but yet at his best, Jack is stream-of-consciousness good. Is he our generation's Jimmy Buffett? Let's wait and see if he gets fat and opens shitty chain restaurants.

Then Shaggy's moved downtown. My audience numbers dove and the night soon died. At least I got some crappy furniture out of the deal.

I moved my residence as well, renting a small house in Sugarhouse where I was not immune to the missionaries' knock on my door. Living in the Salt Lake Valley, I knew it was only a matter of time before a pair of them would hit my front porch. They walked right past the Darwin-fish on my Isuzu's bumper.

I'd been curious as to the mission selection process, how arbitrary it must be for a green and terrified teenager having just completed his training, stressing: *Where will I be shipped off to for two years?* If you're born and raised in Utah are you relieved — or disappointed — if you are assigned your service in Salt Lake City? *Oh my heck, I wanted to learn to speak Tagalog!*

On one flight back from a weekly Vegas gig, I found myself surrounded by a gaggle of these young theological foot soldiers. Worker drones for God. When the kid in the seat next to me introduced himself, I thought he said "Elden" something. A nice, farm-boy name, right? He was 18 and stereotypically polite. He was still mid-mission and seemed enthused about the whole deal. I glanced at the nametag pinned to his suit. Then I looked around at his buddies' tags. Either all of these guys had the same first name or this kid wanted me to call him "Elder." *Fat chance, Skippy.*

The two kids on my porch that afternoon in Sugarhouse were from Virginia and yes, Salt Lake. No frequent flyer miles for you, buddy! (The LDS Church keeps all frequent flyer credits anyway.) There were two teenagers in ties standing on my steps. "We're here to talk to you about The Church of Jesus Christ of Latter-Day Saints. Do you have a few minutes?" Absolutely I did!

"Sure! You guys fascinate me."

They looked surprised. "We do? Why?"

"Because," I said, "you guys are 19 years old and you have The Answer."

I unsuccessfully offered them a beer — I figured getting told to fuck off all day was likely thirsty work — and we picked each other's brains (which would have been infinitely more fun after that beer). The kid from Utah was steadfast in his beliefs: *Yes, mine is the correct religion. No, our prophet's conviction record is not relevant; the important thing is the message he*

147

brought us... Through seer stones, yes. Which nobody else ever saw. Sorry, kid. I think I'm a *no-buy.*

The missionary who had been raised in Virginia, however, was far more open to my perspectives, having been undoubtedly exposed to Southern Baptists, Evangelicals and Born Agains, equally unshakeable in their convictions. Being brought up LDS in America's South must have been a daily pain in the ass. But ditto, being non-LDS in most of Utah.

I used to take a friend for motorcycle rides; growing up, hers was the only Catholic family in a homogenously Mormon Sandy neighborhood. Her older brother would be beat up regularly for having a different set of fairy tales. On New Year's Eve 1999, her whole block threw a Millenium Party. In a pseudo-Biblical, Y2K techno-panic, all of the LDS families surrounding hers distributed survival kits in loving preparation for the impending Armageddon. But no supplies were offered to the Catholic heathens. When the sun *did* in fact rise that next morning, I can't understand why her father didn't go door to door through the neighborhood with a loud knock and a big, stiff middle finger.

My missionary visitors and I bid each other well that day and no one was converted on either side.

I would have other uninvited visitors in Sugarhouse. I wasn't renting in its hip, gay section by Wild Oats. But rather around 21st and 7th, in the middle-of-a-weekday burglary area sometimes referred to as "SugarHood." And my place did get hit pretty badly. Back door bashed in, cushions overturned, the whole nine. Guitars, stereo — gone. The pricks even took my hippie doorway beads.

All of those were replaceable. But they had also nicked the one possession I still miss deeply today: my collection of military coins, given to me over dozens of DOD tours. About thirty or so company coins from service people in Kosovo, Egypt, Macedonia. The Okinawa coin was from a medic. Also amongst the pilfered was a Kuwait Liberation Anniversary coin, inscribed in English and Arabic, "If Allah gives you victory, none shall defeat you." Which when you think about it, belongs in the Department of Redundancy Department. But I digress and defer to the Kuwaiti translation. These coins were shows of appreciation from people I entertained while they were doing shitty jobs far away from their homes and families. I still cringe knowing they're gone.

The Utah penal system has a very forward-thinking program, arranging criminals and their victims to meet face to face. My two burglars were caught not long after they ransacked my place. I met with the younger kid, about 17 years old, and his tattooed and scraggly father in a small conference room inside Salt Lake County's juvenile facility. He looked his age, if that — red haired and still rocking baby fat. He and an older partner were randomly breaking into homes for drug money. I know, it's all too clichéd. That day I was given the opportunity to tell him what he took from me. And who gave them to me — how there are people in places he can't pronounce that bust their ass for him daily. And that if he wanted to do them or me some karmic payback, that he should kindly visit some pawnshops upon his release (he hasn't). I soon bought out of my six-month lease in Salt Lake. There were too many drives up the I-80 freeway to either gig or ski in Park City. Plus I needed to escape the box elder bugs.

- - - - - - - - - - -

So I'm on the table at the Planned Parenthood, legs apart with my nuts shaved. The nurse has numbed me. The nurse's assistant — also female — is just standing there taking notes. On a clipboard no less! The doctor asks me, "Ok you're here for a vasectomy. You're positive you want to do this?"

From a very vulnerable spread-eagle position I grinned: "I loathe children and have little faith in the species." We all giggled and before you knew it, snip snip. Best $450 I've ever spent.

Now I do admit that on that afternoon with my jewels hanging out, I mainly went for comic effect and I certainly don't "loathe children." I do, however, hope all these monkeys lose all that "go forth and multiply" shit before we all run out of water.*

* Note to self: try not to refer to children and your testicles in same sentence. I gotta move some units at Deseret Books, dammit...

PS - probably also lose "unit."

I should start a Utah Chapter of the V-Club. People need to blow more carefree loads. Parenting: hardest job to do, easiest job to get. I met this Midwest hillbilly once who was a complete *no-buy* on vasectomies. "No one's touching MY balls!" What, your seed is special? Let the reader know, this guy was unemployed with an incurable, degenerative disease. All five of his kids are looking at a hard row. But children are miracles, right? And China's off base with their two-child policy? If only my civil libertarian and Malthusian sides could meet and play nice.

It was a fine sunny June Sunday morning and I was exploring downtown Salt Lake, in the long shadows of The Temple. I'd only lived in Utah for a few months and had no clue how difficult it is to find a latte on the Lord's Day. After a decade and a half in Los Angeles, where you can get anything at any time, I was still adjusting. But it was a warm morning, I had a few quid in my pocket and — *is that music coming from the end of the block?*

A few hundred feet in front of me there are police motorcycles turning the corner around a tall office building. Then, if I recall correctly, a convertible of some sort. Then, and of this I'm very certain — a float with several shirtless guys dancing suggestively in short-shorts.

It seems Salt Lake has one of the biggest Gay Pride Festivals in the American West. The demographics seem incongruous and the politics can get fierce, but it's true — we have a very active Gay community in Utah's capitol. I performed for their Gay Pride Festival one year. Pulling up to the event entrance loaded with gear, a chain link fence was lined with a small group holding signs. "God hates fags" and similar hate-fueled clichés. These guys might as well wave copies of *Mein Kampf.* Inside the fence people of all colors and nationalities were dancing, holding hands and enjoying a joyous day together. The contrast was stark and I wondered whom we've allowed to define good and evil.

During the 2011 Sundance Film Festival, that unmentionable "church" from Kansas staged a protest against Kevin Smith's film, *Red State.* Much to my glee, students from Park City High — including a handful of my School of Rock students — organized a counter protest. They waved slogans such as: "God Hates Homework" and "Automatic Doors Make Me Feel Like a Jedi!" One student told the press, "We are taught tolerance and acceptance. This is offensive to us."

Ain't *that* America?

As a kid in Aurora, Illinois, I wasn't clever enough to know I was being bullshitted. I had a strong sense that I was being bullshitted. But bullshitted by centuries of very smart and deceptive men — when people were positive the world was flat. So for that I guess I am Forgiven. An hour at Mass seemed beyond a mere waste of time. Although I was ignorant of Church history and unexposed certainly to any real options outside of Christianity, I was very sensitive to two aspects of Mass: a pervading sense of negativity and its obvious clashes with reality. The former, I learned, is called Catholic Guilt. Most religions have an equivalent. At least the lucrative ones do. Forced to attend CCD (bible study on Wednesday evenings) I was also being taught twice a week that God is fair and just — but that I am also to atone for Original Sin… which I didn't personally commit… and for which I have zero hope of atoning. Like the stories being sold to me, the whole concept hit me as illogical. The Garden of Eden stuff — was it strictly metaphorical, or was it literal? *Well it must be literal because somehow it's putting me to work, dammit!* But I figured the Old Testament was just full of allegory, probably because it was too old to be factual — like when the Jewish God was pissed and got to smiting people with lightning bolts and festering boils.

No teacher in my formative years gave us any real intellectual options. Not even "Murph" in senior year who was apparently hip solely because he was young. Not too hip, though, for platitudes of anti-intellectualism like: "Catholicism isn't like Burger King, you can't just have it your way."

My family is paying you for this shit?

It was his teen-catered allegorical equivalent to that weakest of prayer addendum, "If it be your will." Another monotheistic cop out which completely negates both the efficacy and the purpose of prayer. *A god's gonna do what It's gonna do.* So you might as well get off your knees, right? Nope. Stay down. Stop thinking, start believing, and you're bad if you can't do it. Stop seeing and close your eyes, and somehow you're the fool if you don't.

But periodically through my youth, I would give it a shot. Some schmuck at school would convince me to attend this or that Jesus Meet & Greet at a strange church across town — Born Again recruiting seminars honed in to a teenage demographic. Sure, kids are in need of guidance and direction. Sure, we're fucked up. But maybe it's because you're teaching us to believe in fairy tales. For a while back in junior high, after one of those awkward and emotionally dishonest days — marching to the front of some room full of strangers, their arms raised, maniacal smiles through closed eyes — I began receiving calls from my new "sponsor." He was in his early 20's and had that story similar to so many young and insistent Christians: partied too much, got in trouble, found Jesus, *yeah yeah yeah.* If finding God requires hitting bottom, I'll just avoid hitting bottom, thank you. These pep talks for Christ would sometimes catch me on my way out the door to school. He was calling me at 7 AM? I just wasn't feeling it, and I wasn't amused. I found myself in the position of telling the guy, as politely as a kid can do at thirteen, to piss off. "I'll keep on the path, I will. I just don't think your church is for me." *I'm going to be late for class, buddy.* I was spiritual Play-Doh, surrounded by propagandists.

Popcorn Night, Summer 2008: I should have seen the writing on the wall. One of those cosmic moments when the universe tells you: *This gig is over, pal.*

My first weekly gig in Park City, Utah was Bistro Bar (fka Miletti's). Initially the bar manager was Jimmy "JB" Bowers — he would soon become my percussionist and the dearest friend a guy could want. I signed a weekly agreement and JB started marketing "Tony Tuesdays" at Bistro Bar. The run lasted over 4 years. From sardine-packed ski season insanity to tumbleweed nights when I'm only singing to Tommy behind the bar: *More Franti!*

For a few fat years there, pre-housing collapse, it seemed every cougar in Park City had her real estate license. They could be Parkites or skiers from Los Angeles — look down and there's Silicon Valley representin' on the dance floor. Single mothers out looking for love, or a reasonable facsimile, many beginning to resemble Nicholson in Batman. Alien anthropologists are going to exhume our caskets and find pairs of clear, perfectly intact bags of salt water. I don't get it. But then again, I dig on the mosquito bites.

Local MILFs would bop into Main Street clubs in gaggles and request "Brown Eyed Girl" — "Yeah but change the lyrics to BLUE eyed girl, cause my eyes are BLUE!"

Right angel, but if I do that it's not about taking it up the ass anymore, is it?

I was up in the corner, by the window, on a bar stool amidst Bistro's inevitable patch cable-spaghetti. JB was on his trap kit, to my left. It was an average Tuesday early evening — a few couples on dates, some random tourists. There's a kid at the far end of the bar, maybe twenty feet away. Wobbling. And sneering. I'm catching a vibe during the last few songs, but I don't know this guy. Mid-Stealers Wheel, this kid stands up, shuffles across the room and plants himself a few feet from me. He starts tossing popcorn at my face...

Ever.

So.

Slowly.

Kernel after kernel. I look over at JB, who's fuming and dumbfounded. I cut an end chorus but finished the song.

> *"Clowns to the left of me, jokers to the right..."*

"Thanks guys, I'm Tony and I'll be right back." I set my guitar down and asked my new buddy to talk outside.

"What, you want to fight?" He barked at me.

"No I'm just curious what your deal is." We headed down the stairs.

"You play shitty cover tunes and you're not funny."

I asked him why the hell he was there, then?

He shrugged. "Cheap beer."

Remember the scene in *Spinal Tap* with the amusement park marquee? "I told them a hundred times, put Spinal Tap first and 'puppet show' last!" It was a *Beavis & Butthead* light bulb epiphany — if Bistro Bar had a marquee outside it would have read: "Cheap Beer & Tony Oros." Hmm, yes. It's time for a new Tuesday gig.

But I did gather myself to counter my critic: "Well. I promise you one thing — I'm a better entertainer than you are a drinker."

> *Shuck it, Trebek! You mess with the bull young man,*
> *you get the horns!*

There was also Harmonica Night. A rowdier room that had me furiously multi-tasking: take requests from the regulars, mention the drink specials, keep the dance floor moving — appeasing all where possible. A local rummy hangs out between JB and I, clapping and singing along. He's leaning on the piano. It's all good. I love when JB gets pissy about our space — he's shooting this guy the evil eye. But hey, we're white guys and we'll take the rhythmic help I guess. The room is slamming, girls are dancing, then — oh no. Aw no...

Do NOT tell me that old cat just picked up my harmonica, and... *eeewww...*

"Hey bra," I lean over to him after the song, "You can keep that harp."

Come on, pal! Blowing into a man's harmonica? It's gauche — like going to an orgy uninvited. I mean hey, there's saliva involved.

KPCW radio superstar and Renaissance Man Randy Barton would periodically wander in with a lovingly predictable request: "Do something YOU wrote!" This is one of the suggestions I would rarely fulfill. Randy and many a tourist will ask for "original music" in respect and deference. But I haven't written a song in many years, nor have I felt any desire to. Some cats get up in the morning with awesome melodies and hooks that are just screaming to get out. I never did. And I never enjoyed the process. Besides, in a crowded bar, original material isn't what I'm getting paid for. If a guy's playing strictly for tips and angling for a record deal then sure, knock out a few songs no one has heard before. But when there's a room full of drinkers singing along to Neil Diamond, first-listen songs are just "Old Testament Tunes" — the dance floor parts like the Red Sea.

Now, for some karmic balance, two happy Bistro blogs from that off-season:

Blog: **Radiohead Night @ Bistro!**
Date: **16 Apr 2008**
Current Mood: **Blessed**
Category: **Music**

Last night was roughly my 4-year anniversary performing at Bistro Bar on Main St. in Park City. Sometimes our "Shoulder Season" provides fantastic evenings and last night qualified.

Jimmy (Bowers, Plays Well With Others) brought his trap kit just for fun. Warming up to an intimate room of tired and happy locals, JB and I began with "Reckoner," a floaty track off Radiohead's latest, In Rainbows. I've been working at home on Track 2, "Bodysnatchers" and we debuted that. Ski to that song some time!

After a bit of The Floyd and a solo Colin Hay, the room began filling a bit. I hit the B minor to start "Faust Arp," a very mellow In Rainbows tune, and the back booth of Brits yelped their approval. Game on, Jimmy!

"Airbag," the opener to OK Computer turned into a Park City sing-along, as we watched two or three known RH devotees walk in...
"An interstellar buuuuurst... I'm back to save the universe!"

The last chord of Track 1 fades, and screw it — "Paranoid Android"! JB's been working on it and it felt like buttuh. The natives were IN. So let's go:

"Subterranean Homesick Alien"
Someone sang, "Waaaaake...."

"Exit Music"
We hope that you choke…

"Let Down" into "Karma Police" which Jimmy & I usually segue into "High n Dry." Too much fun. A request for Oasis, so we took Coldplay's "Yellow" into "Wonderwall."

Approaching last call on a cold & snowy night, I kept the capo on and sent our peeps home with Roger Miller's "King of the Road."

I almost always end my acoustic shows with Louie's "Wonderful World," but when the last request is "How To Disappear Completely?" Well then!

THANK YOU Park City, for another fantastic season!!!

- T.O.

Blog: **20 Days, 24 Shows!**
Date: **04 Aug 08 Monday**
Current Mood: **fabulous**
Category: **Music**

Usually my crazy runs come during ski-season, but thanks to Prime Steakhouse (5x), Thursday Club (6x), and NYPC Pizza (7x) my Utah summer has been one big gig since mid-July!

Jimmy Bowers and I finished the run with a fantastically fun wedding at The Spur — Eric Sopanen of Guitar Czar and Mike Rodgers rounded out the Plays Well With Others line-up.

THANKS Kati for making us part & CONGRATS!

VIVA LAS VEGAS!

I love working in Vegas.

Weekend casino runs in Sin City give me a sensory one-eighty from my beloved mountains and moose. We Utes can access fireworks and real porn right over the Nevada state line. Both must be handled with care however, as they can explode in your face upon returning home.

Las Vegas showroom sound crews contain true Union Men, usually donning uniforms. They are both punctual and highly conscious of their next 15-minute coffee break. Occasionally even, they are happy. But the older cats will tell you stories.

One crew had just returned from a stint with the recent cast of *American Idol* runners-up. These techs were still fuming from the tour, and enjoyed venting to a bunch of wig-wearing jokers during a Tuesday afternoon soundcheck: "They were nightmares, most of them. A bunch of prima-donnas. They'd just won a karaoke contest and they expected to have their asses kissed."

Some bookings would send me cabbing it from McCarran Airport, its Southwest terminal replete with Nascar fashion statements, up North Rancho Road to casinos in shadier corners of town. We'd pass empty lots with homeless guys huddling around bonfires, knocking back cases of Natural Light.

In an August desert, loading docks of Vegas casinos smell like cheap buffet meat.

My bandmates and I would grab every opportunity to study and enjoy Vegas pros up the Strip like classic rock show Yellow Brick Road and Beatle tribute The Fab Four. The latter show's Paul McCartney, Ardy Sarraf is a natural righty now playing *left-handed*... WTF??? *Hate you!* Years ago, my brother was out visiting me in California and we caught a Fab Four show at Santa Monica's Scruffy O'Shea's. Our jaws dropped from the back of the room as we took in their sets. *They're doing "Yes It Is?"* Later in 2005 I was doing a weekly metal show at a Station Casino, The Fab Four (their Christmas album is a MUST for Beatle-heads) were headlining the Las Vegas Hilton nightly. That room was subsequently taken over by Barry Manilow. Hey, if you're gonna lose your house gig, lose it to the guy who wrote the songs that make the whole world sing.

During one of my Friday night Metal Show runs I was taking liberty with my wireless mic and hopped off the stage onto the dance floor. I jumped on a few chairs, shaking my goods at the clientele. I gave our waitress a smooch. Well, I *was* being "Nigel" after all…

A bigger Hispanic guy was standing by the bar, snapping pictures with a cheap little disposable. Running around like a deranged metal-monkey, I snagged the camera and took a pic of him and then tossed it back. He gave me a shove as I laughed maniacally and turned, jogging back to the stage. It was a hoot. *Nearly* everyone had a blast.

After the show, Don, the head security guy came backstage and pointed at me. "Hey Tony, I need you for a minute." He motioned me outside. The band room got quiet.

"Did you grab a guy's camera?" He asked me as we walked through the casino's service areas and snaking hallways. I'm dodging cocktail waitresses and bus boys, still wearing my leather pants and Judas Priest spike bracelets.

"Yeah," I admitted. "I took his picture."

"Well he's saying you hit him. He wants to press charges for assault."

Punch in the guts! Indignation!

Followed by resignation. Yeah. I can get carried away with the *mach schau.* Let the chips fall and all that. Security Don led me back to a small, stark room straight out of Law and Order (sans-cheese-ball Mike Post soundtrack). Our photographer was sitting there, arms folded with a very coy look on his face. Don turned to him, "So tell us what happened again, sir?"

"This dude." He pointed at me, standing there semi-costumed. Yes, I had taken my wig off. "He grabbed my camera as I was taking a picture. He pushed it into my face. Like this." He made a thrusting motion with his heavily tattooed arms.

Don looked at his colleagues and summoned one of them to join him in the next room. They returned after a long few moments, during which I played eye-chicken with this probable gang member. I was less physically intimidated than concerned about losing my fucking gig.

Dan returned and asked meathead: "One more time? You're claiming this man assaulted you?"

"Yep," replied tough guy.

"Well, we just looked at the surveillance tape. It's very clear that you, in fact, shoved our performer, Mr. Oros." Don turned then to me.

"Mr. Oros, would you like to press charges of assault against this man?"

Now *that* moment is the videotape I'd like to see. Which of us had the better poker face, because I know I just about dropped a deuce in my drawers. I played it cool enough to wait a second and stare the guy down one last time before declining Don's offer.

After this guy was banned from the casino for life and escorted out, Don explained to me how often casinos are hit with frivolous lawsuits, and this guy was just after some payout.

"Nigel don't pay, baby! You pay NIGEL!"

Who? More on that clown later...

Performance Schedule, Sundance 2006

FRI 20   Après ski @ Park City Resort's
             Corner Store, 4-7 PM
          JB Mulligans Club & Pub, 804 Main St., 9-1 AM

SAT 21   Solo acoustic après ski @ Cisero's 6-9 PM
          80's Geek Show, Salt Lake City, 10 PM

SUN 22   All-70's Redneck Rock Re-view:
             MULLET HATCHET (as Tayler Parks) at
                Cisero's, 306 Main St., 10 PM

TUE 24   "Tony Tuesdays" solo acoustic @
             Bistro 412, 10 PM

WED 25   T.B.A.
             (schedule posted at ParkCityProductions.com)

THUR 26   Metal Show (as Nigel Tones),
             Salt Lake City, 10 PM

FRI 27   Après ski @ Park City Resort's
             Corner Store 4-7 PM
             Ringo Bar (under Claim Jumper), 10 PM

SAT 28   Solo acoustic après ski set @
             Cisero's, 6-9 PM
          80's Geek Show, Salt Lake City, 10 PM

SUN 29   Plays Well With Others: Acouschtick with
             JB on congas @ Cisero's, 306 Main St., 10 PM

GYPSY KIDS AND CAMP FUCKEDUP: EGOBALKANS I

January 2001: There was a fantastic lunar eclipse when I first took Egodog through the Balkans. I doubled on singer and tour manager duties. There were post-show midnight trudges through bitter cold for our fifteen minutes in the email tent. There was *Queen II* on my Walkman.

Guitarist McLefty (currently Musical Director and portraying Brian May in the killer-accurate tribute show Queen Nation) still sported the remnants of a Hawaiian tan he obtained while visiting his in-laws over Christmas. He recommends that everyone find a woman from Hawaii. McLefty was faced with the daunting task of walking to a frozen porta-potty to have a piss. Grumpily, he put on his flip-flops to do the miserable walk through the frozen mud. As he closed the door behind him the rest of us heard him mumble, "Two weeks ago I was fucking parasailing over Kona..." Minutes later he arrived back at the barrack with his teeth chattering so badly that all we could make out was the word "shrinkage." We all woke up in pools of our own sweat thanks to our thick military-issue sleeping bags. When they finally decide to thaw out Ted Williams, MWR's gotcha covered.

JOE HIGGINS
"HIGGIE"
DRUMS
EGODOG, COVERDOGS
RATTLE & HUM

My Musicians Institute and Illinois buddies had spent the previous decade pursuing different stylistic paths, yet a few of us had remained tight. Higgie had a break from his alt-band Gingersol. His drumming breathed new energy to our songs and Higgie is a riot to travel with. Even at his coldest and most miserable his dry one-liners make us howl. Higgie was patient and accommodating although Egodog was a bit heavy for his tastes. He would soon land in a band called AM Radio, managed by Weezer frontman and Musicians Institute graduate Rivers Cuomo. They signed to Elektra Records and hit the road via minivan across the States. AM Radio played stadium opening slots for Third Eye Blind and opened for Weezer at

Budokan in Japan. They worked two years on the road pushing their record but accrued little "buzz" or unit sales. When they returned from their last road stint, Elektra had been bought out and was no more, and AM Radio was unceremoniously "dropped" from their label deal. Higgie would eventually turn his energies toward motorcycle racing, but we'll gig together whenever logistically possible. To this day, he remains my favorite drummer on the planet.

Bassist Lars had parted amicably with Egodog and moved back to Norway. On Ego-bass was now high-energy funk-meister Damian.

It was LAX to Frankfurt to Budapest and much jet lag for the Egokids. Perennial Point of Contact Mac, true to form, gave us a mere twenty minutes at Hotel Kapos to "just splash some water" on our faces before Mac whizzed us off for goulash at his favorite haunt a few blocks away. We drank "bull's blood" — a deep, red wine that Hungarians drink chilled. Yes, *ick*. Mac often arranged the touring entertainers' schedules around what he wanted to do that week. He was a biker with a Bosnian wife who lived in Germany, and was certainly a character.

"Where are you from, Mac?"

"I'm from everywhere."

Our first SFOR Ego-gig was a few miles outside of Kapesvar, Hungary at Taszar Base. We had the next night's act in tow with us. The Kevin Banford Band were good, true, old school country. That guy lived it, man — big hat, belt buckle, skinny jeans and all. Kevin probably slept in those horrendous cowboy kickers. Once on a tour through Korea, Fab took Kevin golfing and *yes, he did* — he wore the boots on the golf course. I wish I could have seen the little Korean greens-keeper, just losing his mind from behind a shrubbery. Egodog and The Kevin Banford Band were square pegs enough strolling through a Balkan military base but the juxtaposition of the two bands' fashion senses was a sight.

We introduced ourselves around the MWR tent at Taszar and did our last minute show preps. For a base that size, the turnout was looking solid at 60 or

70 heads. The soldiers who really looked forward to DOD bands were always eager to chat you up about who had previously come through. Occasionally they'd be treated to big celebs via USO, but more often it was MRW peons like Egodog. The previous summer while touring the Middle East my Coverdogs were about a month on the heels of a classic rock trio called Raven. Entering a new camp, all we'd hear was, *Raven this, Raven that...* But after our shows, they were often referred to as "Raisin." Soundchecking now at Taszar, an older soldier was blowing smoke up the ass of some band that had come through camp the previous year. "Yeah they did Zeppelin, Stones, some Sublime. What were they called? *Cover*-something..."

The Hotel Kapos lobby was swimming with prostitutes. Egodog had an evening off, and we decided to check out the local strip club — or Kapesvar's equivalent, anyway. We sipped Stella Artois and chatted up the working girls. One was from Greece, but most were Russian or from a former Soviet republic. Always the heavy, I eschewed a lap-dance from a young and sad Serbian girl who shouted her life story to me in cliff-notes, point blank over thumping Euro-house music. As we were talking (see: stripper not making money) two young men knocked at the door of the basement club. The bouncer stood from his stool, peered through the window of the door, and waved them off. They left visibly irritated. I asked my little Serbian friend why those guys weren't allowed in.

"They're local."

Like an undiplomatic slap in the face it struck me: *Soldiers and tourists, fine. But no Hungarians.* Rough.

That evening's last imagery was our bassist punching an ATM machine while his hooker stood impatiently behind him. She might have even been tapping her foot.

Women in Hungary. *Mmm, mmm good.* KFOR soldiers referred to the Hungarian capitol as "Bootie-Fest." By my first Balkan run in September '99, Fab had already been through some half a dozen times. While we were sightseeing one day in Budapest, a blonde on a bench waved and winked at him, then patted the empty seat next to her. Mac and I howled as our usually composed tour manager drew red and stammered incoherently.

Now, I certainly do not mean to imply that a large percentage of women in Hungary are prostitutes. Just saying the prostitutes they do have are generally

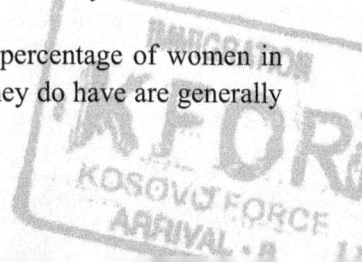

damn attractive... can I get an endorsement deal from their local union? Or maybe it could be the next huge reality show craze: *Hungarian Hooker Idol!* I'm an idea man.

The next morning Egodog was scheduled to check out and meet in the lobby at 0700 for our bus down into Bosnia. If there's one thing that makes me appreciate America, it's a hot shower. I don't know what Euros as a culture have against the concept; most cheap European hotel rooms offer only a tub with the dreaded hose. And water pressure? *F'getaboutit!* That morning, for the life of me I could not find the magic knob configuration which bringeth forth the hot water. Perhaps they were rationing for Tito Day, I don't know. But after several minutes and multiple attempts I had little choice but to rock me an ice shower. I took no solace in knowing that devout Sikhs rise to this misery every morning. I was a pampered American, and *this just sucks.*

Egodog was scheduled at Camp McGovern where I did back-flips to find their guest quarters had at last received actual beds. When you're psychologically prepared for cots and sleeping bags, a mattress is a big fluffy bonus from The Universe. Or from Jessica in MWR, anyway.

Then off to a venue everyone was calling "The Thunderdome" at our next stop, Camp Dobol, also in Bosnia. Our expectations were raised by its nickname and we envisioned an enormous theater packed full of rowdy, rock starved Army Joes. But alas... it was a tent. A big, echoey tent, holding maybe forty guys on folding chairs. Like McGovern two nights before, the appearance of Egodog was at best a mysterious event, perhaps to be explored if there wasn't a ball game being televised on Armed Forces Network.

It was an occasional source of frustration through DOD tours, knowing there were soldiers, sailors or airmen and -women reading in their bunks, bored as hell and unaware there was entertainment in camp. More communication up and down the line would have optimized our presence there. Well, at least the soldiers had their cappuccino. Even in the summertime, one of the few visceral pleasures your soldiers can look forward to is a latte from the base's local-run cappuccino hut. A shot of liquid give-a-shit in a drainingly mundane existence.

Not that the native Balkan employees had it a whole lot better. Impoverished and thankful to dole out fried chicken and lasagna to Alabamans and Texans holding M-16s, local workers were subject to stringent and sometimes arbitrary rules — American soldiers would throw away entire trays full of food but if a Bosnian DFAC worker took home a can of Diet Coke, she was fired. The advantages afforded us, by a sheer fluke of fate or geography, was at times unnerving.

Most local Bosnian and Kosovan civilians employed on base worked for a company called Kellogg Brown & Root. Whenever soldiers or entertainers were served meals, whenever we had our clothes laundered, it was being done by KBR. Up until 2007, Kellogg Brown & Root was a subsidiary of Halliburton. During the Clinton presidency the CEO of Halliburton was Dick Cheney. And when Bush II invaded and occupied Iraq, which company received no-bid contracts — tallying in the billions — to provide the civilian labor? Anybody?

Bueller?

You guessed it, Halliburton was handed the gig. But Eisenhower did warn us:

"We must guard against the acquisition of unwarranted influence, whether sought or unsought, by the military industrial complex... Only an alert and knowledgeable citizenry can compel the proper meshing of the huge industrial and military machinery of defense with our peaceful methods and goals."

Yet. We the People have dick for long-term memories. We're too busy watching game shows to give a shit.

German *Busfaher* Rudy wound us up through snowy mountains that led us to Sarajevo. We stopped for pee breaks at roadside homes/cafes where Bosnian hillbillies roasted goats on a spit. Checking into Butmir and meeting some new MWR staff, Egodog quickly learned that little if any advertising had been done for our shows at Sarajevo. In fact, the head of MWR's first words to us were, "What do you guys do? I was telling people hip-hop cause I didn't know." *Ouch*. With a substantial African-American presence at Butmir, I thought: *There's one disappointed audience waiting to happen.*

Undaunted, we took the initiative to wander the camp, which led us to that evening's venue, Charlie's, to do some last minute promotion. The formula is: McLefty + beer = PR Machine. "Yeah we're playing tonight here at 1900, then tomorrow in the MWR tent — American rock and roll, man! *Merci...* Or, um... *Tusen tak!*"

Like Comanche Base a few nights before, Charlie's was packed and rowdy for Egodog. Attendance was certainly bolstered by the presence of alcohol. We set up our backline in the corner, plugged in and kicked the shit out of that place. There's drunk soldiers from half a dozen countries singing along to Foo Fighters and Beastie Boys.

> *"I'm gonna set it straight, this Watergate... I'm tellin' y'all it's Sabotage!!!"*

The American contingent had organized a 5-mile run for the next morning, Martin Luther King Day. Seizing both the change in my exercise regimen and a chance to do some promo for that night's show, I rose early and bundled against the winter morning. The racecourse wound through the base and soldiers from multiple nations participated. We received yelps and cheers from camouflaged Danish and Austrian soldiers, leaning against the DFAC and having the day's first smoke. I finished the course at a time of 24:30 and promptly buried any hopes of becoming an NFL wide receiver. Off to a shower and breakfast (DOD Touring Hint: when available, shower in the MWR buildings — they are always cleaner and less crowded with large Bulgarian men).

I know it's incongruous as hell, but the fact is — you could get a fine massage at Sarajevo's Camp Butmir. Local Bosnian girls were rubbing down soldiers for a few Deutschmarks. And damn straight, we indulged! Their hut was right across from the Italian Carabinieri headquarters. All the Brits suspected the Italian military police of homoerotic activities but we witnessed nothing quite that enlightened, and we weren't going to down enough Peronis to find out.

Egodog humped through the snow up to an old Turkish fort and the Olympic stadium — an unused reminder that Yugoslavia had recently played host to the world and its athletes. Now it was surrounded by tombstones. In addition to a shared Olympic history, Sarajevo and Salt Lake City are similar in their geography. If my Ute readers can imagine — one day a huge segment of the population runs up into the East Bench and begins lobbing 50-calibur shells toward apartment buildings in Sandy. Substitute Atheists for Serbs in our local, theological analogy (don't worry, we have no attack plans at present) and you get the picture. We paused for somber photo ops and our new bassist Damian shot video.

At a monument to Josip Tito a gaggle of gypsy kids surrounded us, begging

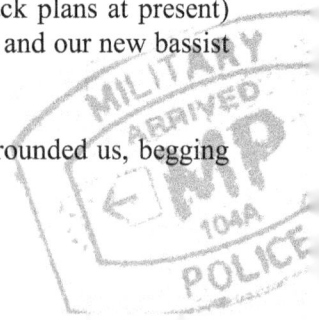

cheerfully. Higgie had some Hungarian Forints in his pocket and he doled out a handful to the pre-teens, who were dressed in t-shirts in the 30-degree weather.

Roma!

The kids hand the devalued local currency back to Higgie, pleading "No, no! Deutschmark, Deutschmark!" We debated later, driving back to Butmir, whether or not their shabby clothes were just for show — a sympathy play for schmucks like my band and me? Our military guides and my Hollywood tree lot experience told me those kids likely would be picked up in BMWs and driven back to comfort, even opulence. I can claim Romanian blood, but I won't defend gypsies. Or vampires. Vampires really do suck.

Sorry, couldn't resist.

Back to Eagle Base for an interview on Armed Forces Radio, broadcasting to the entire SFOR theater, and that night over a hundred soldiers crammed into their sports bar-equivalent, Triggers. Another dry base, yet another crazy room. Mike had caught The Crud yet he somehow kept smiling. Damian's back was bothering him. Being an uninsured but opportunistic cat, Damian took an afternoon and saw the medical staff. Within an hour, he had been x-rayed and diagnosed with scoliosis. The kid was already in his mid twenties and he never knew what the hell was up with his back.

We reached Camp Able Sentry in Macedonia a few days on the heels of an R&B act, which had failed to impress, evidently. Good Department Of Defense acts spend much time fighting the reps of the weak ones. "You're the DOD band? Oh. Well maybe I'll check you guys out." That translation, in our circles? Let's face it: *they ain't comin'*.

- - - - - - - - - -

In the middle of a military tour nothing refreshes your body and head like a night in pseudo-civilian lodging. Even at the tail end of NATO's mission in the Balkans, entertainers couldn't fly directly from Bosnia into Kosovo. We strapped on the Kevlar and helmets, squeezed into a frosty C-130, and were flown to Ramstein Air Base in Germany. We had single rooms in North Billeting and I surfed American Forces Network on the tube.

AFN is a riot. Not unlike Mormon-targeted media in Utah, military television programming is a window into a wacky, foreign culture. AFN doesn't broadcast normal commercials but instead fills program breaks with service and family-related spots. These mini skits at best provide an outlet for aspiring actor / soldiers, and at worst are sermons to the proverbial choir. However cheezily produced, I enjoyed the spots about American and military history. I was encouraged to know that our service people were being versed on Thomas Paine and FDR. More service-centric segments fascinated me, like AFN's admonitions to be mindful of security breaches — Operations Security:

"OPSEC: it's everyone's responsibility!"

In civilian speak this is: "Shut the fuck up, you're going to get us killed!"

I thought some messages could use more direct approaches, as military time is valuable. How about these themes for AFN ads?

"Quit eating the crap and have a salad, fatty!"
Or,
"Stop hitting your kids, asshole!"
How about:
"Don't fuck the locals."

I'm hoping they'll hire me. I'm here to help.

The band and I rented a car and day-tripped into Heidelberg for beer and lunch. Mainly for beer. That night, exhausted as I was, it was a pleasant respite when Karla's sister and Air Force Major brother in law dropped by for a brief visit… All right, maybe I could've done without the screaming toddler. I tend to frighten young children. But these folks had saved my ass a few years prior when I was broke and backpacking though Europe and here they were again, just checking in on me, bewildered two year old in tow.

With barely enough time to fire up our little coffee pots, we departed the next morning for Kosovo. The multinational base in Kosovo is in Pristina. They call it "Film City." Our energies were running thin despite our one night of comfort, and humping our guitars and rucksacks through the freezing mud Damian grumbled, "Where we going now, Camp Fuckedup?" He wasn't far off. Film City's billeting was full up for the night. We'd have to crash in "the big tent" across camp. We schlepped gear and PA over to the little tin box we would perform in, then more mud, more freezing rain over to our dreaded sleeping quarters. We peeled back the vinyl flap to see dozens of bunk beds, sardined like a smelly submarine. Ukrainian soldiers sat on their bunks in polyester short-shorts and black socks. The men were large and strong. The funk was stronger. The backs were hairy. We was a-scared.

NATO bases allow alcohol, so Americans serving in SFOR or KFOR generally welcome an assignment at Butmir or Pristina. We set up our gear in an acoustically impossible room, another anonymous and flimsy structure where the volume was determined mainly by Higgie's oft-heavy drumming. Word was spreading around base that afternoon, even to the non-English speaking contingents. Shit, you're cold, you're miserable and bored on your bunk, a million miles away from your family in Bumfuck, Finland but hey — there's an American rock band in camp? That's two or three hours you don't have to be a soldier.

The Heinekens and Grolsches flowed, quelling some homesickness as troops from a dozen nations threw shoulders into each other in a happy, green and gray mosh pit. Captain Stephanie, Shannon and our new American friends threw an after party in their tent. We all drank together and pissed on a Czech tank. They Sharpied their wishes on a NATO flag and ended up following us around KFOR the next two nights to Camps Monteith and Bondsteel. Groupies in Kosovo!? Like we were Phish or something!

POC Glenn of basketball fame arranged a meeting with the Colonel who nearly nixed our KFOR shows. He was very honest and told us that months before, upon first getting word of our trip, several people at Bondsteel attempted to check out our website, ostensibly for promo purposes. It was apparently blocked by an anti-porn firewall at KFOR. We're guessing it was due to our drummer's reference to his favorite porn star on his bio page... Nice job, Higgie. A cyber cock-block! Colonel Gross then went on to say that after pulling the plug, "Ten or so people — including apparently one at the Defense Department — screamed bloody murder and came to your defense saying you were pro, very patriotic, and that the troops should get this show." So he told us just to do our thing, and he stopped by the well-attended gig briefly, later sending a positive review on up the line.

The band had a stopover at the Astron Hotel, Munich. They had a free shuttle and we were in our rooms within an hour of landing in *München*. Then one more flight back to girlfriends, day jobs and correspondences at our LA home base.

From: C████████████████
Subject: ████████
Date: ████████
To: T████████

CLASSIFIED

Chris here, I'm writing you from Camp Bondsteel me and my friend
Rodney saw you guys last night and you brought the pain!!!!!!!!!!!! Rodney
(not really a rocker) can't fucking shut up about EGODOG. I might have to
shoot his ass. I have seen just about everyone live, you guys kicked half
the bands asses I have seen and you did it in a Tin building in Yugoslavia.
That's just cool. Most famous bands sound like shit live even with the best
equipment i.e. Blink 182. You guys are gonna be even more Famous
than you already are. I think what you are doing for the army is unbeliev-
able. Rock bands are usually liberal fucks who think we are baby killers
and Big business republicans. How did you get this way ,were you
dragged from a burning building by a soldier or some shit? Regardless its
cool.

I play guitar and I would like some of your TAB ,is it on the net? I would
like to play your shit. Your music hard but still keeps the melody and tone
not as to over harden as so many people do now days great lyrics too.
Anyway enough praise I don't want to sound like a bitch. Please add two
email addresses to your mailing list. We will be in LA for x-mas and Vegas
for new years and would love to see you play again, maybe you could
hook us up with some passes.

— Chris and Rodney
PS the CD is great... and can i get an EGODOG sticker for my Guitar
Case?
SPC Christopher Culberson
HHC 2-1 AVN (AVN TASK FORCE)
Camp Bondsteel Kosovo
APO AE 09340

From: Pe
Subject: C
Date: A
To: To

CLASSIFIED

What's up dogs, you guys rock! I was happy to see that you managed to make another trip to the Balkans. I was at your first Balkan Tour in Taszar Hungary from 20 Aug 2000-13 Mar 2001. My name is Peter Ramaglia from the 119th MP Company Warwick RI. I live in Providence RI (What up Mike!), and trust me - all my friends that listened to your CD "Words Are Kerosene" were very impressed and wondered why they haven't heard of you yet. I told every single one of them the web address for your band. A few made the purchase (as I did on "The Pleasure of Action"). I am just trying to get your name out to the ones who haven't heard of you. If you ever make a trip up here to do any shows I will be one of the first to buy a ticket. I wish all of you the best of luck in the future and will be looking forward to your next cd. Tony... Happy to see the picture of you and the torch. I was also deployed to the 2002 Winter Games in Salt Lake. It was great to see your pride! Keep it up guys."
— SPC Peter Ramaglia, Hungary

From: 08001920
Subje
D
To

OPSEC
OPERATIONS SECURITY

How is the rest of your DOD tour going? I hope you are having a good time. I wasn't sure how I would like Egodog. What I experienced last night was, for lack of a better word, awesome!! Your sound kind of mixes old school with the new. I like it. I am officially (drum role please) A FAN!! I have gained a lot of respect for your vocal ability. I have a lot more to say but I need to get it all sorted out first. I hope you don't mind me rambling about it. Good luck on the rest of the tour!!"
— Daniel J. Thompson, Bosnia

From: Ke
Subject: E
Dat
To:

CLASSIFIED

EGODOG: Tony and All - can't tell you how great it was to meet all of you on the plane to Kosovo. Wish we had been there long enough to hear your concert. You are true patriots, and raise the morale of our troops deployed in far-away lands. I am very grateful for that. Please stay in touch, and let me know if you ever have some time to kill in Germany. Sincerely, Kevin

— COL KEVIN G. TROLLER
CDR, 266TH FINANCE COMMAND
FIRST IN FINANCE SUPPORT

WHO'S IN CHARGE?
OR,
ARABS ALSO SHOOT POOL

September 2001: The Coverdogs were on our third run through the Balkan theatre. It was my fifth time through Bosnia, Kosovo and Macedonia, having also done a few tour-managing stints with Egodog and other AKA acts. Somehow we had weaseled business class seats to Frankfurt, which makes everything yummy when you're over 6 feet tall. All four of us on this run were big guys, ecstatic not to be crammed between restless children in coach.

As per usual, this MWR Balkan tour began up top and headed south: Taszar Base in Hungary, then the bus ride through Croatia into Bosnia-Herzegovina for a couple of remote camps and the multinational Eagle Base outside of Tuzla. Through the mountain passes to Camp Butmir, a short drive from Sarajevo's partially functioning airport — underneath its main runway remains a narrow tunnel that shuttled besieged and starving citizens to freedom during the war.

Mac was on vacay in Germany. Our new POC Bill was thinking outside of the connex and had found the band some lodging off base, in the wooded hills above Sarajevo. We were thrilled enough to be crashing anywhere but Butmir's cramped multinational billeting, and Bill had found us the most fantastic A-frame bed & breakfast. We had individual rooms — warm little cocoons to where we all retired for our late afternoon power naps before that evening's gig on base. I had drifted off to Travis on the Walkman: *The Man Who*. There was a knock at my door and it was Fab, looking dour. "You gotta see this. We have CNN on in my room." POC Bill and Spark were on the edge of Fab's bed, and Moose soon arrived to gawk at the live coverage with us.

When the second 747 struck the World Trade Center one ambiguity vanished — we were most certainly being attacked, while my buddies and I found ourselves civilians in a combat zone. We turned to our POC and asked what our status as civilian DOD entertainers would mean should something, well, who knew at that point? In those initial hours, outside of perhaps Dick Cheney and Don Rumsfeld no one was sure of the attack's scope. New York and D.C. were hit — but would they strike Eskan or PSAB in Saudi? Why not target our troops in Bosnia? Bill said he'd look into it and soon excused himself to touch base with Butmir's MWR staff. Our show that night was postponed within a few unsure hours, and all non-essential travel (that means rock bands) was frozen throughout SFOR and KFOR. We were unfortunately ordered to report to Bumir, and report ASAP.

After a few days of rumor and impatient distractions — gym, video games, emailing family and girlfriends — The Coverdogs were ordered to fly out to Ramstein Air Base in Germany. We would do a few shows in Kosovo but our remaining shows in Bosnia were sadly nixed. Camp Bondsteel in Kosovo is home to a handful of European soldiers, including a contingent from United Arab Emirates. Following the attack, American and Emirati Commanding Officers were quick to meet and then instruct their troops not to view each other suspiciously. When the band arrived, we sensed little if any tension. Emirati guys were even in the MWR hall playing pool much of the time, next to the Yanks and Krauts.

The longest waiting lists at Morale Welfare & Recreation tents were always for the computer rooms. As we shot e-updates back home to Cali, sandwiched between GIs, we pondered the concept of the old school mail call. For decades, soldiers and their families hand-wrote letters which were put in bags on a boat and took weeks or months to arrive — *maybe*. In wartime, soldier-to-Stateside electronic communications are replete with security nightmares to be sure, but anyone really intimidated by the progress of information technology is an idiot. The satellite age allows people to remain closer. No more crackly LAN line calls from a crowded phone bank. Dear John letters have become Dear John emails. We performed in KFOR later that week, serving as a timely distraction for our troops while the geo-political landscape was being redrawn and Dubya was reading *My Pet Goat* upside-down.

The push of gear up the ramp exiting the Bradley International Terminal is always a joyous exercise. Coming back to a different and more frightening America, I spotted Karla waving us in. Right next to her was a chauffer with a big white sign in black sharpie: "Steve Lukather." Wow, nice. Toto in the house. That solo to "Hold the Line," baby! Fab, Karla and I lingered a few minutes but we didn't bug him. No one needs to be perky and sociable after a long international flight. All of our Dogs were simply relieved to be back in

The States, however irrevocably changed it would prove to be.

In the ensuing weeks I spent far too many hours flipping between the news networks, absorbing both coverage and propaganda. The country knee jerked and cowered. Clueless George told us to keep shopping. The Seventh Inning Stretch went from "Take Me Out to the Ball Game" to "God Bless America." Rummy told us he was *on that shit*, and we were encouraged to see our Special Forces going up Afghani mountains on horseback. Pat Tillman quit the Arizona Cardinals' defensive backfield, took one for the bigger team, and was summarily fucked for it. Bin Laden told us why he attacked us and we plugged our collective ears, singing *la la la…*

MELTDOWN IN KUNSAN
AND FREE BIRD SEED

Independence Day 2002: Decidedly not my finest hour. I was returning to Korea fighting a malaise. I'd been bashing my head against the same walls for much too long, with few tangible results. But that weekend at Kunsan did provide some amazingly sublime moments.

The Coverdogs would hit the stage that July 4 in the parking lot of the air base's main watering hole, the Loring Club. I attempted to pump myself up for our first set while The California Girls played their surf rock standards. Hey, a little T&A for our fightin' boys! After a long intermission the girls would return, then Coverdogs would close the evening. Our huge, temporary stage faced the club. Behind it, the golf course and flight line.

The Air Force's color guard arranged itself in the July humidity under a thin cloud cover. A female cadet sang the National Anthem. When she reached the song's climax, a break in the clouds sent a perfect shaft of light down onto all of us. Fab, Bart and I turned to each other from across the stage, jaws dropped.

Most of my angst had dissipated when we began our first few tunes. Sans-rehearsal due to travel logistics, we stuck to our standards: Stones, Beatles, Doobies. We began CCR's "Traveling Band" and its first verse lyric:

> *"737 coming out of the sky..."*

Then the sky roared, and rising from the flight line behind the club an F-15 launched into the air.

We'd save the heavier and newer stuff for set two: Soundgarden, Foo Fighters, Lit. We added "Sunday Bloody Sunday" and "Pride (In the Name of Love)" as we were laying the groundwork for a future U2 tribute tentatively named Rattle & Hum.

Kunsan Air Base had become a pretty regular destination. During one trip we had a KISS tribute in tow. They were setting up to soundcheck behind a big thick room divider as Ross, Fab and I ate lunch. After the sonic beeps and farts of a line check, their drummer counted off "Shout It Out Loud" with its dual guitar lead solo. Ross turns to Fab and I and cringes, "Jesus! It sounds like two cats in a bag!" It seemed their Gene Simmons was beside himself. Apparently Korean Air misplaced one critical bag from their band's flight: the Gene costume. Oh man. Without the big 70's alien suits there *is* no KISS show (just ask the 80's lineup of KISS). This poor cat was forced to play that night's gig in borrowed black sweatpants and shirt, Gene makeup on his understandably pissy face.

A blitzed and enthusiastic crowd was there to greet us on that 4th of July. They'd scream for Stones, hoot for Hendrix. The Coverdogs as we'd been doing it was beginning to burn me out. Every situation eventually runs its course and even with setlist additions and the occasional change in personnel, it was nearing time for different directions and outlets. I had nightmarish visions of myself and The Coverdogs twenty years down the line, weathered and beaten, taking offers from MWR reps like old Eugene in Seoul — six months runs as a sequestered house band playing six nights a week at some dive bar he ran in Itaewon. "You guys have a nice combo," he would pitch to jaded and hard drinking bluesmen, their aspirations of glory long since dead. The money was garbage but Eugene would pay your rent and you can discover the culinary delights of kimchi for a winter. As a long-term career scenario, I was a *no-buy*.

My biggest mistake that day was checking emails between sets. I hadn't yet grasped the Buddhist concept of being in the moment, yet I also had to be on top of things: what if there was a work-related mail in my inbox? And indeed there was.

We knew Higgie would be busy with Gingersol, so we had lined up The BongBoys' Paulie on drums for *Egodog-Balkans II*. But now I'm half the planet away, reading a panic stricken email sent by McLefty. He's scouring to see if there were any drummers interested in going to Bosnia with Egodog. All it entailed was a valid passport, clean criminal record, mini-disc player — and the ability to learn three hours of new music in two weeks.

About a month prior we'd had held a refresher jam with Paulie. We hadn't recorded with him for nearly a year (amazing drumming on our *Words Are Kerosene* album) but he snapped right into place from the rehearsal's first hits and our musical concerns were allayed. Lefty and I began looking forward to really enjoying the upcoming tour. It would be summertime back at Camp Fuckedup and we thought we had a fresh bro with whom to share the experience. Even the political industry pressure was off. Hell, if VH1's *Military Diaries* wasn't interested in Egodog's second tour of the Balkans (I pitched them, they declined) I felt we had truly had exhausted all potential media and industry avenues — we would be able to simply enjoy the travel and the performances. Yet now with Paulie backing out all I could think about now was damage control. Auditions, additional rehearsals and significant angst were now looming on our schedule — *makework* is a drag. My mind raced but found no answers on the drummer front. I'd rather send Coverdogs to Bosnia a third time than bring SFOR a sub-par Egodog lineup. As I sat on a rock in Kunsan and scoured my mind for potential remedies to our predicament, I hoped that Paulie's opportunity was substantial enough to warrant the scorching of our bridge and passing up a tour of a combat zone (his gig would last about a month).

The Coverdogs took the stage again at dusk. I'd just run inside the club to hit the head and been accosted by another inebriated airman: "Dude! You GOTTA do something from this century."

"Gotta?" I love an imperative in a request. Yet, in retrospect — a pretty funny line on his part.

I shook off the exchange and went into game-mode, immersing myself in the C-Dog standards. The give-a-shit does tend to kick in, usually when you're farthest from home. Or farthest from knowing where the hell you're going next.

One airman ran up on stage at Bart's side of the four-foot riser mid set and motioned to his buddies — he was going for it. They held out their arms to encourage the coming leap. In one fluid motion we watched in horror as our stage diver crouched, jumped, and all his friends promptly jumped aside — SPLAT! His pride was bruised harder than his face and he dusted himself off, to much kudos.

We left the stage to sell a few CDs and meet some folks. I gravitated towards the older service people, better on this night at handling their liquor. Mid-set I had noticed a girl pressed against the stage and crying uncontrollably (Fab says *Oh GOOD*). While approaching me for a CD afterwards she explained that her brother just died. I stopped the conversation I was having and expressed my sympathies. What an indescribably rough situation, especially being stationed overseas during the loss. But this girl was beyond sloppy drunk and while other people patiently awaited my attentions, she was getting grabby... *Yes, your brother just died. Yes, I am sorry. Yes, I do care. Please let go of my shirt. Right now. I'm asking you nicely.*

Our two remaining shows were inside the Loring Club, on the floor of the bar area. The previous night was fairly sleepless as my mind chased down possible resolutions to the very significant hitch in Egodog's upcoming return to Bosnia and Kosovo, now less than three weeks away. Mentally drained and eager to escape my room, I headed to the club early and killed a few vodka tonics. No matter how fantastic your job is, at one point or another everyone can feel like a whore. That night in Korea, I was there.

Another huge bee in my bonnet around this time was the occasional assertion from a serviceman, "You look like the guy from Creed." Now, to any agnostic priding himself in having some modicum of musical taste, this is an insult of the highest order. I winced visibly and pressed on.

Showtime: Bart broke a string during set one and I began a solo version of a mellow Chris Cornell tune, which I thought would be a nice interlude. "Preaching the End of the World" is a track off Cornell's first post-Soundgarden release, heavily influenced by the late Jeff Buckley's intricate and unorthodox chord changes. Aside from the blank stares, all I got was one drunk at the front who yelled, "Are you gay?"

Really dude? That's all you've got? But allow me to retort!

"Shut up or I'll fuck your girlfriend!"

Sure it's an old 80's line — Steven Pearcy of Ratt if I'm not mistaken — but I was basically heading towards a *fuck subtlety* night. We weren't far into the second of our three sets when another guy shouts for the oldest of all rock clichés. "Free Bird!"

So I kinda tore into that dude as well. My guys had never witnessed this... nor had I. "Alright pal! You got it. Only now it's your job to tell the next guy that he's too late and we've already played it."

"Do some Godsmack!" from another Air Force cat in civvies.

"Godsmack? I told you last night: no Godsmack, for the same reason as no Megadeth and no Slayer. Because no one gets laid. Not that you had a chance anyway."

And the band cringed on.

I had hit a wall. After some years of accepting anything and everything from The Audience, I let my pendulum swing the other way and told some drunk guys where to stick it. The coming years of gigging would help me hone more diplomatic counter-punches, but I would no longer stand there defenseless.

At least there was one person that night that found me amusing. After the show I ended up walking back to my room with a blonde who'd been buying me vodka cherry collins all night. The band had been calling her Pamela (as in Anderson, but any attractive blond on a far away military base could induce such mirages). She gave me her "And that's why I joined the Air Force" story as we traversed the base golf course towards my billeting. Accommodations are the most cushy at Air Force installations. The band members all had our own rooms, sharing a small entryway and bathroom. I flipped on the little clock radio. Pam and I made out a bit. After a few minutes she excused herself to the restroom. I laid back, dizzy with Stolichnaya and my ears ringing from three hours of amps and drums. I closed my eyes, although I was in no danger of drifting off with this beautiful girl from somewhere or other who was right over...

Hey she's been in there a while now... I'm going to give her another minute.

I called out to her. Nothing. I got up and opened the door to the entryway. Both the bathroom door and the door to the hall were open — and she was gone. I was stunned. And obviously, pretty worked up at that juncture. I closed both doors, shuffling back to bed, defeated and deflated. I tossed and turned a while and I pondered my life...

I smelled something.

Over here, by the window next to the bed. Oh. There's vomit on my floor. And there's a fitting end to my weekend in Kunsan.

Yet, from my discontent a seed had been planted. One too many shouts of "Do some Skynyrd, maaaan!" careened around my head like hillbilly buckshot and had broken my tenuous grip on reality. I began to see visions at night...

I was on a mountaintop and I was visited by a great Buddhist monk. He was clad in red, white and blue. He glowed like a book burning. And his hair... His hair was long in the back. But kind of short on top, you know? Kind of like a Kentucky waterfall. The great and wise monk said his name was **Yeah Man Woo**, and he would teach me the ways of Southern Rock. As I thought I heard a banjo playing down in the valley, he said I should git me some bibs and form a great band. With two drummers, of course. "You will cover Skynyrd while smiling through your tooth. You will play ZZ Top, Doobies, Allmans... In order to sing the redneck, you must **be the redneck**. You must embrace the unemployed father of seven that lives deep in your double-wide. Your name shall be Tayler Parks. And you shall call your band: **Mullet Hatchet**."

And so it were.

HAVE PIPES, WILL TRAVEL:
EGODOG BALKANS II

August 2002: After a frantic drummer audition process back home in Los Angeles, Egodog settled on a quirky cat named Kenny. He lived in his rehearsal studio but he hit like Keith Moon. Once we had arrived in Hungary Kenny also picked fights with our regular Point of Contact, Mac. It was like the Southern Baptists protesting the Disney Corporation — I couldn't decide who *not* to cheer for.

We were handed off to Big Shirley, our Sarajevo POC. Remember the 70's sitcom, *What's Happening*? Right! Shirley schlepped us through Sarajevo for a guest appearance on Bosnian-language Radio MIR. During our van ride to the station MIR spun "My Wonderful World," a tune beautifully written and sung by McLefty who beamed from the back of the van.

Camp Morgan was a smaller outpost, a larger Forward Operating Base. Our tour bus was en route to a show that night at Camp McGovern, near Brcko. It was early afternoon and we had scheduled an optional stop at Morgan to shake hands with those guys. Sometimes during DOD stints that's all you have time to do. Those are awkward or occasionally sad stops, as the grunts we were meet-and-greeting had little idea who these random entertainers were. They were essentially being teased — yes that's the MWR band, bringing a show to *other* soldiers.

Having less than an hour before we needed to split for McGovern, Lefty and I grabbed our guitars and our smallest amplifier and headed toward the DFAC. A smattering of Army Joes were eating lunch, and as we'd become accustomed, looked at us quizzically. But the word didn't take long to spread around camp. Within a few minutes it was Standing Room Only at Camp Morgan's dining facility. The soldiers kept coming and you could just see the relief in many of their faces: a half hour of anything to break the monotony! *Help us forget where the hell we are!* Lefty and I did some stripped-down classic rock covers and an original called "Spinning Round" which I'd written for Grandpa Lew. With Damian and Kenny banging time on the cafeteria tables, we gave them Petty's "Free Fallin'" and Mellencamp's "Pink Houses."

Most soldiers were singing along, smiling, happy. But a few were more somber, like it was just too hard being reminded of things back home, even if it's only music. After a few songs the emotional contrasts in that room had me feeling decidedly cloudy. Once again, I would be heading home within a few weeks while these guys were stuck here in the middle of Nowhere, Bosnia for months, sometimes years at a time.

Getting the wristwatch tap from bus driver Rudy, we wrapped up and shook hands with our latest group of ephemeral friends. Loading back onto the bus, I headed for one of the cozy and private sleeping bunks in the back. I just wanted to lie down and ingest it all. We were about to pull away and the band and Rudy were talking, but then there was an unfamiliar voice: "Is the singer here?" I poked my head from between my curtains. Sergeant 1st Class Moore headed back toward me holding his camouflaged jacket. It had been signed in Sharpie by, essentially, the whole camp:

Sgt Thompson

SPC Garcia "Gunner"

SPC Beasley, "Buzz"

SPC Parker

SPC Motsinger

2nd Lt. Baer

Sgt Smith

PFC Walls. SPC Clark. SSC Inklebarger

CPL Bond wrote "Play the originals they were good"

SPC Woebkenber. "Rock On"

PFC Kleeman

Sgt R. Brockin

"Camp Morgan. 5th Platoon, SFC Moore"

I've worn Sgt. Moore's BDUs just once since that day, while participating in Park City's 2006 4th of July parade atop the Park City TV truck and resurrecting "Pink Houses" with JB on congas. Well, and also Neil Young's "Rocking in a Free World" — hey, we *are* the "Independent Republic of Park

City" after all. That jacket was handed directly to me but it belongs to McLefty, Damian and Kenny as well. It hangs in my costume closet, the coolest piece of clothing I own.

Egodog ended our second Balkan run on 9 August 2002 at CAS: Camp Able Sentry. We set up our gear on the basketball court against a fantastic Macedonian sunset. After our set closer — again Beastie Boys' "Sabotage" — Damian smashes his inexpensive bass on the concrete; a Norwegian troop named Morten promptly buys it from him.

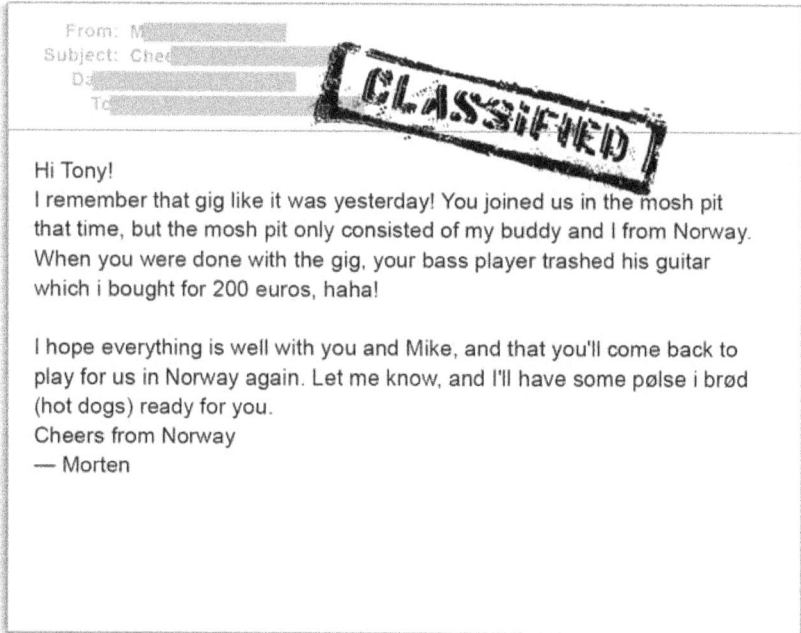

> From: M███████████████
> Subject: Che███████████████
> Da███████████████
> To███████████████
>
> CLASSIFIED
>
> Hi Tony!
> I remember that gig like it was yesterday! You joined us in the mosh pit that time, but the mosh pit only consisted of my buddy and I from Norway. When you were done with the gig, your bass player trashed his guitar which i bought for 200 euros, haha!
>
> I hope everything is well with you and Mike, and that you'll come back to play for us in Norway again. Let me know, and I'll have some pølse i brød (hot dogs) ready for you.
> Cheers from Norway
> — Morten

RETURN TO SASEBO
OR,
YOU CAN NEVER GO HOME AGAIN

On Friday afternoons, Hesh would pick me up from grade school and I would retire to my grandparents' house for my weekly overnight. Hesh is unrivaled in the kitchen and she would indulge my Friday night menu requests: spaghetti, steak, arros con pollo — all consistently brilliant. Lew would relinquish the evening's TV programming choices to me as well: *The Sonny and Cher Comedy Hour. The Donny and Marie Variety Show. The Dukes of Hazzard*... The man was a fucking soldier.

LEWIS POPP
UNITED STATES NAVY
U.S.S. TROUSDALE
WWII

Lew and Hesh would religiously attend just about every little league game my brother or I ever played in — or rode the bench in. On Saturday mornings I would join my grandfather in his garage workshop. I'd tune Lew's paint-splattered radio in to WLS AM, and we'd work side by side on our respective projects. "Puttering," Hesh called it. I relished every hour until one of my parental units would pull up the drive to take me back to a house that was never really happy. My folks' relationship was tense and tenuous; they would divorce when I was thirteen. *Home* was always Lew and Hesh's house on Kingsway Drive.

CHICAGO-MIDWAY, SALT LAKE CITY, CHICAGO-MIDWAY LOS ANGELES, TOKYO-HANEDA, TOKYO-NARITA, YOKOSUKA, ATSUGI, SASEBO, TOKYO-HANEDA, LOS ANGELES, CHICAGO-MIDWAY.

March 2003, Aurora, Illinois: I'd been living back in "A-Town" for a few months following fifteen long years in Los Angeles. I set up home base on Kingsway Drive, in the same warm log cabin-like back bedroom where I'd spent so many lovely days throughout my youth.

My suburban Chicago winter of 2002/03 was a move prompted by two motivations: promises of weekly work from my then-booking agent (little materialized) and my Grandfather Lew's failing health, his need for help being beyond what Hesh could provide, for all her Old World strength. He was being eaten away by a nasty 4th stage cancer and my profession allowed me the flexibility to live with them, hopefully making some final stage logistics easier on the two people who taught me more than I can convey.

Every week I'd fly out of Chicago-Midway to Salt Lake for my Thursday Metal Show gig. During these ambiguous months I was also in professional limbo as a serious candidate for a lucrative vocal slot in an ex-80's supergroup — let's call them "Satin Pistol." They had sent me three instrumental demo tracks on CD, two of which I thought were funky and interesting. I set up my Boss recording unit in a spare bedroom and spent a few days tracking the melodies and lyrics I'd written:

> *"I will not play the rat in a maze today. Gridlock victim, commuter slave... Part of me's gotta still believe everything's gonna be alright."*

Rumors were flying back in my LA circles as to which amongst the half dozen or so finalists had the edge. I was happy with what I was sending the band. A few weeks later, they held auditions for the singers whose CDs they dug and I flew back out to Cali for a few days. The band was gracious and made it clear they were far from a decision, so we noodled a few times each through my three prepared songs through a very *very* loud sound system. The band was still toying with arrangements and I'm not sure those riffs even became anything and made any cut.

"Anything specifically you need to hear from me?" I asked the frizzy-haired guitarist late in the jam session.

"Um... I like when you're in the high shit."

I wasn't surprised when I began hearing word that the band was going with a known commodity from a platinum-selling 90's band. Listening some years later to their two albums together, I bow to their eventual choice's brilliant and superior vocal and melodic skills. While I was certainly chewing my arm off for new professional directions (insert Def Leppard joke here) the music I was given to work with didn't really move me. I had never been a fan of their infinitely successful 80's band, and although I might have eventually found a creative place with those guys, essentially I would have been doing my Metal Show character "Nigel," without the wig. Besides, Utah was rife with possibility and I was enjoying myself.

Some years later Satin Pistol would come to Park City for a show during Sundance. They arrived minus their singer who reportedly "missed his plane." I was down the street with my Martin acoustic, obliviously working the steakhouse as the four more travel-savvy Pistols put a jam session together up Main Street at a capacity Harry O's nightclub. The drummer did come in for dinner before the show and tip me ten bucks, however. So I got that going for me.

- - - - - - - - - - -

"We're getting you a shot or two of brandy," Karla told me as we boarded the elevator up to the bar at Encounters. For all our trips through LAX, we had never been inside that distinctive restaurant that serves as an internationally recognizable landmark for that airport. This was very much a medicinal binge. I had a probable bronchial infection and my voice was nowhere to be found, a few hours from boarding a plane for three gigs in Japan — the rest of my band had already arrived in Tokyo and I was a day behind.

Karla has seen my greatest victories and my lowest moments. This was to prove dark times for me, and an ignominious debut tour for my new U2 tribute show, Rattle & Hum.

This was to be my third trip to the country where Lew Popp got his battle star during WWII. Although I never served in the armed forces, Lew recognized the contribution my entertainment efforts made to the country he served in war as a sailor. Now he was gone, having mercifully passed a few weeks before, a shell of the physical man he once was, writhing in pain and holding on stubbornly much too long for his own good. I figured, hell, I travel so much anyway, I can kill two birds: work from the Midwest and help Hesh take care of Chief.

If he liked you, Lew called you "Chief." It's a Navy thing, a nod of respect. He called me Chief long before I approached deserving it.

In preparation for Rattle & Hum's week of naval bases in Japan, I had flown from Chicago to LA with all my Bono gear yet tragically without the first item on every tour's checklist: my passport. "No worries," I thought, "we'll have it overnighted." Well, I won't mention the company whose driver failed to *completely* unload the truck that night but let's just say they "absolutely, positively" fucked up. So I missed my flight from LAX to Tokyo-Haneda and had to purchase a ticket out of pocket to the tune of over half my paycheck for the week.

Money, however, was a secondary concern as I sat at the bar with Karla and hoped a few shots would open up my bronchial passages. I was uninsured and desperate to get my instrument back.

Few things feel more emasculating than not having my pipes. You wake every morning wondering if your body will allow you to do your job that night. To be certain, there are steps we vocalists can take to mitigate the capriciousness of our instruments, proper technique highest atop the list. But some days, even with care and hydration, rest and a good warm-up, the vox just aren't there.

Let's face it, they ain't comin'.

I bid Karla goodbye at LAX's Bradley Terminal, accepted a handful of Xanax and found my way to the jet. Asian aircrafts' coach sections are far from accommodating to tall Westerners and I was more than happy to down the aforementioned pharmaceuticals with much complimentary whiskey.

I landed groggily on Japanese soil with guitar and bag, not relishing the navigation required to get my butt to the naval base in Yokosuka: bus to the domestic airport, across the vast city, then bus to train. The train proved harrowing, if only for the uncertainty of its destination. As I quietly tested my tenuous vocal state and tried to visualize getting anywhere near the notes in "New Years Day," I scanned the line's map on the wall. After a few educated guesses and dubious directions from an annoyed American sailor, I saw the shipyard and the base where my bandmates awaited. A quick call to our POC and I was whisked to the All Hands Club, a small venue on base where the band had just finished setting up in preparation for soundcheck.

They turned to me in faces mixed with surprise, laughter and more than a trace of relief after wondering if their singer would arrive at all. I shook my head and hopped on stage. After some brief travel mishap recaps, they launched into a song. I opened my mouth for the first line and… nothing. *Ok I need more warm-ups,* I thought. Instructing the other three to run through our rustier songs, I found a back room and tried to sing. And tried. And nothing. The band's levels were set and we adjourned to our lodging with our POC and driver. After a restless yet heavy nap, I hit my pre-show yoga routine and shower where I began more vocalizations. Still no luck. Still no chance of a show for me. I'd been flown halfway around the world, and for the first time in my career I was unable to do my job. I was shattered.

I informed the band of my state, of which they had been vaguely aware. We devised a plan utilizing the bassist's vocal abilities and decided it was best to have the other three ad-lib a set for what would surely be a disappointed crowd, as for weeks we had been advertised as a U2 tribute show. Our driver took me to the infirmary where I was looked over and given some antibiotics and anti-inflammatories. Defeated and spent, I forsook the show and went to bed. *Well, here's one way to get a free doctor's appointment,* I thought.

The next morning we boarded another bus, taking us to Atsugi for show number two at Club Trilogy. I felt only marginally better, although the band informed me of an understanding audience and a decent show the night before. I probably should have done the injured quarterback thing and stood on the sidelines with my band. But I was just devastated. That next day's soundcheck produced a few more notes than the previous day's attempts and I resigned myself to pushing through that night. The possibility of diminished paychecks for the rest of the guys was a superfluous motivation. The Atsugi show was indeed rough, but fortunately for my pride, sparsely attended and there wasn't three hundred sailors hearing me croak and cackle. Our original setlist was again scrapped, but at least this night the Department of Defense got a four-piece band.

The following morning I watched Armed Forces Network in my room as I re-packed for a short flight to the naval base at Sasebo. I had been playing Salt Lake for over six months and was following CNN reports about the return of abducted Mormon girl Elizabeth Smart — a sad and nasty page in Utah's history. Meanwhile, I was fighting my demons of disappointment and doubt half the planet away. A limp to the finish line to be sure, and a relief to have the three shows and travel hells behind me, but Rattle & Hum's Sasebo performance proved a relatively acceptable conclusion.

Each show, each tour, to me was either a victory won or a defeat in battle. This had been neither. Hamstrung by swollen vocal chords, I struggled for every single note. Zero fun but we got the job done. I'd done my job to the best of my ability, no more, no less. I hate the gray areas.

Sasebo, Japan was familiar to me from a few years before. During the steamy summer of 2000, Egodog was booked for five consecutive nights at the base's only nightclub. Also flown over by AKA that week was Brooklyn-raised, LA based comic Dwayne Perkins. Being funny and clean is the hardest job in entertainment, outside of doing triple penetration porn (aww, see?) and Dwayne does it brilliantly... The clean humor, not triple penetrations.

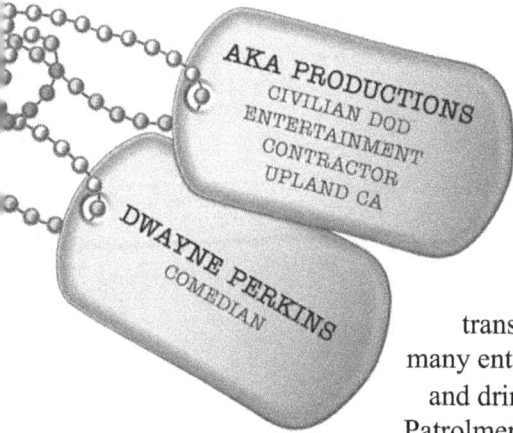

I was wary of a weak reception and assumed attendance would drop as the week went on. Outside of Deadheads, who wants to watch the same band five nights straight? However, Egodog and Dwayne were in fact brought to the island that July because the Navy was conducting its largest ship-to-ship troop transfer since WWII. Thus, Sasebo contained many entertainment-starved sailors ready to laugh and drink and rock. And man, they drank. Shore Patrolmen tried in vain to break up an enthusiastic mosh pit, with civilian-clad off duty sailors cutting loose by throwing their bodies violently into each other. Damian hoisted his bass above his head and ran to the stage edge, ready to smash a second axe to bits, but was tackled by a sailor in the front row.

That tour had one of my most memorable exchanges, as a base medic informed me their suicide prevention visits were sharply down that week, a fact he attributed directly to our presence at Sasebo. That was the first story I related to Lew upon my return to the States that summer.

From: Do...
Sub...
Date...
To...

I just wanted to take some time to thank you again for coming to Sasebo and playing the shows. The small touch of home that you provided really lifted the spirits of many sailors and I have had to medevac less people the last month than I ever have before due to mental health issues and I am thinking it is because your shows allowed them to expel some energy and also enjoy themselves in an environment that would normally cause stress and home sickness. Is there any plan to come back to Sasebo? I am sure that I would not be the only one that would enjoy seeing you again. Well I will keep this short for now when I get back to LA I hope to take in one of your shows. Thanks Again.

— Jason "Doc" Glasgow, Sasebo Japan

OPSEC
OPERATIONS SECURITY

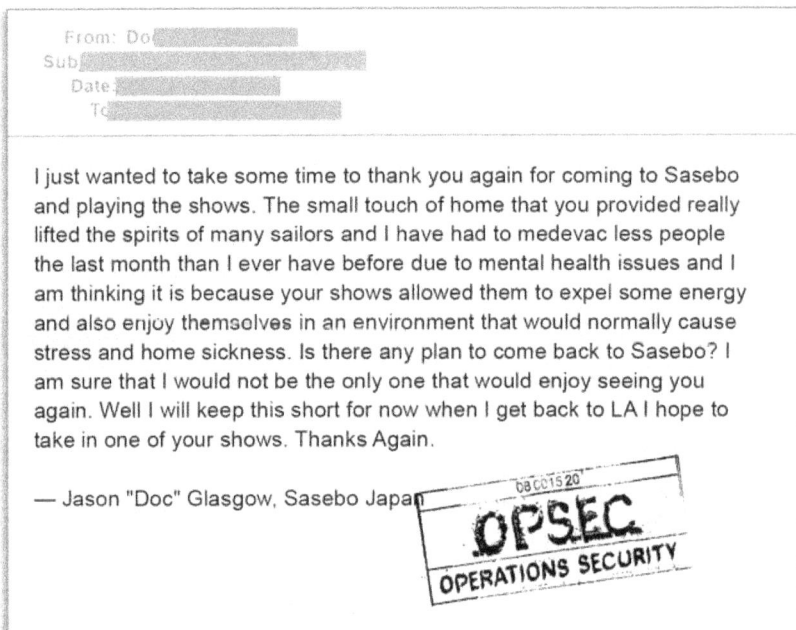

The next morning, before we were due to depart for the airport, I rose before my colleagues and had breakfast alone. Solo breakfasts in arbitrary places are one of my favorite things in the universe. It was a gray and foggy morning. Japanese ships sat in dock beside American vessels quietly awaiting their reactivation. I walked my off breakfast, attempting to shake the stink of my travel errors and physical failings.

Lew had been here some six decades before, perhaps in the hills surrounding me. Trudging through December Japanese snow to cut down a Christmas tree for his ship, he likely found his visit to Sasebo no more victorious than I did this one. But I allowed myself to talk to him on the pier that morning. It was the first day I really grasped that he was gone.

My family and I had just spent months ensconced in the day-to-day logistics of watching him die a horribly painful and demeaning death. There was a man who labored all his life and had work standards that bordered on obsessive. However his last days, for the sake of his honor, I will not detail.

I would rather think of Lew as he was a few years prior, on the sidelines of Soldier Field with me on Anthem Day. Or in my youth, planting his lawn chair at my baseball games. I'll remember him maintaining a swimming pool he rarely used yet kept up every day through the Illinois summers just for his grandkids, neighbors, and sundry pool-moochers.

My dreams rarely make any sense. They're either Dali-surreal, or I'm being chased by baboons. Hey, I'm an odd cat. But every so often I'll have a brief and happy dream about Lew. He's healthy, having somehow recovered fully. He's even fat again, as he looked through the 90's before he got sick. I've never been so happy to see somebody overweight. He just suddenly appears every so often, sitting back in his recliner, telling me, "Oh the cancer? Yeah I'm ok now, Chief."

And Hesh is still kicking ass, by the way. She's one of the top ladies in her Wi-bowling league.

British Metal Show veteran Nigel Tones and I have a love/hate relationship. Countless times have I been cock-blocked by a guy who wasn't even there. Nigel does the deed and I catch the shit. Somehow, his reputation precedes me.

Nigel asked me to allow him a chapter of his own. He did ask politely, and hell, who can resist that accent.

THIS GIG WILL LAST SIX WEEKS OR, SEVEN YEARS OF BAD ROCK

By Nigel Tones

Oi! Enough of that wanker then! Your friendly neighborhood Nigel here, and I'll be taking over for a bit. We need to set a few things straight. Too many bloody rumours. Got to protect the brand and all that.

No man knows me history.

- **Number of times I've copulated in the dressing room at the weekly Salt Lake gig (2002-2009):** One.

  Close quarters, not built for comfort. But sod it, right? I was practicing for the Mile High Club on some future Southwest flight. Why only one session of Hide the Salami, in some 370 odd weeks, amidst all that Thursday night metal mayhem? Basically, when (insert name here) and I emerged from the bathroom, sweaty and hoarse, the club owner had been camped on the couch — the whole bloody time, "Really? You couldn't get a room?" she asked.

- **Number of Thursday Club employees bedded:** Zero.

  Don't shit where you eat, my son.

- **Number of times Nigel has been detained by foreign customs:** One.

  Well, Canadians, anyway. I had a weekend gig up in Edmonton (in February? Why can't my agents send me to Cabo in mid-winter). That Thursday night was late and crazy enough to find me carelessly leaving some metal accoutrement in my travel bag. These included several syringes, which I apply for accuracy under my leather studded bracelet during "Sweet Child o' Mine." My Kanuck border guards were decidedly NOT amused.

- **Nigel's first date in Utah:**

  With an Olympic athlete, actually. We met at a show. I let her pick the restaurant. When we arrived, the lobby was adorned with her pictures and medals in a glass case. "Smooth move," I thought. Just then, the hostess turns and coyly asks me, "Aren't you the singer from Metal Show?"

Right. It's September of 2002. I've got a flat in Hollywood, having just relocated from the UK. One smoggy day one of me booking agent calls and says, "Nigel, do you want a fly-away show on Thursdays?"

"Yeah!"

"It's in Salt Lake City."

"Great!" quoth Nigel.

"This'll be a nice little six-week run," said Booker Man.

"I'm there, baby. I've got a new German character. He's called Klaus Von Steinberger."

(long pause...)

"Ok great, dude. I'll email you the flight info."

The band and I were van-shuttled from Salt Lake International that first Thursday afternoon. The I-80 freeway curved past downtown and The Temple. "That's where God lives," the driver told us.

Enter Frisky Pussy. Yes, the Barmitvah-gigging has-beens from the credit card commercial... kind of. Ok, *not*. Our Los Angeles-based production company owned that band name. Which is also why I'm using a pseudonym and referring to Frisky Pussy as Metal Show. Aren't I a cheeky monkey?

Our agents (we're all independent contractors, after all) assembled a "B-band" to take on bookings the TV spot lineup was turning down. Of the original four, only drummer Blackie remained from the commercial. Our leftover lineup started off doing most of their schtick, as directed by said production company. Although out of respect for what those blokes had already built, I did stipulate from the start that I wouldn't be doing a Xerox of that show's singer. Nigel and his alter-egos had their own bag, baby.

Well, my Klaus Von Steinberger character was soon shelved and I ended up doing the show as me-self because, let's face it — you can goose-step to Scorpions in front of one too many Jewish club owners. Besides, being a Brit allows me more discernible one-liners than any German could deliver:

"You're the ones with the accents, mate. It was our language first!" or "This song's by an Italian from New Jersey, where mommas let their babies grow up to be cowboys, apparently."

Sure, it goes largely under radar. But those who miss the really good bits are mollified by our song selection. Nigel and the Metal Show would bring you all of those lyrical masterpieces, a la:

"Love me like a bomb, baby, come on get it on."

We came, we conquered, we came again. I flew in early from LAX every Thursday to join Mick & Allen on KBER 101, Utah's top-rated rock station. Our spin on the old Match Game was a hoot. Utah opened its arms and legs.

The night of the first show, one band member befriended a local fan and they had a little slumber party. She was named after a soda, if I recall. At the next week's soundcheck, our bartender leans over with, "Hey, I hear the band took a girl across the street and gang-banged her."

Wink wink, nudge nudge.

Naturally, I was aghast. "Well... right!" I replied — and thus our Utah bar was set. We were armed with plausible deniability.

Week 2 in Utah, and we were asking each other if the mullet at stage right was real or a wig. "Joe Dirt" was an under-the-radar hanger-on with that real roadie aroma. His padded press kit's resume included a first place finish at a karaoke competition — and a stint drumming with Cinderella. Wot? We were equally dubious of both claims. He insisted he played drums, yet while hearing his alleged demo on the stereo, Blackie noticed that Dirt's air-drum performance wasn't matching the CD. Complete and utter porky pies. *

The locals raised their steins to approach us at set break: "I'd die without my Thursdays!" Local love was generally exuberant, although the Metal Show did have our early detractors.

"Way to go, assholes! Ruin it for local musicians! Just fly in, take gigs and fly out. Fucking cover bands..." This silly git was at a table a foot behind me, while I was facing the opposite direction engrossed in a completely different conversation with a married couple who were presently using Nigel as confessor: "My husband and I fight all week, except for our Thursday nights here!" I'm accepting heartfelt compliments while wearing leopard-skin spandex. But I excused myself to turn around to Johnny Localband. "Hey mate! Don't dig what we do? Learn some songs somebody's heard before and stop staring at your Docs. Then maybe you can take *my* gig."

* *porky pies = Brit slang for "lies" — Editor*

Unless you're extraordinarily brilliant, no one wants to hear you mumble your misery, mate. People are trying to get laid here... *Dance, monkeys!*

The cue out the club door foreshadowed the evening's head count — usually quite meaty, with averages over 300 paid, barring a Jazz game or finals week at The U. The beer on tap in Utah is about 1/3 the alcohol content of even your standard American piss from a tap. Until early 2009, every Utah establishment that served alcohol was technically designated as a "Private Club." First timers and tourists who wandered into Utah bars had to go through a sad and twisted charade about "sponsoring guests" and it was all just nonsensical: *Yes, come visit our beautiful state and give us your money — but we're going to treat you like a right bastard if you even think about ordering a cocktail.* It was a source of constant angst amongst club owners, bar managers, and entertainers. But it did provide me with additional radio schtick — Utah law decreed we were to state after every bar's name: "A private club for members." This, for me of course became: "A private club for *my* member." I won't expound on the demographic make up of Utah's 10-member, unelected board that establishes liquor laws. Suffice it to say, you'd do as well to have eunuchs regulating a brothel.

Our Thursday Metal Show had its rules as well. Bloody well right it did. First and foremost: No cock in the front row. You could always spot the new blokes — the Virgins — as they were unceremoniously elbowed back behind our zoo of lady fans, whose Jack Mormon boobs pressed lovingly against the stage...

"The front row is a pizza, people! It is to be ALL tomato and NO SAUSAGE!"

Most were compliant. But a few messy tarts somehow couldn't gauge the acceptance-level of grabbing the singer's testicles mid-performance. Or touching a guitar during a song. *No, sweetheart, don't worry about it. It's just a prop.* Better to get sloppy love than none at all, we supposed.

Our stage show had evolved from blatant crotch tweaking and intentionally bumbled Poison choreography to 80's metal tributes — the Ozzy/Rhodes guitar solo with Maxx on my shoulders was a personal favorite. The old bit of riffing on "Here I Go Again" chord changes — a long time gag by our predecessors (now of Steel Panther infamy) was replaced with our Iron Maiden-to-Zeppelin-to-Maiden segue, "The Flight of Immigrant."

"His eyes are ablaze, see the madman in his gaze...
Ahh-AHHHHH!!!"

Again, it was our own bag up in Utah. Everyone at the LA booking agency wanted Nigel to do The Script. Fuck that. I might as well join *Les Mis.*

In time, Salt Lake's Metal Show lineup was finding itself. And thanks to an enlightened local media, visa versa. A live broadcast on Fox 13's *Good Day Utah* brought us instant cred after Nigel's 7 AM morning remote fondling of local affiliate Allie MacKay. A dead hottie, that one. The **Salt Lake Weekly** referred to our Thursday shows as "butt-rocking," and we were pleased to no end.

"We love our bottoms. And they do rock, actually."

The **Weekly's** editor Bill Frost offered me an advice column, which he titled "Dear Rock Star."

Excerpts from Nigel's advice column
Salt Lake City Weekly 2007

Hey there, true believers! It's your friendly neighborhood Nigel, here once again this month to dole out my little heavy metal turds of wisdom. But before I get to your questions, I must address a rather disconcerting issue…

A few of you ladies have pulled me aside at Thursday Club asking why I've stopped posting to my MySpace page. Well the answer is simple: I don't have a MySpace page! Oh there's a Nigel Tones page all right, but I hate to break it to ya — you people are dealing with an imposter. He has cut and pasted articles and quotes from the official Metal Show site and he picked some flattering live shots of me (damn I'm cute), but I can assure you — it's not me.

Now. This disturbing revelation brings certain questions to light. Namely: who is this bloke? And more importantly: is he skimming off my groupie sex? Are any of you girls falling for this? If you plan on meeting "Nigel" at a Starbucks in Logan at midnight on a Tuesday, don't be shocked when you end up naked and wet in a basement pit of some deranged psychopath. *It rubs the lotion on its skin!!!* You have been warned. Now get off the computer and find a date the old fashioned way!

Q: Hey Nigel, I'm dying to meet you & your band. I'm underage so I'm still working my way to get into Thursday Club. Anyway I hear you play all 80's metal. If Metal Show can play a lot of those songs, do you guys write your own songs? I mean are you ever going to release an album of your own? You guys got rhythm so I think you could pull off making an album. — *Jessica SLC*

NT: Well, Jessica, when you're old enough to see the show you will realize that Metal Show has compiled a setlist of most popular 80's metal ever put to vinyl. Oh, vinyl? Never mind. But while Nigel is an accomplished and esteemed songwriter (big in Japan, major label interest, etc.), the Metal Show is paid handsomely to give you only the stuff you know… Unless you're requesting Megadeth. Nothing dries out a pair of panties like some Dave Mustaine vocals. Oh and Jessica? Let us know when you turn 21 and make your first show. We'll be sure to give you a good Thursday Virgin welcome. But don't ask for a "birthday shout out" during the show — this isn't Chuck E fucking Cheese.

Q: Dear Nigel: I've been seeing the lead singer in a band and he's not a very nice person. Last week at their show he ignored me and kissed another girl. Tho drummer rescued me and is much nicer, how do I go out with him instead? I'm not a groupie! P.S. He even gave me VD on Valentine's Day!

NT: Oh bloody hell. Where do I start. Well let's begin by establishing that drummers are cock-blockers. Notoriously and with very rare

exception. Swooped down like the vulture he is, eh? Anyway… Look, we singers are not only the most important instrument in the band, but off stage we also serve as politicians and diplomats. Hey, there's a lot more that goes into rock stardom than you can possibly imagine. Some people have to be schmoozed. If the band needs a place to crash for the night, who warms the ugly girl into the idea of four long-hairs on the floor of her vacationing parents' house in Bountiful? We do. The singers. Always taking a bullet for the bloody team. So sometimes you see us talking to — or heaven forbid touching — a female client or fan club member. Deal with it. But here now, angel. You blew it. You were seeing the singer and now you will settle for the DRUMMER? Two steps back down the food chain, dumb ass! Besides, you said you were "seeing" the singer… Define "seeing."
PS And you made up your postscript cause that's just too funny.

Q: Nigel, I do worship you as the Metal god of God. However, I've noticed that Nigel's column is a little hit and miss. I haven't recognized any consistency yet. Is this inconsistency indicative of your performance with the ladies, life of a rock star, and/or other rituals you perform? Or, are you simply that damn busy and that good? — *Moto, SLC*

NT: Ok, people. You haven't been paying attention. Nigel's column is the last week of every month. The reasons for this are varied: #1, they can't afford to pay me every week. #2, yes I'm that busy. I have manicures on Monday, pedicures Tuesdays, massage Wednesday… you get the picture. If I'm spending any additional time at my computer it'll be surfing midget porn. Thirdly, are you questioning Nigel's sexual performance? Look, mate — to Nigel, the female orgasm is kind of like God: if it exists, I'm unaware of it and it doesn't concern me. By the way, I'm not sure what you meant by "The Metal god of God" but I like it!

A cocktail of instinct and boots-on-the-ground research can assist in weeding losers out of one's circles: single mothers out clubbing nightly, mental midgets bragging about not paying taxes, and the like. The number of people Nigel won't do business with in Utah is happily short. When attendance started increasing at Thursday Club, their first booking guy got chummy with our bassist Trevor during a couple late night hotel room reach-arounds. The exchanges went something like this:

TREVOR: Hey, now that the numbers are up, we can probably get the original band from LA up here.
BOOKER: The guys that turned it down a few months ago? *(sniff sniff)*
TREVOR: Dude, don't bogart that. *(sniff sniff)*
BOOKER: That's a good idea bro. Let's get on it.

An honest club owner and a couple loyal patrons helped me piss in those cornflakes, posthaste. Trevor was soon out, and a new bassist was in, whose axe rode up high like a jazz player but incongruous with 1980's glam metal — irritating the hell out of people who actually gave a shit. So he rocked a curly black wig and beard stubble as Rip Stinger. *Poetry.*

Expanding southward through the great valley, Metal Show added an occasional Friday gig and penetrated deep into the darkest crevasses of Lehi where the locals inform visitors that yes, *Footloose* was in fact filmed there. Mind you, corrupting previously pure and innocent townsfolk then sauntering away laughing carelessly? That's what Nigel does best, and Lithgow was nowhere to be found. Some of our regulars now find themselves questioning their spiritual and philosophical paths. Others have had really fantastic sex because of us... well, us and Jaegermeister.

"Welcome to the Metal Show, where last week some chick passed out with her mouth on a toilet seat... but don't worry, we changed the toilet seat!"

(cheers)

One night the band and I were sprinting off stage at the end of our first set when I was intercepted by a most stunning girl. Her first words, "I'd take you backstage and fuck you now if I wasn't going to have Mormon guilt issues in the morning."

I took her hand, and we headed backstage. "Come on, luv." But instead of making a b-line for the club's tiny and infamous backstage area, we hooked a right at the aquarium and I led her up to the sound booth and grabbed a pen. "Here are the titles of two books and a comedy CD (likely Richard Dawkins, Fawn Brodie and Eddie Izzard). This is your homework, darling. Go home and soak in these, *then* come back and fuck me — but fuck me guilt free."

She took my scribblings and turned to go, somewhat confused. Alas, she never did return. Sometimes Nigel leads a horse to water and it still goes to Temple.

I must say: if the ultimate purpose for Mormons' "magic undergarments" is to turn a bloke off and deter fornication, then score one for ol' Joe Smith. It took only a few awkward moments investigating one such pair of *Jesus Jammies* and Nigel's penis was "magically" flaccid.

Our seventh Salt Lake Thursday fell on Halloween of 2003. I strategically applied stigmata blood and wore a crown of thorns... Nigel *is* messianic complex in Technicolor after all. A known and admitted LDS member was in the front row, dressed as the devil. She kept shaking her fist and pointing her pitchfork at me. I actually missed the irony for a few songs — I was probably looking at her tits. So sue me, they were quite lovely. A couple years later, I would resurrect Nigel-Christ while participating in a local ski resort's Pondskimming Contest. Pondskimming is an annual tradition at a handful of ski resorts across the country. Picture the Polar Bear Club with silly costumes and more lager. Contestants don skis, snowboards and some bloody ingenious outfits. They are then assigned numbers and cue up a couple hundred yards up-slope from a makeshift pool of slush, about 75 feet long. Winners are those with the best costumes or those who make it across the water. Prizes are awarded in both categories, although the latter accomplishment's reward is that you stay dry and avoid a dose of pneumonia.

Amy from Park City TV interviewed me atop the bunny hill's staging area at The Canyons, where I shivered next to: Dynamite Man (with exploding head), Viking Chick (very hot), Creepy G-String Guy (sorted). Amy eyed me up and down. It was April but they'd just caught a blustery cold front with snow blowing sideways on — I was fairly naked under the Biblical garments. Amy opened the broadcast with: "That's an, um, interesting costume. Want to tell us about it?"

I replied, in my best New York Hassidic accent: "I'm a migrant worker from Galilee! My fatha' said I could walk on water, so I figured no big whup!" Any thoughts of annual pondskimming re-appearances were nixed as soon as Nigel of Nazareth hit the ice water. My nipples never need to be that erect without involving clamps of some sort.

I would occasionally invite nationally touring comics to open our show, while promoting their weekend appearances at Wiseguys, out in the dreaded West Valley. Dwayne Perkins, big Griff from Atlanta, and Craig Gass, introducing us with dead-on impressions of Gene Simmons and Sam Kinnison! Local stand-ups Guy Seidel and the fabulous, highly musical impressionist Marcus cut their comedic teeth at Thursday Club. There were costume contests, and costumes without the contest. Some fans would stiffen up their bang-claws and hit the club, 80's-style. We should have petitioned the capitol for a state holiday, each Thursday — naturally to be celebrated on Friday mornings whilst hung over from vodka-Red Bulls.

Touring bands would at times hear about our Thursday debauchery, sometimes jumping up to sing a tune. Young country studs Rascal Flats were in town and closed our show one night to a surprised and excited crowd.

A slap-together lineup of metal veterans was playing down the street from us one week. I'd heard about the show while in studio at KBER 101 that afternoon. We'd finished our last set and were headed back on stage for the encore, when I noticed a guy sitting on the drum riser. A little bald chap, just having a lounge on our stage. "Hey, where's security," I thought. He was just sitting there, smiling. "Screw it," I silently concluded, we'd planned "Highway to Hell" so let's go, squatter or no!

Backstage, five minutes later, we learned it was Chris Slade. Yes, the drummer of AC/DC. Aww! He got "The JACK!"

EMAIL: Called Out By a Cougar *(no, not THAT kind)*

With Nigel & Utah's Metal Show celebrating our sixth year in Salt Lake, many Utes have been asking about bits of our history. One fan email covers much of it, so I thought I'd share our exchange:

From: Eric
Subject:
Date: Sep 8, 2008 4:51 PM
To: Nigel Tones

It was me who waved at you yesterday when you were getting off the long term parking bus at the airport. It must have driven you nuts to have ridden out with all of us BYU fans. ha ha.

Incidentally, I'm a BYU alum and a long time Metal Show (Back to the Frisky Pussy days) devotee. You also called me out from the stage when I had the temerity to wear my BYU hat to a gig. I promptly flipped you off and laughed. You were cool when I came over to say hi afterwards.

You would be surprised (or maybe not - I get the sense you're a smart fellow) how many Mormons are regulars at your show. That number includes some BYU students and alumni.

The Pussy days were a loooong time ago. I remember seeing you guys play with the bassist from Metal Skool or whatever they are named now. I'd guess he was filling in. Yes, I saw Metal Skool at the Viper Room.

Interestingly my first Frisky Pussy experience was with my BYU buddy who was then in med school at the U of U. It would seem that the med students (a few of whom were former BYU guys and active LDS) loved to come see you guys and wind down with a few beers, Red Bulls, or whatever they liked to drink.

I'm going to admit to you I kind of miss Max Steele. He was a nice guy and was impressed when I correctly guessed the make and model of his guitar. (I had a few Kramers back in the day) Every so often we'd talk guitars at the bar during a break.

Anyway, you looked a bit bewildered when I waved so I though I would explain.

Regards,
Eric

Aaaaahhh, Eric. Thank you for the clarification; I thought I was getting one of those Missionary Waves. You know, the ones that say, "Hey, we're nice — and we don't need caffeine."

BTW, Excessive Celebration??? Weeeeeeeak. What Ward does THAT ref attend?

Love technology. We are now acquainted. And as I have entertained you, you can enlighten me: Did BYU place the Science and Theology Buildings as far, logistically across the campus as possible? Do those professors eat lunch together? I envision food fights.

Courage,
Nigel

Behind the scenes every week at Thursday Club, the *real* show was on…

Bassist Rip once skipped his meds and began inexplicably shooting Nigel and Maxx the ol' evil eye on stage during our first set. We got backstage for break, and Rip is still skulking, not looking at me directly. Then Maxx bounces in. Rip grabs Maxx and whips him violently against the wall.

"Don't you EVER disrespect me like that or I'll beat the shit out of you!"

"Dude, I'll fight you if I know what I'm fighting you about!" Maxx yelps. Nigel placed a call the next morning. Bloody hell. Two down.

The early Metal Show lineups included several personality extremes just pulling a Huey Lewis, *workin' for a living.* Most of us could play well with others. When we didn't have Friday or Saturday gigs in California, we stayed out some weekends and skied The Canyons. Having carved the French Alps as a child, I appreciated what Utes have deemed "The Greatest Snow on Earth." Maxx knew Big Bear and Mammoth like the back of his fret-hand, but he was also extremely blitzed by the time we hit the Cabriolet and Nigel spent some quality hours on Apex Ridge sloshing him back into his skis.

Maxx Steele wasn't our first call for the Thursday Club Metal Show guitar slot. Via a local SoCal referral, I'd emailed an invitation to a player named Ty Longley who politely declined — he'd just landed a touring slot with 80's real-deal glam band Great White. A few months into our Utah run, half the country away in a bar in Rhode Island, Great White's ill-advised pyrotechnic effects set the club ablaze, killing 100 people, including Longley.

Sacking Metal Show's first guitar player, my mate Maxx Steele, broke my heart. His recent family history had been brutal, and he'd weathered a lot. However, he weathered it through a bottle, and after a while it just became too much. One Thursday he was wobbling noticeably on stage left throughout the first set. The guitar playing suddenly ceased mid song and we looked over to see Maxx in a heap on the dance floor. He'd just fallen off the stage — and broken his arm. I doubled up on some weak rhythm guitar to cover the second set, but Maxx Steele would be out of commission for six weeks. He returned, wrist in a brace and all was good in the SLC once more... for a while.

A few months later, as his stress and ergo drinking increased, Maxx would fall off the same stage — and break his other wrist. I had done the show in Las Vegas every Friday with a versatile guitarist called DD, whom I approached to substitute. The gig was still Maxx's — providing he went through a detox and came back sober and ready to rock. He and I spoke by phone the day he went into the clinic, then again thirty days later, when he emerged. He sounded strong, happy and ready to return. He really is a genuine cat, and was emphatically grateful about my promise to keep his guitar slot warm for his sober return...

Right. You know what's coming.

Maxx Steele's first night back fell on our 4-Year Anniversary Show. The band was staying at the Holiday Inn on 9th and Main. I hear it's a homeless shelter now. My routine was to pick the lads up in the lobby following my radio appearance and drive us to the club for soundcheck. When I entered the lobby that Anniversary Show Day, Maxx was prone on the couch with his feet up, watching the big screen. I thought, "Please let him be tired and napping." But no. He had stopped at the airport bar and was now hammered at five in the afternoon. We were all livid. I poured coffee down his throat and told him, "Sober up and enjoy this show, mate, because it's certainly your last."

Working technically as a "cast member" for a production company, hiring and firing wasn't my responsibility. However, it was easier for all parties to have a point man on the ground in Salt Lake City. I was the only member of these lineups to move to Utah, while the other three players flew back and forth from Vegas and Southern California. Band personnel messes were generally mine and the club owner's to clean up: drunk guitarists kicking a hole in the dressing room wall, stealing beer from the cooler, bad attitudes from under-appreciative trust fund babies, and players still warped from fat weekly work during the dot com boom: "Man we were doing disco in San Francisco every weekend at a grand per guy, per night. This is bullshit!" Now, playing little old Salt Lake City, their paychecks were a fraction of their former glory, and in their ignorance of economic realities, egos were bruised.

But the guys I became close to were the ones who walked off that Southwest flight every week with smiles on their faces: *Look what we do for a living! Hazaar!*

Right. Dig it or get the fuck out.

Maxx loved the gig, every Thursday. Our first Metal Show had been a private one-off in Buffalo, New York. During an Ozzy tune he hopped his skinny bum up on my shoulders. His ankh necklace proceeded to tangle itself in my hair, and when the solo neared its conclusion and I squatted to let him down, Maxx and I were still attached like psychotic Siamese twins. I'm trailing him around stage left until finally extricating myself right at the chorus.

Straight off the bloody rails!

After that surprisingly clam-light inaugural show, we're on the chartered bus ride back to the hotel. The driver was spinning Journey, and when Maxx and I instinctively stopped talking to focus on Neal Schon's outro solo in "Who's Crying Now," I knew I had found a new chum. Letting him go from the Salt Lake show was a drag, but even Maxx knew it had to happen. Up here in our odd little corner of the entertainment business, my modus operandi was to handle our mini-dramas in-house. When a situation finally reached untenable levels, only then would I phone the higher-ups. With the powers down in Vegas visiting the club a grand total of never, I had the necessary autonomy to keep the train a' rolling.

Establishing and maintaining a show's presence in the local media is a key component in making a weekly gig successful. However, Nigel's adoption of those responsibilities eventually became a source of resentment among the more insecure and myopic band members. My aforementioned weekly appearances with local radio giants Mick & Allen, plus articles and interviews in the *City Weekly* were sources of strife — any time The Singer worked to garner press, out came the pissy faces and back-biting.

I had written a script for a Utah Metal Show mockumentary, to be debuted on a projector screen at our upcoming 5-Year Anniversary Show. The club's owner and I coordinated a video shoot out at the Salt Lake International Airport. We wrangled strippers and missionaries to greet the band. That afternoon's endeavor required the three guys from Vegas changing into their costumes upon landing and before they cleared security. We would then film all four of leather and spandex-clad metal dudes greeting our throng of Utah love. Yet, there were *issues.*

The club owner turns to me halfway through the filming to ask, "What's up with him?" pointing to our then-bassist. "It's like pulling teeth — is it such a pain in the ass for him to do this today?" Nigel would eventually thin the herd again.

The logistics of filming a leather-clad heavy metal band walking through TSA could only happen in Utah. Our cameramen, missionaries and strippers were gathering while I was trying to determine how we could get a shot of all four metal men coming through the security checkpoint simultaneously, since the video crew and I were already on the other side next to baggage claim. Just as I'm pondering our predicament, a younger TSA agent sidles up behind me, nudges my arm and says, "Thursday Club... Metal Show... rock on, dude." And we were in. Through security and out again.

We're rolling! Pile in the limo, bimbos!

In September of 2003, our bookers landed the film premier party for Jack Black's *School of Rock* at The Hollywood Athletic Club on Santa Monica Boulevard. "We need to put together a metal lineup of our funniest guys," our agent instructed me. I suggested DD from the Vegas Friday lineup. He was a better ad-libber between songs than Maxx. Ditto the Vegas bassist — a touch funnier than Rip Stinger on the repartee (this was pre-Rip meltdown). JFed was hungry for gigs and had the best comedy timing/pacing of all the company's drummers. JFed and I worked a weekly Vegas room for an agent who somehow couldn't comp a room for the singer from Salt Lake. I crashed on a mattress in his extra bedroom, right under a drum head signed by director Cameron Crowe. JFed had played the drummer of Stillwater in Crowe's *Almost Famous* and his understated performance was spot-on.

The Thursday following my recommendations and dear, was that a tense drive from the airport! The regular Utah band, Maxx, Rip and Paulie were furious for being passed up. Well, hard cheese. My employer asked for my objective opinion: The funniest guys. Not "Who are your best mates?" Not even, "Who's the tightest band?" But rather, we are to place tongue firmly in cheek for this one. I had long been a Tenacious D geek, from their HBO mini-series days. I was completely floored meeting Kyle Gass (and his mother!) and a few moments of conversation with stand-up stud Patton Oswalt was infinitely more satisfying even than my substantial paycheck. All young and brilliant American comedians.

It was one of the few times our booking agents had seen us perform as a unit. After a few weeks of phone preps we lunched on bangers and mash at the Cat & Fiddle across the street, listening to our booking agents saying, "Yeah, just do what you guys do." However. That evening we stood backstage, seconds away from starting our set when the same guys run up to us near frantic and throw us a one-eighty: "Hey don't do any schtick. Don't try to be funny, just play the songs." Perhaps they had been mingling and recognized the caliber of comedic talent in our midst. They left us, standing back there in spandex, mouths agape at our employers' lack of confidence. "Fuck that," I said when they left our sides. "Let's do what we do." Not to insinuate that Metal Show's level of comedic chops came anywhere near those in that room, but during

"Welcome to the Jungle" Jack Black rocked a long, hard metal-slide up to the stage and godammit we were vindicated.

One week I began receiving a series of text messages, Facebook messages and emails. "Hey Nigel, someone's looking for you on Craigslist."

Craigslist? I rarely use that site, and never for gigs. The ad was in all caps: "NIGEL TONES, WHERE ARE YOU?" I guess some Poison tribute was seeking a Bret Michaels. What, was I suddenly difficult to find on the internet? Facebook, Twitter, MySpace even? YouTube. Yahoo. Google, maybe? Whoever was chasing me down truly redefined not doing their homework. Factor in an email full of misspellings and syntax errors, and the whole exchange was exactly what you'd expect from guys that ostensibly enjoy playing Poison's attempts at music.

One night at a gig, the club's TVs were tuned to VH1 and I was able to experience, sans sound, that train-wreck of a reality show featuring Bret Michaels. I didn't know its title and I didn't care, being satisfied to comment on pop culture from a safe and sanitized distance. The premise of the show appeared simple: a washed out singer holds court for a parade of bimbos, each trying to out-shallow the others and thus, win his affections. Even with the sound turned down, the scene exuded banality. But should I have expected more from the show's star? Listen, people. In the hey-days of his career and at the peak of Poison's success, in his youth and in his prime — Bret Michaels was *awful.* There is absolutely nothing redeemable anywhere near that band's catalogue. I gave those songs to my guitar players to sing on Thursdays while I cut the crowd and nicked strangers' beers. Poison was arguably the straw that broke glam rock's back, ushering in a decade of un-melodic, heroin soaked gloom from America's Pacific Northwest. Thanks, CC DeVille. I went from wanting to punch your face to wanting to slit my wrists.

I caught the progression of dim botox queens on the screen being assessed by an equally vapid no-talent, and I watched in even further horror as the club's patrons followed every scene with rapt interest. *Oooh, which one will he pick?* I turned to a bird next to me at the bar: "Why do you allow this into your consciousness?" I asked a girl engrossed in the show.

"It makes me feel better about myself," she admitted.

I know it's a gross generalization, but here at the dawn of the Information Age, there are two types of media consumers: those who wake up and check BBC to see what's going on in the world, and those that check TMZ to see what's going on in the world.

So look, Sunshine — the next time Nigel turns you down for a shag, don't take it personally. It just means Nigel's not naïve... I know you'd probably be thinking about Brett Michaels' bald melon while I'm giving you the old *in-out.*

Poison was co-headlining Salt Lake's Usana Amphitheater one night in the summer of 2009. But backstage, thirty minutes to downbeat, their bassist was nowhere to be found. Managers and crew flew around the hospitality trailers in a panic, trying to find their missing *member.* "What are we going to do? We have a half hour and he's not answering his phone!" One astute tech pointed a few feet away. "You *do* know Hugh McDonald from Bon Jovi is standing right over there." Hugh had recently moved to Utah and was on a break from Bon Jovi recording sessions back east. Hugh is the consummate player, with Jon Bon as the *least* impressive notch on his resume, having performed with the likes of Ringo Starr, Willie Nelson, and Gladys Knight. Poison's manager ran over and frantically asked Hugh if he would bail them out — in front of 10,000 screaming Ute metalheads. They would have perhaps fifteen minutes for a run-through of chord changes and arrangements. "How much would you need?" Poison's manager asked Hugh.

Hugh put a pinky to his lips a la Doctor Evil and sneered, "One MILLION dollars!"

More from Nigel's *Salt Lake City Weekly* advice column, "Dear Rock Star"

Q: Dear Nigel, due to your extensive experience with women, I feel you would be the perfect candidate for an experiment I have been contemplating. Since the sex in committed relationships seems to grow more and more enjoyable as time goes on, (until the relationship fizzles of course) then I wonder if it is possible to have the same effect in an unattached situation, regular intervals = great sex. Interested? — *Ella*

NT: *Dear Ella, although my libido certainly tempts me (I surfed your home-porn site, nice!), my head is not currently in a place where I could fully enjoy the experience. You know — been busy pushing for Third World debt relief and such. As advanced intellects and souls, we must be cognizant of our mind frames in order to pursue the right situations at the right moments. Oh wait. Was that not a question for the article?*

Q: Dear Nigel, have you seen the Metal Show rip-off band across town? You must be pissed! — *Eric, SLC*

NT: *Copycat bands, ah yes! The sincerest form of flattery, as they say! Hey, if they're making a few quid and getting laid, who is Nigel to complain? Salt Lake is smart enough to know who first brought high-class, Vegas-style entertainment to Utah. And no, I haven't seen their show. I have better things to do than go see bands.*

Q: Ohwee, is religeous behaviour a reaction to sin? In the absence of sin would religeous rituals and behaviour still be nessisary in order to be a saint and live with god? Help!!!! — *Jimbo*

NT: *Well, the first thing you need in order to find god is spellcheck. Then you need to realize why religion exists: to keep the bad sheep in line. Oh, how I long for the day when humanity can be moral and ethical strictly for morality's sake. Until that day, you'll all be fighting and killing and dying over whose book of fairy tales is right. Which, to me is infinitely hilarious.*

Q: Nigel, why haven't you been selling panties lately? My friends have the thongs, sexy baby! — *Tara, Sugarhouse*

NT: *That was a limited run of stuff (t-shirts, panties, etc.) but we'll do more for the 3rd Anniversary show (Sept 15 — hundreds of registered voters, Rocky Anderson — wink wink). Other stuff, too. Bandanas, bumper stickers... yeah, car decals… know which ones kill me? Worse than the Calvin piss-on-whatever stickers? "Anarchy." Gimme a bloody break. I'm sitting in traffic behind a Toyota Land Cruiser with an "Anarchy" sticker in the back window. Mate, if there was anarchy this afternoon, you wouldn't have that SUV by nightfall. You'd dance around for an hour to Rage Against the Machine albums, then it's "Waaahh, why won't my toilet flush?" Sure, the whole system's a mess and in dire need of an overhaul, but the solution is certainly not anarchy. Power is a void waiting to be filled. And the people rushing to fill those voids are the LAST wing-nuts you'd want doing the job. So hey, here's an idea: I'll lead you. You just overthrow The Man and I'll slide right in. I'll make it fun, I promise. Come aaaan. You can trust ME!*

Nigel Tones is lead singer of the Metal Show, appearing every week at Thursday Club (a private club and so on) since September 2002. He is a weekly guest panelist on the Match Game with Mick & Allen on KBER 101, Thursdays at 5 PM, and he sincerely hopes you all find the oneness of your being.

All good things cum to an end.

I retired from Thursday Club in the Fall of 2009. Rumours have been numerous and varied as to the whys. Utah — the big sewing circle. Don't let our other author tell it. He'd give you some girly bollocks about being "burned out" or "needing to move on." So Nigel himself will set things straight here. You cued up and paid your fare, right? Right!

Acclaim. Accolades. Jealousies... become schisms. Duplicity. Disappointment and disillusionment...

After some increasingly nasty political battles, I decided to get on me bike. Why do disappearances happen? Who is John Galt? From far, far away, Nigel was fully prepared to give his continued support to the club and to that show. I even agreed to walk away without any announcements: no retirement statements, no explanations on the radio or on line. The old Thursday show could just keep on trucking with another singer. I could get in some much deserved beach time, and then (per weekly conversations with the club owner) return with our new, twice-as-excited band and complete Utah autonomy. However. Everybody talks a big game about laissez faire economics — until someone builds a better mousetrap.

And loyalty is not a trait adhered to by your average booking agent or bar owner. It was never my intent to deceive Utah's metal-hungry legions — I did intend to return to that stage. But, *C'est la vie* (that's French for something).

> *"Give not that which is holy unto the dogs, neither cast ye your pearls before swine, lest they trample them under their feet, and turn again and rend you." — Matthew 7.6.*

Some Utah mates and I eventually launched Nigel and The Metal Dogs, assembling a group of Utah players I still enjoyed performing with. We chose a home. We painted me face up 15 feet tall on the side of the building, and flyered the free concert series across the street from our new room, with video rolling the whole time. Unfortunately that club didn't have the advertising dollars to compete with Nigel's former cronies, and we were unceremoniously banned from local radio. Factor in also our new venue's local rep — not of chick-friendly good times, but rather of joyless Cookie Monster bands *(Grrrrr, grrrrrrr!)* and Nigel's grand relocation was doomed. Bill Frost and *City Weekly* went to bat for the local Dogs, but alas, no amount of ass-busting could bring substantial numbers to our new Thursday venue. We pulled the plug in nine weeks.

Nigel is dead, man, miss him miss him.

For a while, the tired, old Metal Show pressed on at Thursday Club without me. It would grind to a slow death in a sad fizzle of low attendance. Rest in peace and you're welcome. If I wanted to work with tools, I'd have become a carpenter.

> *Kisses!*
> *— Nigel Tones*
> *Banshee vocals and sundry mischief, Nigel and the Metal Dogs*

And what of Nigel these days, pray tell?

Whether he's fighting off birds in Knightsbridge or meditating in a Tibetan monastery, Salt Lake City Thursdays will always remain in his barren attempt at a heart.

Perhaps Nigel disappeared into the mountains like Ted Kaczynski with a nipple ring. Perhaps he's plotting his glorious, megalomaniacal return to the Valley, clad in leather chaps, Aviators and a codpiece.

Perhaps, at this very moment, he's trying to bang your sister.

MYSTIC PARROT
OR,
THE OTHER SIDE OF
LEAD SINGER DISEASE

At the tail end of a recent ski season I received one of those last minute calls that tend to fly around Park City in April: "Hey Oros, we're driving down to (insert Southern Utah desert destination) tonight, wanna come?" In this case, it was a natural hot spring in Monroe, Utah, a three-hour road trip from the Salt Lake Valley. One of my ski buddies was following a regionally touring jam band down to Mystic Hot Springs where they could all soak in natural lithium-heavy waters, overlooking a gorgeous but certainly quirky valley below. And oh, by the way, per drummer JB: "Stu doesn't have a bassist, do you want to sit in?"

I had cabin fever. Screw it. Mail me the charts.

Monroe! Wasn't that Jim J. Bullock's character on that Ted Knight sitcom? *Too Close for Comfort*!

"You know how I know you're gay?" asked JB. "You can name Jim J. Bullock's show!"

I packed swimming trunks, my bass, guitar tuner and assorted cables and awaited Freeskiier41's BMW in my driveway (his real name is Steve but I figured he'd want the Tweets). Freeskiier is a pudgy ex-Marine, who now does all his ass-kicking on a pair of Dynastars. We caught Stu's opening set at a Salt Lake club — decently attended for a Sunday night — and hung out for a few tunes before packing in the Beemer and heading off into the darkness.

There was a heavy skunk aroma, minus actual roadkill... there were mushrooms, sans pizza…

215

We arrived well after 3 AM and found the band cabin, a raw and quaint single roomed pine structure containing one each: a bed, a couch, and a mattress on the floor. Bandleader Stu had the bed deferred to him, while being the new guy I grabbed a sleeping bag and couch while Freeskiier41 hit the chilly pine floor.

Always the guy on tour to sleep lightest and wake first, I decided on an early morning stroll around what we soon were calling The Compound. An April sunrise was illuminating the scene before me: remnants of old, wooden carts and rusting pitchforks, old pickups on blocks. It was a cross of 70's TV sitcom sets, somewhere between *Little House on the Prairie* and *Sanford and Son*. When humanity finally calls it quits and the planet swallows all traces of our existence, Monroe, Utah will have had a head start.

The Deadhead who owns Mystic Hot Springs also had permanent tenants in an adjoining trailer park. Dogs barked from behind makeshift kennels and a shirtless fat guy leered at me from his porch. On the side of one trailer its owner had stenciled, "Don't laugh, it's paid for." Hearkening back to my recent Wells Fucko refinancing nightmares the point wasn't at all lost on me.

Stu, Freeskiier and I ventured through chain-linked neighborhoods and found what was likely the only place for breakfast. We bounced in and I felt like Dafoe in *Mississippi Burning*. The Cowboy Corral is owned and run by the uncle of Rodeo legend Layne Frost of the *8 Seconds* film fame. He and his cheerful, bee-hived wife worked the grill right behind the counter. Freeskiier drifted off upright in our booth while Stu and I ordered their Cowgirl Breakfast on dares.

As we were squaring up the bill and chatting up the local farmers, an older cat in a ten-gallon opens the back screen door and humps in an amplifier and guitar. *It is me, or is it 11:45 on a Monday morning?*

Yes! This guy was setting up for his luncheon set at the Cowboy Corral! Cowboy Ken and I bullshitted for a few minutes while he set up his mini-PA. He has a local trio called Latigo. They do classic country around town. As we chatted, he gets the power up and begins strumming. I bowed a *namaste* and he started singing. His voice was just beautiful! A pure and uninhibited old-school country twang, his high range was effortless. I'm sitting three feet from him and he's just *owning* some C&W standard — which admittedly I didn't recognize. We dropped a tip into his jar while bidding him a killer set and a Park City "Muchluv."

Stu's band and I had a nice soak in a chilly and brutally windy early-spring morning, after which Freeskiier and I hung back in the cabin. The remaining band members, whom Stu has positioned strategically around the Intermountain West for creative (but mostly for budgetary) reasons, were sequestered a few hundred yards away in our aforementioned trailer park. They were billeted in a big, old hippie bus, painted sky blue — complete with murals of whales on one side and a portrait of Utah's Arches National Park on the other.

> *"C'mon baby, take a chance with us*
> *And meet me at the back of the blue bus!"*

Our only other mineral-bathers that weekend were a young lesbian couple en route from Somewhere, USA to Las Vegas, and a shaggy couple from Colorado; the guy looked like the singer from Spin Doctors, his girl was dreadlocked — they were straight out of a tent at Burning Man.

The spa's office tripled also as a concert venue and home. The stage was in the living room, a few short feet from where folks paid ten bucks a soak in slick volcanic rock and their rusty, strategically placed bathtubs. We wondered aloud where the tubs had been pilfered from, prior to their present function.

The owner of this groovy little crash-pad had furnished his living room-cum-concert venue with not only a very competent sound system, but he'd also scoured E-Bay for old cameras from TV stations — those big, bulky units on round, wheeled platforms, each large enough to hold a man's weight. Bill had three of them and I'm sure Stu was stoked at the prospect of catching one of his shows on video — especially on a stage that had been graced by the likes of The String Cheese Incident, Moe, Wisebird, and a dozen other jam bands I can't tell apart. Mystic's owner had apparently been the merchandise manager on many of the Grateful Dead's tours throughout the 80's and 90's. The office / venue and adjoining Hot Rock Café were adorned with Dead concert stickers, t-shirts, muumuus — a barrage of tie-dye stimuli.

I must state for you here, good reader, in full disclosure: I *detest* jam bands.

As with heavy metal, hippie rock certainly boasts a few moments of inspired goodness. But for the most part, both genres are self-indulgent and fairly rudimentary at their base. However, I had never soaked in a natural hot spring and was experiencing some serious wanderlust. What better way to indulge in both than this odd weekend unfolding before me in central Utah?

A couple of discussions in the band cabin, in the absence of their/our boss *du jour* Stu, made me privy to a familiar and common thread running through various circles of musicians: a mild yet ever-present resentment of the Lead Singer. Now to be sure, on this short run I found Stu completely reasonable and easy to work with. But his long-term players were airing a dozen little gripes when given the opportunity to vent.

My ears have been burning for twenty years.

After a delicious pre-show meal courtesy of Bill's girlfriend and daughter a few local teens began arriving. Even as a hired gun, I was getting excited at the prospect of an actual audience on the living room floor before us. But no such luck. These kids were Bill's camera crew, two local high schoolers who I think were there primarily to hit on his daughter.

Undaunted and fresh from a band cabin rehearsal, we hit the stage. Freeskiier watched the first set vegging on the big couch, ten feet from the band. He ended the second set giggling on the shag carpet, his skull full of fungi.

We ran some of Stu's twelve bar jams to warm up, then into cover tunes by Neil Young, The Black Crowes, and of course, The Grateful Dead. I'd been looping Stu's CD on the drive down, and cheat sheets on the floor never hurt either. JB was on our company trap kit to my left with Greg on djembe and backup vocals sat upstage with Stu. Salt Lake keyboardist Raymond is a dead ringer for Greg Allman. Or Rick Wakeman. He was to my right. I was chilling in the back, up against a projection screen scrolling tie-dye graphic streams. Stu was shouting out changes and polishing turds. I was in the back, multi-taking and catching pockets with JB who shouted during the second tune, "You've never played bass with me!"

After assessing Bill's lack of promotion, Freeskiier had earlier suggested longer, true *jams* that night. I discouraged him from the idea, especially in light of the evening's promotional potential for Stu's band (see: video shoot). But by night's end, Freeskiier was shouting from the floor, "Longer! I'm gonna time you!" He did. Our next jam clocked in at 4:15 (or was it 4:20?) while Stu segued our next progression. The musical marathon was on. "Over seventeen minutes, yeahhh!"

We knew we had about one more song in our last set. JB and I locked into a groove and after Stu's very tasty acoustic guitar solo, I look up to see venue owner Bill between Stu and the mic stand.

What happened? Is he pissed? Have we passed a Monroe curfew of some sort?

I then noticed the bird on his wrist. Green and yellow, gorgeous. A big ol' parrot on the guy's arm. And the parrot is squaking. No...

It's *singing.*

Bill is cueing the parrot and the parrot is singing along into the microphone. JB and I are in stitches. Keyboardist Raymond is concentrating quite hard, looking quite Allman-like. We finish the tune. Freeskiier cheers wildly. As do the two or three residents of Monroe in attendance.

Later we're loading out and I peek back into Bill's video and audio control room, which was quite impressive. He has two video screens up, splitting images from his teen crew's various angles. We were listening to the audio...

And the parrot was *killing it.* I'm serious. It sounded awesome.

Post-show in the band cabin, we were adhering to Mystic's no drinking, no smoking rules — *yeah, okay* — and Hammond player Raymond was assessing that closing tune: "I was watching the bird. It would sing louder when I hit certain notes."

I'd bet that if you were to put that vocal track into Pro Tools, Polly's performance was twice as accurate as an early Offspring demo. The bird had mad skills.

UTAHPALOOZA!

The summer of 2008 should have seen my 20-year high school reunion, but no one back in Illinois was on the project. I was more surprised than disappointed, as they all seemed pretty chummy back in the day. My thought was: I had little in common with these people when we were young and we would likely have less now. But the non-anniversary of my escape from Catholic education planted an idea in my skull that I would pursue with Fab over the next several months.

Wouldn't it be infinitely more interesting to assemble all the disparate clowns with whom I'd traveled and entertained throughout the years — a class-*less* reunion, if you will!

Many of the guys in our cooky little musical universe are working players, fluid in multiple genres and shows. The Utahpalooza setlist would almost create itself. We'd all get to swap musical spit with old mates as well as introducing people from our various circles.

Summer 2009: Park City non-profit Mountain Town Music offers Park City Productions two outdoor dates. Therein we saw the seeds and began assembling the puzzle pieces. A few brave sponsors helped our baby production company cover flights and rooms for our performers from Vegas and LA but all musicians would essentially be playing for free. Here in the boom of social networking, our logistics and communications were easier than ever.

Flights were booked and lineups congealed in a gradual and enjoyable process. My Mullet Hatchet (Southern Rock) guys were available. The Metal Show would co-headline with a "Coverdogs All Star Jam," playing a bunch of guilty pleasure tunes: "Band on the Run!" Perhaps Rush, "Limelight." Pink Floyd? Some Zeppelin, of course!

"It's all part of my Rock and Roll Fantasy!"

Our new Ute bro, Paller got the ball rolling with gear and cash endorsements. Comcast donated director Kevin and their crew who would broadcast the day *OnDemand*. Park City Productions's street team Lori and Lexi sold NYPC Pizzas, and our little journalism major Sunshine worked the merch booth (biggest seller: Vinyl Williams). Danny Marz at Rockin' Northern Utah printed our posters and postcard flyers. Guitarist buddy and Bear fan Hatz donated a guitar amp via his music gear company, Line 6. Rehearsals were held in LA for the guys based down there while I emailed sets to our Utah guys and worked the promo in Utah.

For the day's opening slot, I rang up Utah's School of Rock. Involving the school would throw even more flavor into this reunion stew.

- - - - - - - - - - -

When Utah's branch of the Paul Green School of Rock Music (the documentary on which was a Sundance Festival film entitled *Rock School*) opened its first branch in Salt Lake, I was intrigued but my gig schedule was too tight to accept a teaching position. Eventually I would jump in head first and dig every second of it. I was cosmically rewarded with exchanges such as: "My brother Ian thinks Ronnie James Dio is a better vocalist than David Bowie but I told him Bowie has a richer low range," vocal / guitar / drum student Lydon tells me during a lesson.

There is *no way* I was this rock-savvy at thirteen.

Playing in rock bands is rapidly becoming this generation's little league baseball. For thousands of teens and pre-teens, weeknight trips to the batting cages have become evenings dissecting David Gilmour solos and Thom Yorke lyrics. You're showing a ten year old how to play a Gmaj chord one day and a few months later he's ripping the lead to "You Shook Me All Night Long." A couple of years after that, one student is attending Berklee in Boston, another has set up shop at Musicians Institute in Hollywood.

I took on the director position for Park City's AC/DC show. After our three-month semester, those kids absolutely killed the auditorium at Ecker Hill Jr. High School. Stunned early-on by both their musicianship and showmanship — both miles and years beyond where I or my mates had been at that age — I devised a motivational device wherein three or four students would get to join me onstage at an upcoming outdoor concert. The Canyons Resort, right in our back yards, was holding their Spring Grüv free concert series and the scenario was ideal for all: an all-ages venue and a guaranteed packed audience as the shows began right at 4 PM when the ski lifts stop running for the day. Besides, I knew their performance on stage with us would absolutely *slay*. I informed the kids of AC/DC tunes scheduled for our Canyons set and a handful of them got to work. Decision Day was rough, but I knew we'd be able to get many students involved at show time. They were given their pre-gig prep notes. A few kids hadn't yet played a single thing in front of a crowd.

They arrived punctually with their axes, cables and tuners. And costumes. Oh yes. You ain't getting on stage in your civvies. Little Anthony rocked a wig and rasta hat. Pat, having won the "Highway to IIcll" solo, was clad in his Angus-best velvet suit coat, tie, and knicker shorts. Soundcheck was a bit of a cluster, with the kids taking in new stimuli while trying to set volumes and tones. We ran thru half of two AC/DC selections, letting our guest players get out a few bugs and nerves. They hung backstage, punching each other in the arm and last-minute cramming with their iPods while the band and I hit the stage, costumed and nippy in the afternoon chill.

The crowd was a sea of loudly-colored gapers (atrociously dated one-piece ski suits) as it was 80's Day at The Can. The PBR was flowin' and the audience swayed on late-pow day spaghetti legs. We "adult" players got things heated with an onslaught of 80's hits. On Metal Show drums for Spring Grüv was Angelino Dwight, father of two and my favorite Mod on the planet. Although he was in a band with the late Jani Lane, Dwight was more impressed when he met Joni Mitchell.

Toward the end of our 90-minute set, just when the energy couldn't get stupider, I announced the School of Rock kids and amphitheatre erupted. The boys were well-rehearsed and fell right into the moment featuring guitarist Pat doing a perfect Angus-Young-strut right across the stage like he built the place.

Jogging toward backstage behind a roaring local crowd, I was intercepted and bear-hugged by Dwight: "In all my years of doing these shows, that was the best moment, EVER!"

September 2009: I checked schedules; many of the School of Rock All Stars would be available for Utahpalooza. At one show I'd had my ass kicked by a kid named Chris who absolutely *owned* Oingo Boingo's "Dead or Alive" on vocals and lead guitar. He was excited to participate, as were SoR parents and staff. *Bring it!*

I was fluttering through the tent that early afternoon while the kids were on stage. My Mullet Hatchet and Rattle & Hum guys were sitting with mouths agape. The All Stars were out front, dead-on nailing Steely Dan's "Reelin' in the Years" then covering The Who's "Baba O' Riley" — with actual violin, mind you...

"These kids are opening for *us*?" Drummer Cam asked me in mock panic. Teenagers Sami and Dom were picking each others' guitar solos in "Hotel California."

I had scanned the All Star setlist a few weeks prior, made sure it didn't clash with any of the seven other shows contributing to Utahpalooza, and headed down the hill for a rehearsal in Sandy. To close SoR's set, I thought it'd be enormous fun to join them on Radiohead's "Paranoid Android," the beautifully epic and complex track from their rightfully acclaimed *OK Computer* album. I plugged in my acoustic and ultra-tight drummer Matt counted us off. My first time playing *OK Computer* material with a full band, and they were half my age. When we ended the tune in a perfect dead stop, thirteen-year old multi instrumentalist Maddie approaches me tentatively:

"Um, there's one difference in that acoustic voicing."

In other words: *You're fucking up old man!* She showed me the proper way to play Thom Yorke's guitar part and we ran it again.

Utahpalooza created multiple scenarios where initiative was taken and bars were raised: players, event sponsors, neighbors, local press. The fun factor couldn't have been higher.

The big show at The Canyons was on Saturday but most Palooza players arrived Friday for a small Park City BBQ in the afternoon, followed by a warm-up gig at Sidecar Bar on Park City's Main Street. Saturday morning was rainy (weather being the biggest variable when putting on an outdoor show) but when Fab's Caribbean pan drum band Trinidadio hit the mid-afternoon stage, the clouds parted and the sun shone down on Utahpalooza.

The whole weekend was a beautiful blur.

Ute players met Vegas and LA players. Students met new friends. The Metal Show guys planted themselves respectfully in front of second act Vinyl Williams while Chris ogled Lionel's NASA-esque foot pedals. Pops met

Mullet Hatchet's Cuzin Cleotis who waltzed up and obliterated the talk-box solo in "Rocky Mountain Way." Our new Ute pal Hugh McDonald of Bon Jovi's band jumped up for "Dragon Attack" with McLefty on guitar and Paulie of Queen Nation and BongBoys on drums. Guitarist Paller joined me, bassist Seaton of Royal Jelly, guitarist Hatz and my first drummer ever, Higgie. It was a *Summer of The Barn* reunion.

"The Boys Are Back in Town!"

Attendance was acceptable for our first real shot at concert production. Fab and I lost a few bucks. But. It was a cream-dream.

All-day music festival to rock the Canyons

By Alisha Self of the [Park] Record staff

Looking at Park City's vibrant music scene, producer/entertainer Tony Oros thought there was one thing missing: an all-day, all-out rock n roll festival. So he decided to create one.

The concept for Utahpalooza came about last year, when Oros was slated to attend his 20-year high school reunion in Illinois. "I decided I'd rather get together with all the guys I've played with over the years," he explains. "I've got these circles that go to half a dozen states and a couple countries, and I said, let's have a reunion on stage."

On Saturday, September 5, Oros' fellow musicians from his shows in Utah, Los Angels, Las Vegas and around the world will come together for an afternoon of free, live music at The Canyons Resort Village. From 3 to 9 p.m., seven bands will take the stage, filling the mountain air with the sounds of classic rock, 80's favorites, and hair metal hits. Food, drinks and libations will be available.

The festival, which is presented by Oros' company, Park City Productions, and Mountain Town Music, is focused on rock. Six of the seven bands specialize in covers and fans can expect to hear everything from Lynyrd Skynyrd to Journey. "With the exception of a couple songs through the day, you'll know just about every song we play," says Oros.

The show will start with the Paul Green School of Rock Music All Stars, featuring some of the best young instrumentalists in the program playing the likes of Steely Dan and Led Zeppelin. Then 19-year-old Lionel Williams, a Midway native, will take the stage with his band, Vinyl Williams. "That's the only original band of the day, just because I love his stuff so much and I want him to get heard," says Oros.

The festival will also feature acts from Skinny Tiez, a local 80's costume band, and Fab Rodig of Trinidadio, who will mix up the set with Caribbean steel drum music and a bit of reggae flair. Between sets, local comedians, DJs and even an opera singer will provide the entertainment.

The headliners of the even include Oros' own creations, Mullet Hatchet and The Coverdogs. Mullet Hatchet features Oros in his redneck glory as lead singer Tayler Parks, crooning to Southern Rock classics such as "Sweet Home Alabama" and "The Devil Went Down to Georgia."

As British rocker Nigel Tones, Oros has lead the Metal Show in 355 weeks of shows in Salt Lake City. "We don't do that show outside very often and we rarely do it outside of that club," he says.

Utahpalooza will conclude with a mashup performance with musicians from different groups coming together under the umbrella of Coverdogs All Star Jam. "Everybody from every band swaps in," explains Oros. The musicians will cap the outdoor portion of the night with the sounds of Queen, Paul McCartney and Wings, Bad Company, Pink Floyd and Journey.

Around 10 p.m., the festival will shift gears and head to Cisero's for the afterparty, where Skinny Tiez and the Coverdogs will again grace the stage.

Oros says he plans to make Utahpalooza a yearly event and sees potential for it to grow into a larger festival. "We've got so much talent between the guys that I work with in Utah and the guys from L.A. and Vegas, we could have easily done two days of bands. There are a hundred reasons to do it every year."

He adds that Coverdogs will remain the centerpiece of the event, giving musicians from all different areas and genres a chance to jam together.

Oros encourages everyone to come out and celebrate one of the final outdoor concerts of the season. "There's going to be lots of great tunes all night and it's free, so we just want everyone who's in town to pile out there and enjoy the show," he says.

LET'S FACE IT,
WE AIN'T GOIN'

Late December of 2010 was icier and snowier than usual even by Park City standards. Fab picked me up for the airport at 6:30 AM, in full knowledge that most East Coast airports had been closed due to heavy snow. These included New York's JFK, our domestic point of departure for three Coverdogs shows in Europe for Armed Forces Entertainment.

Honestly, I was unsure which half of this little run I was looking forward to most: my return to the Balkans after eight years (Kosovo, specifically) or New Year's Day's comped ski rentals and lift tickets at Edelweiss Resort. America's military presence had dropped sharply since I took McLefty and Egodog through KFOR and SFOR back in 2002; only Camp Bondsteel near Urosevac and "Film City" in Pristina remained. Even my globally-astute Pops was surprised to hear Coverdogs would be playing for Yanks in Kosovo. "We still have guys over there?"

Yes Pops, we do — and they're BORED!

We loaded my guitar and my gig bag (see: ski gear and wigs) into Fab's '98 Ford Explorer, but alas, in the absence of any pre-dawn Summit County salt-job "The Gigster" spun its rear tires impotently on my street's significant incline. *Ugh.*

Plan B! We squeezed our gear into the spacious trunk of an insomniac friend's Mercedes and thanks to all wheel drive and studded tires (German engineering!), we were off for Salt Lake International.

Since I woke that pre-dawn I had been attempting to re-route us via phone, however "Due to extreme weather, no one at Delta is available to take your call." *WHA???* Did they just all say *fuckit* and go home? All right, Fab and I agreed. We'll just have to head down to the airport and speak to an actual human being.

Despite the holiday season and the airport closures out East, lines inside the terminal were happily short. Our Anton Ono escapade in Fab's truck had set us back some 20 minutes but no worries — as Flight 3 to JFK had been nixed anyway. What are our options? We told a calm and curt redheaded Delta employee named Dan of our situation while he punched up options on his screen and irritated travelers behind us gave us the ol' stink-eye. The Coverdogs are used to it.

"You guys have already been re-routed... but that flight leaves in 10 minutes." Were they planning on notifying us telepathically? *Double ugh.*

Plan C! Dan comes back after some running around with two old-school, hand written tickets. More glaring from the cue behind us. We looked at our itinerary on the bag tags: Dallas to Amsterdam to Vienna to Pristina. We'd be arriving on the continent too late for the first Kosovo show, but if Young Ben, Moose and Spark could get out of LAX to Vienna, the old gang would at least be near KFOR and ready to rock.

Fab makes expensive cell calls to our man in Germany and to "The Captain" in Washington, detailing our dilemma and Delta's significant hoop-jumping to get us over to Vienna. Our three other Coverdogs were on standby from LAX to JFK but we crossed our fingers and got in the TSA line right behind a very weepy Mormon missionary. I tried unsuccessfully to peek at his ticket; either his destination was some place gnarly and terrifying or he'd never left his farm town, or both... tough turds, "Elder!"

We walk up to our gate just as we're being paged and the attendant was ready to close the jetway door. Then my cell rings with a 703 area code. *Isn't that D.C.?* I picked up. "Is this Fab?" asked the female voice. I handed him my phone and gave our tickets to the Delta attendant. I listened to Fab over my shoulder...

"Really. Ok. Yes, we were just about to board for Dallas."

Uh-oh.

"Thanks. Bye." He hands me the cell. "Well, we ain't going," Fab grunts.

To Dallas?

"To Europe. No tour. They pulled the plug."

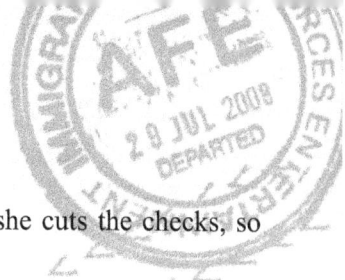

Who?

"The Pentagon. The people *above* The Captain. And she cuts the checks, so we ain't going."

Seems that all Dan's efforts to get us re-routed also cut out our Star Alliance (United/Austrian Air) flights, thus screwing up the whole billing sitch and putting AFE back at square one. "Wanna do breakfast?" Fab said. "Or the bar. I need a cocktail." Now *there's* a professional Tour Manager decision. No New Year's gig. And our bags are going to Dallas.

FECK! ARSE! DRINK!!!

Ok, we'll head down to the baggage office after and see if the lady at the gate got our stuff yanked in time. We were not hopeful. I placed a text to my manager at the steakhouse in hopes of retrieving my gig for that night. After a few $10 bloody marys we hit the baggage office. Ah shit. Who's behind the counter? Redhead Dan. *Sorry, my brother.* All that scrambling for nothing.

More calls to Germany, to Young Ben and the guys in Los Angeles. Well, at least we were paid up front. *Wait…* are we going to have to pay back Armed Forces Entertainment? Indeed, that would likely be the case. And the suckage continues.

I walked into the steakhouse late and with no guitar that evening. The baggage delivery service had called an hour before, but still no sign of them. Tiffany behind the bar said "I'm so sorry Tony." I hadn't been abroad in over five years and it was killing me. My co-workers knew it. No, Edmonton doesn't count. As the families at the piano bar cast puzzled looks my way, I noodled with what gear I could set up in preparation for the *possible* arrival of my axe. Soon, a text from Fab. Oh by the way, there was apparently going to be a VIP at Edelweiss on NYE for us to entertain: General Petraeus.

Fuck *me.*

Not the General, of course but, you know — I was bumming. We love performing for Brass. My guitar and costume bag did arrive in the nick of time and I resumed my piano bar routine of Beatles, Eagles, 70's one-hit wonders.

The next morning I hit Canyons, skiing out my frustrations on a beautiful bluebird day. When I was done floating down fluffy pillows of Utah pow (I never ski with my cell so if it's dumping, don't even call) there was another text from Fab, who had been back and forth with our guy at Edelweiss: we're back ON. New Year's Eve only, but we were re-booked to depart on the 30th. My heart leapt!

Thursday morning and Fab and I are back in the Delta line, halfway hoping to see our pal Dan behind the Delta counter. The line was creeping and we were due to board in less than 10 minutes. We flagged down a Delta employee in a red jacket. He reassured us, "Flight 3 to Atlanta? That flight has been cancelled." He then added, "Yeah. You're in the right line."

Fab and I hop on our phones. We MUST get out! The previous day had seen numerous cancellations and delays. In short, Salt Lake International was a shit-show. Our plane to the East Coast had been grounded due to mechanical difficulties and as we drained our cell batteries for solutions, Fab and I simultaneously discovered our dearth of options. No Delta flights to Munich until tomorrow — several hours too late for a NYE show. Southwest had one available seat to San Francisco, then a direct connection to Germany. Jet Blue? Nada. As Fab spewed profanities within ear-shot of elderly Mormon women, my soul sank with the thoughts of not only my loss of a New Year's gig, but the potential of disappointed folks in Garmisch.

Finally Fab gets a call through to an Armed Forces Entertainment representative. She had a thick accent and we had a weak cell connection. But we gleaned that AFE was on it and we'd have two tickets at the American Airlines counter. Sure enough, to our glee, we were booked. At last The Coverdogs were off to Europe for the umpteenth time.

31 December, Germany: After a restful flight in spacious exit row seats, Fab and I landed in Munich. Drummer Moose, guitarist Spark, and soundman Young Ben waiting for us on a tour bus loaded heavy with sound gear and guitar cases. In the snowy late afternoon we pulled into Edelweiss Resort and set up AKA's sound system in the ballroom for a quick soundcheck before hitting the dinner buffet. Our trusty C-Dog lineup launched into two sets of classic rock, disco and dance tunes while throwing on various wigs and personas. Military families danced with their teenagers and toddlers and we all rang in 2011 with much silliness. I mean, Outkast's "Hey Ya" in mullet wigs and tooth-black? No holds barred!

We set down our guitars to join our hosts and a big crowd for a fantastic fireworks show in the chilly German fog. Then, Coverdogs headed into town. Specifically to a bar named Jameson's. The club has an entrance adorned with swinging doors that look like a service entrance. I should have remembered this detail upon entering (sober) because at 2 AM in a sardine-tight crowd (hobbling drunk) I could find no exit whatsoever. *Where is my band and how do I get out of here??? Alle aus! Mach schnell!!!*

My previous memory was of Young Ben standing next to the club's tiny stage, absent-mindedly plucking the keys on the disco band's synthesizer. The American bandleader sporting a huge afro wig was unamused and wagged his finger at our soundman who should've known better — Lord knows a Coverdog would've been livid at such a transgression. After I finally found my way out of this drunken Bavarian labyrinth, Ben and I stumbled through the frigid and quaint Garmisch streets until a minivan pulled up along side us and offered us a ride. I declined, deciding to enjoy a quiet stroll through a city new to my travels, while Ben opted to jump in the van.

While bundling up to ski the next morning, Moose informed Fab and I that their driver that few hours earlier was in fact a visiting four-star general. Drama had ensued as a sloppy Ben apparently rode in the back seat spewing arbitrary F-bomb-laden tirades while Moose elbowed him with an urgent yet impotent *shut the fuck up* glare. The Coverdogs make friends everywhere we go.

My first day skiing the Alps made me appreciative of that legendary Utah powder; the hill was icy and the snow was man-blown (non-skiiers insert fellacio joke here). While being fitted with our complimentary rental skis and boots I asked a resort employee, "Where are the good trees on this map?"

"Trees?" He asked incredulously. "No woods to ski up there, man." The off-trail cover was indeed thin and crusty, but the groomed runs at Garmisch Classic were long and steep, and the views were just epic. At the resort base it was a gray and overcast morning, but halfway up the gondola we pierced the cloud line and emerged parallel to a perfect white blanket lying gently across the valley. I introduced ski novices Ben (hung-over) and Fab (no skills but fearless) to a new ski-idiom: when you wipe out on the hill and your skis go one way and your poles go another, that's called a "Yard Sale." Fab eventually did locate his wallet and room key, but he limped around pretty gingerly for a few days.

On the evening of January 1st, in order to optimize our trip to Edelweiss, we were scheduled downstairs from the previous night's room at their little sports bar called Zuggy's. Several military families had gathered, enjoying some burgers and awaiting more singalong silliness. We called out a few classic rock standards and began a mellower, more intimate set. Then came the *Request Napkins*. Man, I should've taken a picture of the stage floor at night's end. You couldn't see the wood under my feet for the soggy scribblings:

"Got any Mellencamp?"

"Springsteen! Seger, please!"

Spark Myth and Moose slid in with my and Fab's acoustic set like we'd been rehearsing for years. Which, when you think about it...

Jamming with old buddies! That whole "fits like a glove" cliché really does apply. The little accents, the dance-floor segues. Chorus harmonies from stage left. The drummer's tempo from count-off is just right. Big arena ending, and I flash four fingers behind my back: crescendo on E minor, then *BAM BAM BAM BAM!*

We're out!

ALI AL SALEM. ECHO.
MAREZ. SATHER. VICTORY.

Had I been a USO performer in the early 1970's — who had never been to Vietnam — I'd feel like a complete douche. Thus you can understand my excitement over my first MWR tour of Iraq, late March 2011.

Yeah. When the break from your routine is ten days in Iraq, you're probably not at the most balanced point in your life.

Dwayne at AKA Productions received a Pentagon request for a U2 tribute, probably to maintain a St. Patrick's entertainment theme throughout March's schedule. Rattle & Hum's original Edge and Larry (guitarist Bart and drummer Jorgen) live in LA, so our Utah lineup got the call: drummer Cam and guitarist/attorney Phledge — The Kids! The three of us were Iraq-virgins but Fab had already tour managed through Iraq and Afghanistan dozens of times. Fab was on Rattle & Hum bass — "Fadam."

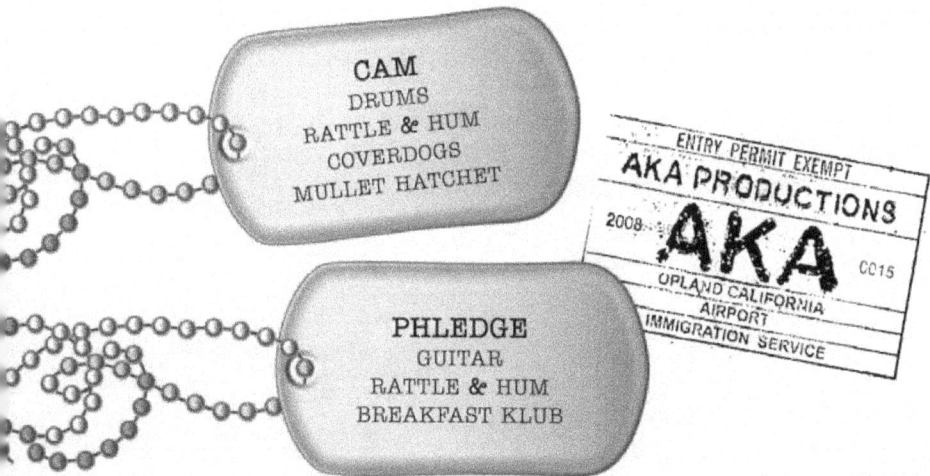

CAM
DRUMS
RATTLE & HUM
COVERDOGS
MULLET HATCHET

ENTRY PERMIT EXEMPT
AKA PRODUCTIONS
2008
AKA
CC15
OPLAND CALIFORNIA
AIRPORT
IMMIGRATION SERVICE

PHLEDGE
GUITAR
RATTLE & HUM
BREAKFAST KLUB

We ran down the documents we had been sent for the Iraq tour. We were given our orders and a long, very specific To DON'T list:

Artist and all support personnel will abide by the following conditions for the duration of the tour.

- Artist may not ▮▮▮▮▮▮▮▮ immediately prior to, during and/or after any performance. Artist may not ▮▮▮▮▮▮ ▮▮▮▮▮▮ or ▮▮▮▮ onstage.

- An acknowledged ▮▮▮ will not be referred to in a manner that would offend a follower of any ▮▮▮▮

- ▮▮▮▮▮▮▮▮▮▮▮▮▮▮or connotations of ▮▮▮▮▮▮▮▮▮▮▮▮ and ▮▮▮▮▮▮▮▮ will not be used.

- ▮▮▮▮▮▮▮, ▮▮▮▮▮▮or ▮▮▮▮▮▮ groups will not be defamed and individual ▮▮▮▮▮▮▮ and ▮▮▮▮▮▮▮ will not be ridiculed.

- ▮▮▮▮▮▮▮ or any type of act which results in participants temporarily losing control of any part of their mental or physical faculties will not be used.

- Artists will not bring guests for ▮▮▮▮▮▮ and will not ▮▮▮▮▮▮▮ in an unacceptable manner with members and guests.

- Artist will not engage in acts of ▮▮▮▮▮▮or threats of ▮▮▮▮▮▮ toward any person. Artist will not possess or carry ▮▮▮▮▮▮ or ▮▮▮▮▮▮ of any kind.

Etcetera.

In short, the document we signed stressed the following: No booze on stage, no drug use and no vulgarity. No racial slurs, ethnic slurs or religious jokes (aww, peas!). No mentions of "sexual depravity or perversion" (that's my favorite) and that we are responsible for set-up and break-down of equipment (duh).

Now does the FBI, CIA, or NSA give a shit about my book or its contents? No they don't. But they do have nano-drones with retina-scanning technology, so if they change their minds I'm covering my ass.

While Cam, Phledge and I packed up our stuff, Fab was already over in Kuwait on a two-day break after Tour Managing the Washington Redskins' cheerleaders. I know, rough gig. Fab hung out at Camp Arifjan, reading, eating at the DFAC and awaiting the arrival of his U2 trib-mates from Utah. Phledge, Cam and I loaded our guitars, electronics and costumes and flew to Denver where we killed time before our Lufthansa flight into Munich.

20 MAR 2011: Layover in Denver, per tour journal:

By the hour, I'm feeling a weight lifted off of me... energized by travel. Energized by 'The hard, exhilarating pleasure of action.'* Energized by my job having meaning. And none of it a second too soon. Back to the first work that made me realize that my profession, the job of entertaining, has purpose.

I'm on the plane, en route at last! Media is unimportant. Exposure is irrelevant. This tour is for me, and for the soldiers I will entertain. I have no one to impress, nothing to prove. I want new sand under my nails, new stimuli in my senses. I want history in my face. And I want to bring my skills to people who need it. I'll sing the songs from my youth and cry in the desert.

I'm flying over the Black Sea. Somewhere below me, Muammar Gaddafi and Charlie Sheen are losing their minds. I'm either betraying too much, or I'm not being honest enough. But I'm here now.

* Ayn Rand

235

Nine hours and three in-flight movies later, Cam, Phledge and I were drinking Paulaner at *München*. Way off in the back of our terminal we sprawled out, cat-napped and read the International Times while families and businessmen boarded flights to New Delhi, Amman, and Dubai. I was nudged out of my slumber by an old pal, the just-arrived Tour Manager Young Ben! After quick intros to Rattle's drummer and guitarist, Ben and I disappeared into the Lufthansa lounge for finger food, scotch, and big leather reclining chairs. Sorry, guys. Ben only gets one guest, my miles have expired, and I'm pulling seniority.

The staging area for the Iraq theatre is Camp Arifjan in Kuwait. There's a big warehouse on base where AKA Productions keeps multiple PA systems. The guys and I picked out all necessary components from the stacks and loaded them into the MWR vans for our first show of the mini-tour, Camp Ali Al Salem, about an hour outside of Kuwait City. We off-loaded and set up the sound system before an ice coffee break at one of the free-standing buildings that house fast food mini-locations: Pizza Hut, KFC, Hardees. One may wonder why a deployed soldier would spend money on crappy fast food when the vast array of Dining Facility choices are always free?

To break the monotony. And certainly, for a visceral reminder of home.

The Green Beans hut was air conditioned, its walls adorned with posters advertising a program that lets civilians State-side comp a cup to a serviceman or –woman deployed in shitholes like Ali Al Salem.

"Honor first, coffee second!"

During our soundcheck one soldier was singing along from the basketball court a few feet from the stage. After running through "Bad" off *The Unforgettable Fire* that kid asked if we do "Stuck in a Moment You Can't Get Out Of." Through the mic I told him we did, and that we'd add it to the set tonight. We had all noticed this guy nailing the lyrics throughout our line check, so later during the show I called him up on stage. He crooned a very competent Bono for what proved the highlight of the evening.

Before flying into Iraq, we had a precious 24-plus hours to kick back in our little single rooms on Arifjan. We shot off some emails and hit the gym. Phledge spent quality time appreciating the vast array of toilet-stall poetry and contemplated chronicling the various scribblings:

"I'm writing on a bathroom stall — take THAT, society!"

And my personal all-time favorite, a drawing of a toilet with comic-book quote bubble proclaiming:

"I eat POOP!"

I would have chronicled additional latrine musings, but Phledge and Ben are presently fist-fighting over who gets to publish that book.

We also did some DVD browsing at the local kiosks. Ahh, those combat zone DVD shops... We've all shopped for movies on line or — Allah forbid — at Wal Mart. But let's say you're staring at a rack of DVD compilation packages: every single episode of *MASH, West Wing,* and *24.* The Robert DeNiro Collection contained over fifty films: *Taxi Driver, Goodfellas, Raging Bull, Midnight Run!* Over on the adjacent wall are the New Releases. This means specifically — films still being shown in theaters back in the States. The price, for any aforementioned box of DVDs? No disc set over $30. Thirty bucks! For every Jack Nicholson film in one package? Rock!

But here comes the moral conundrum. Recent media reports claim these profits go eventually to? You guessed it: Al Quaeda. Their Pakistani branch, to be geographically specific. Fab, The Kids and I were hearing these rumors about a month before Seal Team 6 popped a cap in Osama Bin Laden in an Islamabad suburb. If it sounds too good to be true, it's probably financing Islamo-fascists.

I avoided the temptation to pick up those *Seinfeld* seasons in Baghdad. Although I must say the packaging on said compilation crediting "Michael Richardson as KEVIN!" was pretty damn amusing.

We were each assigned Arafjan billeting's standard rooms — cramped, yes. But a full night of solitude felt like five-star luxury in our knowledge of the logistics to come. I was assigned a room at the female end of the third floor. Initially I was quite pleased with this surprise travel twist. That is, until I realized I'd have to schlep through several hallways to have a piss. Not to mention the shitty looks I was getting from every G.I. Jane I passed.

I caught cable coverage of the freshly-erupting "Arab Spring" on my room's tube. Several Middle-Eastern nations were just beginning to shake centuries of theocratic and despotic shackles: Bahrain, Yemen, Syria, and quite intensely that week, Libya. Egypt had deposed Hosni Mubarak a month prior. Some brave Tunisians had lit the fuse. Steve Jobs, Bill Gates and Mark Zuckerberg unintentionally fanned the flames. Welcome to democracy. Good luck with *your* tea-baggers. From our friendly Kuwaiti confines, I surfed CNN Middle East for coverage of Muammar Khadafi's carnage. I caught a couple panel discussions on Press TV. I felt a part of the planet again. Until, from out in the hallway…

BEEEEEEP! BEEEEEEP!

A loud siren erupts. Then the male voice broadcasts: "EXERCISE!" I'm thinking: What? Like, drop and give me twenty?

The recorded voice then continued: "A chemical hazard has been detected. SEEK SHELTER!" and I immediately felt better. I had already worked out that morning.

At Kuwait's Arafjan we received a detailed mission briefing (their mission, not ours) from highly amusing Alabaman Lieutenant Colonel Crumpton who answered our logistic and political questions (Kuwait is more than happy to pay for an American military presence on their sands) in his Southern drawl while warmly non-sequituring into hilarious, meandering anecdotes, always inserting a loud "Roll Tide!" where he could.

Soon, time to load up the pallet for our flight. This was Fab and Ben's area of expertise. Our cases of amps and drums were strategically arranged so as to fit on one pallet, which slid neatly onto our passenger-unfriendly C-130 cargo prop plane. They called it "Blackhawk Tetris." Our big Rubik's Cube of musical gear would be transferred onto the second of two helicopters later that afternoon, when we touched ground in Iraq.

. . . .

The band and three of our MWR escorts were crammed into a chopper at Adder Air Base, each of us weighed down with Kevlar flack jackets and helmets. A machine gunner hung out the side of the Blackhawk pointing his M60 down at the barren, vast Iraqi countryside. Our route from Adder in Tallil to Camp Echo in Diwaniya had been obviously established years ago in the early days of the war — we found ourselves flying above a few tiny villages, but no major urban centers. Nonetheless, our gunner sat vigilant as we snapped jpgs from our cell phones in an odd and moody photo-op. Central

Iraq wasn't golden desert sand as I'd envisioned, but rather a landscape sparsely dotted by dead-looking shrubbery dissected by the occasional irrigation canal. Civilization's influence was barely noticeable beneath us during our 90-minute flight.

Upon landing at Camp Echo we were promptly informed that our show, originally scheduled out of doors, had been moved inside, to the most solid structure on the base — the dining facility. Camp Echo had taken a mortar round from the city the previous night and their DFAC was fitted with a double reinforced roof. While Cam (happily married and pragmatic) nervously pondered this news, Fab shrugged it all off; he'd experienced live fire before, during his numerous Afghanistan and Iraq MWR tours.

SUVs drove us a few turns through camp, where our driver pointed out an orange highway cone poking out of a hole in the concrete: "That's where it hit last night. But it didn't explode. It just sent some asphalt flying. Last month the same thing happened. One of our guys was jogging and he took a chunk in the head and was hurt pretty bad."

Every day, folks.

We pulled up to the DFAC/concert venue, where in the midst of deployed Yanks and TCN chow-line workers we hastily set up our gear. "Let's put the drums up in front of the soda fountain — speakers next to the salad bar!"

The camp's PA system then suddenly announced: "ATTENTION! The U2 tribute band will be performing at the DFAC in 30 minutes!" Echo's entire population began streaming in. We weren't egotistical enough to think they were all in attendance just to catch the Utah-renowned Rattle & Hum — the dining facility did have the rocket-proof ceilings after all.

Well aware of the lyrical ironies, we opened our Camp Echo show with "Beautiful Day." Being behind schedule that evening we performed one long set instead of our standard two sixties or seventy-fives. As we were to find during the next three shows, the night's biggest singalong was U2's pseudo-gospel "I Still Haven't Found What I'm Looking For." The DFAC crowd was relaxed, most remaining in their folding chairs, some still eating a late dinner. I did a shout out to any possible Utes in the house and sure enough, one Joe from the back of the room hailed from Draper. 801 in the hizzle!

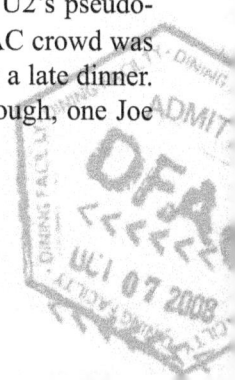

Immediately following our last tune, Lieutenant Colonel Scott Gerber approached us, weighed down with a handful of gifts. I asked him if he's like to use my microphone and he politely declined to many snickers. Oh yeah, I thought standing behind him, he's probably used to this. He effortlessly boomed out to the DFAC: "Camp Echo? Rattle & Hum! Let them hear it, whaddya say?"

At most Army bases, this would have been followed by a loud response of "Hoo-yah!" However, Thunder Squadron's battle cry is "AI-EE-YAH!" and the room responded as such.

"Hey fellas," their Commanding Officer continued, "In appreciation for your performance here today we would like to present you with these company coins. I don't know if you know the protocol, but if you're in a bar with another member of Thunder Squadron and you aren't carrying your coin you gotta buy a round for the room."

I think we're buying that round anyway, gentlemen.

Then came a gift I had never received with any band, on any Department of Defense tour: LTC Gerber gave us the camp's Colors. Even Fab, our jaded Gloom Peddler was visibly moved. We were handed an accompanying plaque, which read:

This flag was flown with honor over Camp Echo
located in Diwaniyah, Iraq in support of

OPERATION NEW DAWN

On behalf of Thunder Squadron, 3d Armored Cavalry Regiment
Let it be known that this flag was flown in honor of those
who gave the ultimate sacrifice. The United States Flag
is presented to you for your excellent support and significant
contribution for those fighting for freedom.

23 March 2011
Guitaud Leandre
CSM, US ARMY
COMMAND SERGEANT MAJOR

Scott R. Gerber
LTC, Armor
COMMANDING

With unsolicited help from various Echo soldiers, we loaded the pallet back onto our Blackhawks and skirted the edge of the town on a dark (minimal lights, for security) and quiet night flight back to Adder Air Base, balancing Styrofoam take-out chow on our laps.

Our Army Point of Contact Gail picked us up for breakfast the next morning. We had a quick pit stop to the billeting office and squeaked out an acoustic tune for an employee Gail said was a "huge U2 fan" and highly bumming there wouldn't be a show for her at Adder. We told the tiny trailer, "It's your call" and opened the request lines for the handful of coffee-sipping staff. Sure enough? They got "I Still Haven't Found What I'm Looking For."

Later that afternoon we took another C-130 to Camp Marez in Mosul. That outdoor show was one of those mildly attended (many GIs were out on patrols) yet thoroughly enjoyable nights — the band was tight, and three particular soldiers up on the hill seemed to know every lyric. Ben had our monitors warm and dialed. We peppered our hit-heavy setlist with a few B-side guilty pleasures. One soldier just kicked back on the bleacher seats all night, filming the whole gig.

Three awestruck patriots under blood red skies.

More Blackhawk Tetris the next day and we were Baghdad-bound. We arrived in a heavy spring downpour and scrambled across Sather Air Base's flight line to two awaiting MWR vans. Our small caravan wound through the expansive compound, straddling enormous walls topped with razor wire that kept all of Baghdad decidedly out. We weren't to leave the vast American-controlled area over the next three days — regular patrols had ceased in the city, it was just too dangerous. One soldier had recently been jogging too close to a perimeter wall and a sniper from a nearby apartment building shot and killed him. Baghdad would soon revert largely back to local control; we witnessed many Iraqi soldiers at Camp Victory working alongside the Americans. It was clear that our guys had one foot out the door.

Camp Victory contains several of Saddam's palaces linked by a series of moats which Hussein created by stealing irrigation water from local farmers.

Asshole!

The whole complex once resembled a demented Garden of Eden, alive with lush foliage and designed to impress lesser despots (or Donald Rumsfeld). It was now an ugly dead shell of its former glory. Sandbags and barbed wire protect the base's privately contracted security guards — mostly Ugandans — and the moat's water had long ago grown murky and disgusting. Yet American GIs spend their mornings fishing for whatever mutant carp survive in that shit-soup, only to immediately chuck them back in. Nothing even close to edible lives in there. We saw a small boatful of Third Country Nationals dredging the moat in front of the Al-Faw Palace. One worker seemed to fall into the "water" and we recoiled in horror as his head went under for a few seconds. Our MWR guide turned to me and said, "That's why we don't fuck the local prostitutes."

Our first full day at Camp Victory was spent touring Saddam's various structures, mouths agape in the nerve center of the American Empire's latest conflict. The Al-Faw Palace was impressive from afar, but upon closer inspection was really a piece of shit. The marble façade was just that: flimsy and cheap. The huge chandelier above our heads wasn't made of crystal and gold, it was glass and plastic.

Also at Victory that week was a rapper called Chamillionaire, who apparently has a hit called "Ridin'." Hey, don't ask me. He was on a USO tour and toured the palace with us that day. He and his crew were nice enough, but I was and remain happily ignorant of his genre. All I knew that afternoon was, I was coming down with a head cold, and I'd venture that of the two guys with microphones that night, I would be the only one concerned with hitting my "notes." This cat likely also had a functioning vehicle back home to return to, while my '99 Chevy Blazer had just eaten an engine the day before we departed for Iraq. At Saddam's throne, a gift from PLO leader Yassir Arafat, our humble little tribute band let the rapper and his posse have the first photo-ops before we slid in for ours like an afterthought.

Ok, there's my sour grapes. I'm human.

The MWR SUVs drove past the nicknamed "Perfume Palace" where Saddam housed his concubines. And his mother-in-law... you gotta wonder if Saddam ever took shit from his mother-in-law. Maybe she would occasionally get mouthy. Now *there's* a reality show I would watch.

The conjoined Victory Over Iran and Victory Over America Palaces are across the compound. They were never completed and stand unused and unsafe. The doorway of the former building was adorned with a semi-circle of green helmets taken from decapitated Iranian generals.

And you may ask yourself: Why does a Victory Over America *anything* exist in Iraq? Because Norman Schwarzkopf and Bush Senior and didn't invade Baghdad after the first Gulf War. Incidentally, what did the U.S. do on the opening day of the second war? Dropped two 500 lb. bombs right on that fucking roof. Fab, Ben, Cam, Phledge and I were standing amidst the fractured concrete and rebar eight years and over 4400 American casualties later, nearly to the day.

Directly across from us was a series of small, squat buildings that our POCs referred to as "Flintstone Village." One of Hussein's sons-in-law was suspected of treason. Saddam had him murdered. But as a consolation prize, he built his grandkids a home resembling a Hanna Barbera cartoon. What a guy.

Our last stop that afternoon was at the Ba'ath Party Headquarters, also cratered with extensive bomb damage. Phledge and Cam jumped down into the empty swimming pool, used solely to machine-gun down party enemies. The theater room took a direct hit in 2003. It's now more ceiling than room. This was where the war's first attacks reportedly missed Hussein by five minutes, yet killed many of his top military staff as they watched *Pretty Woman* on a big screen. You really can't make this shit up.

We rode with a truck full of our gear across the Baghdad compound to Sather Air Base where we off-loaded into a hangar-like structure containing a basketball court, a stage, and several dozen folding chairs. Before we could even make a note of soundcheck, in struts a tall, gregarious guy in Air Force BDUs. He extended his hand, "You guys are the U2 tribute! My name's Tony. I've been looking forward to the show!"

His name, more specifically, was Anthony Rock. General Anthony Rock. Or sometimes "General Tony Rock." I'm sorry man, but that's just plain cool. We all had a photo op together and the good General would return a few hours later to plant himself in the front row and sing along to all his favorite U2 songs.

After the show, the band and Young Ben were invited to hang with Lieutenant Colonel Jay Land and his buddies behind the JVB. The Joint Visitors Bureau is another former palace converted into barracks, conference rooms, and a guest registration area which doubles as a TV and internet lounge. Cam and Phledge kicked my ass at chess before joining Victory MPs Aaron and Brett, Colonel Land, and Fab for Camp Victory's favorite late night pastime:

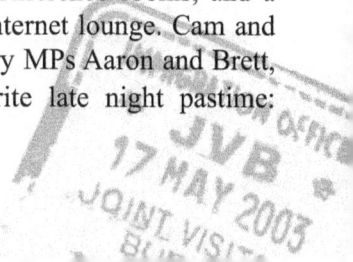

Smoking cigars and driving golf balls into Saddam's moat! I shit you not. They aim their balls at the back side of the Al Faw Palace far across the water. Ori Hoffer back home at Park City TV made my nighttime follow-thru their "Picture of the Day."

Our last show in country was across the compound at Camp Victory's large wooden outdoor stage. Soldiers were already gathering as we set up in the late afternoon sun. They applauded our run-through of "Red Hill Mining Town" before we walked over to the dining facility, passing more intimidating Ugandan security for a pre-show snack with band, crew and MWR people...

DFACs are where our most classic conversations occur. Our guys rarely talk on planes. Ticket agents ask us if we'd like to sit together and we bark huge NOs in unison. But planted at a cafeteria table, mid-tour in some remote chow hall, we can debate minutia for hours. We can argue about the color of oranges. In Coverdog circles, all bullshit is called out and all opinions are respected. One of our POCs put it best: "It's weird — you guys will talk politics and religion, but not music."

When darkness fell the bleacher seating at Camp Victory filled respectably. The MWR peeps counted 450 heads. Mostly Americans but also a few clusters of soldiers from disparate African and South-Asian countries. Most of our audience was in PT issue, perhaps having stopped by the concert after an evening jog. I wandered behind the stage, half-pacing and half-warming my voice with my vocal coach on my iPod. Colonel Land had the evening free and was in attendance. I asked him if he'd like to introduce us, which he did curtly but smoothly as I grinned wide from off stage right. Cam began the intro to our opening song...

- - - - - - - - - -

Twenty-two years ago, my grandfather and I departed Kingsway Drive in our suburban Chicago hometown loaded down for my impending adventures in Hollywood. Pew had taught me how to bust my ass:

"Do it right or don't do it at all, Chief."

Aunt Linda reassured me that being different was ok. Pops gave me the ability to entertain. Ma gave me the ability to visualize the things I wanted. I visualized a thousand possible futures, but could have predicted little of the long and winding road to come.

Hollywood, CA 1989: I found myself waiting outside a movie premier amidst paparazzi and fellow fans to watch heroes of mine emerge from their limousine. Planted alone in the theater I watched the backstory of a band and its tour unfold, absorbing the words of people whose music inspired me deeply.

The screen suddenly shifted from drab black and white into a startling red, with guitars rising and an arena crowd surging in joy. I stepped out into the Hollywood streets, my internal engines on overdrive.

Baghdad, Iraq 2011: I'm standing aside a stage on an Army base. I'm here to bring a few hours of home, to learn, and to share things I've learned. I feel infinitely grateful for my profession and for my path. In the broadest sense of the word, I'm here to entertain. I don't necessarily feel like a soldier. But I do feel like an American. My friends are beside me and my drummer counts us in. There's more to be done.

I'm awaiting my cue.

AFTERWORD
Spring 2013

Well, there it is.

And so what if it took longer to finish than I anticipated? Julia Child spent several years to publish her debut, and she didn't have to chase down lyric clearances. Plus, it's been ski season and a boy has to shred. To my patient graphic designer and co-editor Cheryl, I hereby apologize for every email I ever sent with the subject line: "FINAL CHANGES!"

A handful of folks in our soldier circles must be applauded for their help and their feedback regarding occasionally sensitive military matters (including one quote: *"I laughed, I cringed!"* which I thought was brilliant). Thanks also to the many working musicians, present and past, who shared their gifts with me and became an invaluable part of this little play.

Until next time, good reader! Time to get busy finding new adventures.

Courage,

- The Author

LYRIC ACKNOWLEDGEMENTS

Page 4
Ran Away To Tell the World
(J. Gnecco)
Artist: Ours
Lyrics reprinted with permission by the writer Jimmy Gnecco
© 2008 Misery Head Music (BMI)

Page 5
Maybe Tomorrow
Words and Music by Kelly Jones, Stuart Cable and Richard Jones
Copyright (c) 2003 STEREOPHONICS MUSIC LTD.
All Rights in the U.S. and Canada Controlled and
Administered by UNIVERSAL - POLYGRAM
INTERNATIONAL PUBLISHING, INC.
All Rights Reserved Used by Permission
Reprinted by Permission of Hal Leonard Corporation

Page 19
Fountain of Sorrow
(J. Browne)
Artist: Jackson Browne
Alfred Music Publishing

Page 25
Fish Heads
(R. Haimer, B. Mumy)
Artist: Barnes & Barnes
Music Spazchow
Lyrics reprinted with permission by the writer Robert Haimer

Page 33
Whole Lotta Love
(R. Plant, J. Page)

Page 37
Going To California
(R. Plant, J. Page)
Artist: Led Zeppelin
Alfred Music Publishing

Page 39
Where Is Harrison Ford?
(G. Markell, C. Mathewson, C. Moreland)
Artist: Altered State
In My Room Music (BMI)
Lyrics reprinted with permission by the writer Gregory Markel